THE IDEA OF GOD
AND HUMAN FREEDOM

THE IDEA OF GOD
AND
HUMAN FREEDOM

WOLFHART PANNENBERG

THE WESTMINSTER PRESS
PHILADELPHIA

Translated from the German by R. A. Wilson

Essay 1 from
Terror und Spiel. Probleme der Mythenrezeption
Wilhelm Fink Verlag, München 1971, pp. 473–525

Essays 2–6 from
Gottesgedanke und menschliche Freiheit
Vandenhoeck und Ruprecht, Göttingen 1971

Published by The Westminster Press®
Philadelphia, Pennsylvania

PRINTED IN THE UNITED STATES OF AMERICA

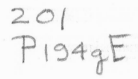

Library of Congress Cataloging in Publication Data

Pannenberg, Wolfhart, 1928–
The idea of God and human freedom.

Translation of 1 essay by the author from Terror
und Spiel and 5 essays from his Gottesgedanke und
menschliche Freiheit. Also published as v. 3 of
Basic questions in theology.
Includes bibliographical references.
1. Theology, Doctrinal—Addresses, essays, lectures.
2. Christianity—Philosophy—Addresses, essays,
lectures. I. Title.
BT80.P34133   201'.1   73–3165
ISBN 0–664–20971–8

CONTENTS

ABBREVIATIONS

ANET   *Ancient Near Eastern Texts relating to the Old Testament,*
ed. J. B. Pritchard, Princeton, 2nd ed., 1955.

AT   Altes Testament.

ATD   Das Alte Testament Deutsch, Göttingen.

BKAT   Biblischer Kommentar – Altes Testament, Neukirchen.

CSEL   Corpus Scriptorum Ecclesiasticorum Latinorum,
Vienna.

ET   English translation.

EvTh   Evangelische Theologie, Munich.

NTD   Das Neue Testament Deutsch, Göttingen.

PG   Patrologia Graeca, ed. J. P. Migne, Paris.

PL   Patrologia Latina, ed. J. P. Migne, Paris.

RGG   *Die Religion in Geschichte und Gegenwart,* 3rd ed.,
Tübingen, 1957–75

ZAW   *Zeitschrift für die alttestamentliche Wissenschaft,* Giessen
and Berlin.

ZThK   *Zeitschrift für Theologie und Kirche,* Tübingen.

PREFACE

THERE IS now a general awareness of the slogan "the de-mythologization of Christianity", yet the concept of myth which underlies it is still questionable; and this in its turn calls into question the demands of demythologization. The intention of the first essay in this book is to bring this situation into the open, and at the same time to develop a more soundly based concept of myth, and to indicate the consequences of applying it to the biblical writings. The study was carried out in the framework of the working group *Poetik und Hermeneutik*, and was first published in the symposium *Terror und Spiel. Probleme der Mythenrezeption* ("Terror and Play. Problems in the understanding of myth") in 1971. I was the only theologian in this working group, and was therefore responsible for putting the point of view of theology as a whole. As a result, I had to go into exegetical details in some depth. I am well aware of the deficiencies of my specialist knowledge in this field, and would prefer this part of the study to be taken as illustrating the concept of myth developed in it by pointing to its possible bearing on biblical exegesis. If this concept were applied consistently by a competent specialist it would no doubt lead to different results. The study also needs to be supplemented with regard to the functions exercised by the mythical consciousness in the context of the life of society. Thus no attention has been paid to the political function of myth as the legitimation of government, or to the tension between this function of myth and the eschatological consciousness of primitive Christianity. But there should be no insuperable difficulties in extending in this direction the consequences of the concept of myth set out here.

The studies which formed the core of the book were

written in the last few years and continue, sometimes directly and sometimes indirectly, my earlier endeavours to identify an anthropological basis for the discussion of the question of God. This basis is as rationally necessary and meaningful as it ever was.[1] This problem remains an open one for anyone who is an inheritor of the lengthy and glorious history of philosophical and theological thought, and who is intellectually aware. This will not be disputed by those who have kept their heads clear of the fog created by the epigrams, usually without intellectual content, of the God-is-dead "theology" and the pretentious irrationalism of mere ("kerygmatic") assertions, and who are also free of the widespread prejudice, easy to understand in these circumstances, but contributing nothing to the issue, against the intellectual seriousness of theological themes in general. From the anthropological point of view, the problem of the idea of God turns, in the face of atheism, on the question of the meaning and the conditions of freedom. Thus the themes of the fifth and sixth articles in this volume are closely connected with the three preceding studies, which are directly concerned with the idea of God, even though this connection may not be evident at first sight. The importance of Hegel for this group of problems lies in the fact that he presented Christian faith and the God of Christianity as an enduring condition of the modern age. My review of Hans Blumenberg's book *Die Legitimität der Neuzeit* has been included because my criticism of Blumenberg's thesis, that the modern age originated in man's setting himself free from the claims of a theological absolutism, is an attempt to corroborate the truth of this insight on the part of Hegel. Anyone prepared to argue that Christianity and the modern age are reconcilable in this sense must look elsewhere than in the fashions of the present day. First of all, he must defend himself against the tendency at work in theology for generations to withdraw into the bastion of an irrationalist understanding of faith. Secondly, he must avoid what seems to be the opposite tendency, but which in

[1] Cf. the relevant chapters in *Grundfragen systematischer Theologie*, 1967; ET *Basic Questions in Theology*, 1970.

reality often goes hand in hand with it, that of acquiescence in the prejudices of the present moment by a facile dismissal of substantial elements in the tradition. Theology has a right to interpret these, but not to conceal its inability by making gestures of supposedly radical criticism, dismissing the problems themselves with second-hand solutions. This no longer requires any courage, but is done merely for the sake of convenience. Even more than by this confusion of the theological situation, what seems to me to be the intellectually inevitable task of theological reflection is made harder nowadays by the fact that the dominant schools of thought on all subjects clearly consider that there is no intellectual loss, when they come to discuss the questions that concern them, in either passing over in silence the contribution of the theological tradition, and with it a large part of the philosophical tradition, with the problems this contribution brings, or in reducing it to simplifications of a kind which in other spheres of intellectual encounter would scarcely be possible. But one must hope that the intrinsic importance of the issues will eventually impose itself upon the general awareness once again.

The lecture which appears as the last essay here was delivered to the conference on the Future of Religion at Nijmegen in March 1972, and represents my most recent attempt at connecting the anthropological interpretation of religion with my model of reconstructing theology on the basis of eschatology.

The text of the individual articles has not been changed since their first publication. Additions have been made to the footnotes of the sixth article.

WOLFHART PANNENBERG

I

THE LATER DIMENSIONS OF MYTH
IN BIBLICAL AND
CHRISTIAN TRADITION

This essay was first published in the symposium *Terror und Spiel. Probleme der Mythenrezeption*, ed. Manfred Fuhrmann, Wilhelm Fink Verlag, Munich 1971, pp. 473–525, and also separately as *Christentum und Mythos. Späthorizonte des Mythos in biblischer und christlicher Überlieferung*, Gütersloher Verlagshaus Gerd Mohn, 1972.

I

THE VIEW that the Christian message has nothing to do with myth is already to be found in the later writings of the New Testament. The second epistle of Peter makes a contrast between myths and the preaching of Christ, which is based upon eye witnesses (1.16). The two epistles to Timothy which have come down to us under the name of Paul already found it necessary to warn against the appearance in Christianity of "myths and endless genealogies" (I Tim. 1.4), and foresaw a time in which Christians would "turn away from listening to the truth and wander into myths" (II Tim. 4.4). This distinction between myths and the preaching of Christ as the truth is not aimed in the first instance against Greek mythology. In fact there is explicit mention of "Jewish myths" (Titus 1.14). It is not certain whether this refers to a Jewish gnosis, or is a broader and less exact use of the expression.

These observations in the canonical scriptures have not prevented modern biblical critics from finding mythical material even in the biblical texts. This does not, however, consist on the whole of consciously created stories such as II Peter has in mind. There, as in the other references in the New Testament, the background is the attribution of myths to the poets which was a commonplace of Hellenistic education. By contrast, the criticism of myth in modern biblical exegesis conceives of myth largely as an involuntary conceptual form characteristic of a stage in human intellectual history which has now been superseded. This concept of myth, which dominates the debate about "demythologization", is that which Schelling called the "allegorical" concept of myth, which conceives of natural phenomena, and represents them, in a mythical form which is not appropriate to them. In his *Philosophie der Mythologie.* Schelling distinguishes this allegorical interpretation of myth not only from the understanding of myth as poetry, as the work of poets, but also from a specifically religious interpretation, which by contrast to these first two views regards the myth as the truth, that is as theogony, the history of the gods. Schelling regards this historical element in the history of the gods as "a real becoming aware of *God*, to whom the *gods* are related only as individual creative factors" (p. 200).[1] Schelling found such a religious concept of myth elaborated in particular in the writings of Friedrich Creuzer (p. 91). He was particularly interested in Creuzer's idea of a "an original totality ... a complex of knowledge descending from time immemorial", which in Creuzer's work is associated with the idea which derives from Bailly of an "original revelation" which took place in the "primal age", as the origin of myth (pp. 90ff.).

Later scholars did not maintain this association of the religious conception of myth with the hypothesis of a primitive monotheism, as defined in Schelling's *Philosophie der Mythologie*. But the association of myth with the "primal age" and with the ordering of the "totality" of the world of man, an order which was based on this primal age, has become firmly established in the study of myth by twentieth-century scholars of comparative religion. An important step towards a more exact and specific

[1] References in the text are to Schelling, *Sämtliche Werke*, ed. M. Schröter, 1925–8, Vol. 6. In the last passage quoted Schelling takes a step further, in his own characteristic direction, than Josef Görres, whose essay "Religion in der Geschichte" (in *Studien*, ed. C. Daub and F. Creuzer, Vol. 3, 1807) helped to establish the romantic interpretation of myth as primeval revelation.

conception of myth was the distinction between myth and other archaic narrative forms, especially fairy tales and sagas. The brothers Grimm still regarded myths of the gods and sagas of heroes as closely related. They actually used the term "saga" of both, and the only form of criterion they had for distinguishing sagas from myths of the gods, and also from the more poetic and more freely composed fairy tales, was that of the historical point of view adopted by sagas.[2] They also constructed a genetic relationship between the myths of the gods, sagas and fairy tales. Since then, the comparison of these narrative forms with each other, and the distinction between them, has become much more sophisticated, and it has been established that in spite of occasional overlapping, they are independent of each other.[3] The main thing that distinguishes myth from sagas and fairy tales is that its subject is the events of the primal age, that is, those things which happened at the "beginning" of the present ordering of life, which constitute this ordering of life and manifest their continuing power in it. The location of the events of the myth in time is intimately related to its function as a story which supplies the basis and foundation of present existence. The period in which the present ordering of the world of nature and society came into being is from the point of view of those who live at the present day the "primal age", at least as long as the present order of things is regarded as inviolable. Neither fairy tales nor sagas have this relationship to the primal age. Fairy tales do not tell of a primal age in

[2] Cf. for example J. Grimm, *Deutsche Mythologie*, ed. E. Redslob, Leipzig, 1942, p. 18. The brothers Grimm stated the difference between myth on the one hand, and saga and fairy tales on the other, in the preface to their *Kinder- und Hausmärchen (Fairy Tales)*, 1822. For a more recent and exact categorization of fairy tales see L. Rörich, *Märchen und Wirklichkeit*, 1956.

[3] In his article "Mythus, Sage, Märchen" in *Hessischen Blättern für Volkskunde* 6, 1905, pp. 97–142, E. Bethe already described the three types of narratives as different "in origin and purpose" (p. 139). But this did not dissuade him from a view of myth as "primitive philosophy" (*ibid.*) and from seeing in the myths "primitive attempts at explanation, the first stages of science" (p. 137). An account of these relationships from the point of view of myth as an account of the primal age is given by H. Baumann at the beginning of his important article "Mythos in ethnologischer Sicht", *Studium Generale* 12 (1959), pp. 1–17, pp. 583–97.

which things originated, but move on the timeless level of typical desires and fears.[4] Unlike fairy tales, sagas have in common with myths the fact that what they recount is regarded as having actually taken place. But it is not seen, as in the case of myth, as something happening in the primal age as the basis of the present world order, but as historical events distinguished by their extraordinary nature, yet lacking the general validity of myth which derives from its function of providing a basis for the present order of things. A relationship must be recognized between the historical nature of saga and its lack of general validity in the strict sense, in spite of the way in which extraordinary historical events are magnified and treated as typical.

The distinguishing of myth from fairy tales and sagas, as well as from other narrative forms,[5] is based in the first instance on the fact that myth can be empirically identified as a particularly archaic narrative form. At the same time the romantic idea that myths are concerned with a sacred primal age or past age becomes less vague, and is limited to its functional meaning. The location of myth in a primal age means neither that it comes down as a matter of fact from time immemorial, nor that its basic and irreducible theme is that of veneration for the past in general. Rather, there is a precise relationship between the location of myth in the primal age and its function of providing the basis for the present world order. And this is the origin of the reverence and cultic veneration expressed in myth for the reality of the "primal age".

This concept of a primal age as the basis of the present order was decisively established for modern comparative religion by B. Malinowski, *Myth in Primitive Psychology*, 1926, and has been further developed by H. Preuss, K. Kerenyi, Mircea Eliade and others. On the basis of his understanding of myth as a

---

[4] Bethe, *op. cit.*, pp. 106ff.; Baumann. *op. cit.*, pp. 4ff. The function of fairy tales as entertainment which is emphasized by Bethe and also by Malinowski is treated by Baumann, following Röhrich, as a subordinate element. In fact many forms of narrative can be used for entertainment in addition to their other and more original purposes.

[5] In particular legends, *Novellen* and aetiological narratives.

"primeval, greater, and more relevant reality", by contrast
with the life of the present time, Malinowski rightly attacked the
view that the myth could be seen simply as a symbolic expression
of something other than itself or as a form of primitive explanation of the reality of experience.[6] The desire to explain, as a
kind of early form of scientific curiosity, is alien to myth. Its
principal concern is not explanation but legitimation. This of
course does not mean a subsequent justification of what exists,
for the legitimation is obtained from the very fact of a reference
to origins. But this shows that the concept of legitimation, with
its association with an argument advanced subsequently, does
not adequately describe the situation. Kerenyi has described
the function of myth better as that of providing a basis.[7]
Eliade understands myth as a "paradigmatic model" both of
the world order and also, and especially, "for all rites and all
significant human activities".[8] The two definitions converge.
The archetypal model provides a reason, not in the sense of a
rational account, but in the sense of a basis or foundation.
Because, to use Mircea Eliade's term, myth possesses the
character of archetypal reality, a distinction must be made
between myth and aetiological narrative, which is intended to
explain the present situation.[9] A true myth has the function of
an explanation only from our point of view, but not for the
mythical consciousness itself. For it is concerned with the self-
sufficient primitive reality.

Modern comparative religion has not only distinguished
myth from other archaic narrative forms. The recognition of
the close link between myth and the cult has also led to a

[6] The latter view e.g. in A. Lang, *Myth, Ritual and Religion*, Vol. II,
1887, pp. 282ff. Malinowski's argument is explicitly directed against
Lang, cf. *Myth in Primitive Psychology*, 1926, p. 39.

[7] C. G. Jung and K. Kerenyi, *Einführung in das Wesen der Mythologie*, 1941,
p. 16; ET *Introduction to a Science of Mythology*, 1951, p. 19.

[8] M. Eliade, *The Sacred and the Profane: the Nature of Religion*, 1961,
pp. 95ff. (citation from p. 98.).

[9] A. E. Jensen, *Mythos und Kult bei Naturvölkern*, 1951, pp. 87ff., 91ff.
H. Baumann, *op. cit.*, pp. 7ff., makes an even sharper distinction between
myth and aetiological narrative, disagreeing with Jensen's derivation of
the latter from vanished myths.

precisely defined empirical concept of myth, which contrasts in particular with the aesthetic interpretation of myth as creative poetic composition. As early as 1825, K. O. Müller emphasized the close relationship between myth and the cult.[10] K. T. Preuss has re-emphasized this aspect in the framework of Malinowski's understanding of myth as an account of the primal age. Here myth serves as the legitimation of the rites.

It points back to the past, in which the sacred action was carried out for the first time. Sometimes it can even be shown that primitive man is not simply repeating the rite on the authority of the myth; rather, the action as it was first carried out is actually re-presented, as something really taking place, with all the beings who took part in it on the first occasion.[11]

From this point of view, myth can appear as derived from the cult, as the product of reflection upon what is done in the cult. S. Mowinckel has formulated this in particularly extreme terms:

True myth is linked with the cult, derives from the cult and expresses what happens in it and what has happened to bring it into being – the "saving fact" which is "remembered" by being re-experienced.[12]

But to derive myth from the cult in this way is to ignore Malinowski's fundamental insight into the original character of the reality recounted in the myth, which for the mythical consciousness at least has priority over all human action and also over everything that is done in the cult. But even apart from the self-understanding of men who think in mythical terms, the question remains whether the cult, if it is the carrying out of what took place in the primal age, does not itself pre-suppose some conception of those primal events, and therefore assumes the existence of a myth, however rudimentary, for cultic action to take place at all. Consequently, Jensen has rightly argued against the widespread derivation of myth from the cult, with the assertion that the reverse is true, and the cult is derived from the essence of myth.[13] Of course cult-aetiological

---

[10] *Prolegomena zu einer wissenschaftlichen Mythologie*, 1825, pp. 236, 372.

[11] K. T. Preuss, *Der religiöse Gehalt der Mythen*, 1933, p. 7. Cf. also Eliade's definition quoted in n. 8.

[12] *Religion og Kultus* (in Norwegian); references to the German translation, *Religion und Kultus*, 1953, pp. 94ff.

[13] *Op. cit.*, pp. 54ff.

myths can be shown to exist, as later interpretations of a rite. But an interpretation can be shown up to be subsequent to the rite only when there are signs that point to a different original understanding of the rite. The subsequent interpretation of cult-aetiology – which raises the question, whether it should not be regarded as aetiological narrative rather than myth in the strict sense – can at once be seen to be a *reinterpretation*. It takes us back not to a cult which can be thought of as completely without myth, but only to another myth, with which the cultic action was linked previously. But whatever conclusion we come to about the priority in the relationship between myth and the cult, and whether or not both can be regarded as independent phenomena, it is certain that they are very closely linked. This can be seen both from the nature of cult and also from that of myth as an archetype. This need not imply that every individual feature of the creation of a myth must have a counterpart in the cult. It is difficult to justify so rigid a pattern. But one must accept that the formation of myths is inconceivable without the "archetypes" of the primal age. With the lack of ritual fulfilment of the present time the vital interest turns away from the vision which is expressed in the formation of myth, even in the transformation of traditional material.[14]

II

In philosophical and theological discussion about myth and demythologization, the concept of myth worked out in comparative religion is not usually paid the attention it deserves. The concepts of myth which are used are those which see it as a symbol, as poetic creation or as the primitive explanation of nature, conceptions which are drawn from periods in the study of myth which have now been outdated by modern comparative

[14] E. Hornung, in his study "Von Geschichtsbild der alten Ägypter", *Geschichte als Fest*, 1966, pp. 9–29, has shown that the pattern of actions carried out, for example, by the Egyptian king does not exclude the introduction of new types of ceremonial action which are then in their turn ritually repeated (pp. 20ff.).

religion. The result of this is not merely a confusion in terminology. In addition, general statements about myth and its relevance or irrelevance to the present day bear no relationship to the phenomenon as it really is. This arouses the suspicion that the arguments they contain have no more than an ideological function.

An example of this can be seen in the theological programme for the demythologization of biblical texts, which has proved so influential. Bultmann thought of myth as a "mode of conception"[15] which was expressed in particular in a "mythical view of the world" which for modern man, whose thinking is scientific in nature, is "obsolete".[16] Bultmann thought the characteristic element of the mythological mode of conception lay not in its relationship to the primal age nor in the function of what the myth recounts as the foundation of the social and world order, but in the fact that myth speaks of "the other world in terms of this world and the gods in terms derived from human life".[17] For this reason, Bultmann considered that he was using the term myth "in the sense popularized by the 'History of Religions' school".[18] In view of the total neglect of the discussion of the concept of myth in modern comparative religion which was initiated by Malinowski, this is a somewhat surprising assertion. The study of comparative religion to which Bultmann appeals seems to be the "history of religions" school to which he himself belongs. Both Wilhelm Bousset, who taught Bultmann, and Hermann Gunkel understood the concept of myth in a narrower sense, as "narrative about the gods".[19] But Gunkel thought that the specifically mythical character of the stories of the gods lay in the fact that "the primitive mind sees the divine as living being and draws it in imaginative forms".[20]

[15] "Neues Testament und Mythologie" in *Kerygma und Mythos* I, 1948, esp. p. 23; ET *Kerygma and Myth* [I], 1953, p. 10.

[16] *Ibid.*, pp. 14f., esp. pp. 16ff. and 23 n. 2; ET pp. 1ff., esp. pp. 3f., and p. 10 n. 2.

[17] *Ibid.*, p. 23; ET p. 10.   [18] *Ibid.*, p. 23 n. 2; ET p. 10 n. 2.

[19] W. Bousset, *Das Wesen der Religion dargestellt an ihrer Geschichte*, 1904, pp. 77ff.; cf. H. Gunkel, *Genesis*, 3rd ed., 1910, p. xiv.

[20] H. Gunkel, *Zum religionsgeschichtlichen Verständnis des Neuen Testaments*, 1903, p. 14. Gunkel also shows a certain vagueness in the concept of myth

Here the spiritual reality of the divine is given tangible form, and the distinction between earthly reality and the spiritual nature of deity is confused. It is only a short step from this outlook to the way Bultmann describes myth.

The origin of this distinctive view of myth as a primitive conceptual form is to be sought, according to C. Hartlich and W. Sachs, in the work of the Göttingen student of ancient languages, C. G. Heyne. Heyne's theory of mythical thought as a *fundus* which was already present as the basis of all the poetry, as well as all the history and philosophy of early man, is accurately typified by them as a description of the "mode of conception and expression" in the childhood of the human race, to use Heyne's words.[21] It displays a series of characteristics which distinguish mythical thought from that of mature humanity. First of all, it lacks an understanding of the true causes of natural and mental processes. Secondly, it is incapable of abstract thought. Thirdly, it shows the susceptibility to sense impressions which accompanies that inability. Heyne stated that the primitive understanding of the world, lacking insight into the true causes of phenomena, attributed all occurrences, and especially extraordinary events, to the intervention of the gods. He derived the personification of relationships of cause and effect from the lack of capacity for abstract thought, and the love of the miraculous and its elaboration in

---

in the fact that he sometimes departs from his narrower definition of myth to classify as mythical traditions which do not satisfy the narrower concept of myth as the history of the gods, and which, like the paradise story, the narrative of the flood or the Babylonian Adapa story, should rather be counted as sagas; in *Schöpfung und Chaos in Urzeit und Endzeit*, 2nd ed., 1921, p. 148, Gunkel speaks of the "myth of paradise" although he uses the word saga elsewhere for this narrative; cf. pp. 151ff., with regard to the Adapa myth (cf. *Genesis*, pp. 29ff., 38ff.). The saga of the flood is also sometimes called a myth in Gunkel's commentary on Genesis (pp. 71, 73ff.). Perhaps this terminological vagueness reflects the influence of the conception of the brothers Grimm of the transition from myth into saga. This vagueness in terminology may moreover have led to the need for a more general characterization of myth in the sense of a primitive conceptual form.

[21] C. Hartlich and W. Sachs, *Der Ursprung des Mythosbegriffs in der modernen Bibelwissenschaft*, 1952, p. 13. For what follows, cf. pp. 14ff.

recollection and oral tradition from a susceptibility to sense impressions—particularly with regard to rare events. According to Heyne, the mythical outlook described in these terms is expressed both in the understanding and handing down of actual events (historical myths) and also in reflection upon natural and ethical phenomena, which were simply clothed in narrative form (philosophical myths). For Heyne, and especially for the mythical school in theology which followed him, this distinction between historical and philosophical myths became fundamental. Where a historical myth was present, the tradition could at least be accorded a starting point in what had actually happened, while in the case of philosophical myth the narrative is no more than a secondary representation of the idea it expresses.

Heyne's views were then applied by G. J. Eichhorn and J. P. Gabler to the Old Testament, and particularly to the first chapters of Genesis. It was not difficult to represent the direct attribution to the intervention of God of natural phenomena such as rain, and unexpected events like dreams, as mythical in Heyne's sense. Since moreover "in the language of un-educated races thoughts are portrayed as speech and con-versation with the things" which evoke such thoughts,[22] not only does God speak to men in dreams or ask Cain about his brother Abel, but the snake in Paradise is represented as speaking and is thus personified. Thus in general terms one should expect from the biblical account "more material conceptions in langu-age, more painting and poetry than bare history and abstract conceptions of language . . ."[23] In addition the "reasoning" associated with the narrative is represented by those who handed on the story, in accordance with "Oriental" practice, as part of what happened: "For Orientals the fact and the way of thinking about the fact coalesced into an inseparable whole."[24] This approach was also applied to the New Testa-

[22] J. G. Eichhorn, *Urgeschichte*, ed. J. P. Gabler, Vol. III, 2nd ed. 1793, p. 173, also p. 154; cf. Hartlich and Sachs, *op. cit.*, pp. 27ff.

[23] Eichhorn, *op. cit.*, Vol. I, 1790, p. 4.

[24] Gabler, *Neuestes theologisches Journal* (1798), p. 239, quoted by Hartlich and Sachs, *op. cit.*, p. 67.

ment by Eichhorn and Gabler,[25] although this was to overlook the link which Heyne made between myth and the preliterary stage of popular history. The analogy between the modes of conception was the decisive element which enabled this approach to be extended to the New Testament. And as early as 1794 Corrodi had also included the eschatological conceptions of the New Testament amongst its mythical parts, because the account of the end of the world was portrayed in the same tangible images as that of the beginning of the world.[26] This view of myth, in which the effects of David Hume's view of the origins of religion can be perceived,[27] although Hume did not use the term myth to describe it, was adopted both by D. F. Strauss's criticism of myth and also in Bultmann's concept of myth. But Bultmann consciously replaces the idea, based on Heyne's view, that myth represents non-material (abstract) subjects in material form, by the statement that myth "speaks of the other world in terms of this world, and of the gods in terms derived from human life".[28] This results from the fact that as a dialectic theologian Bultmann assumed the existence of an other-worldly, divine reality which is contrasted with man and his world as their crisis, and for this very reason cannot be drawn down into the sphere of the "visible world, with its tangible objects and forces, and . . . human life with its feelings, motives and potentialities" (*ibid.*), as in mythical thought. Thus he took up the concept of myth derived from Heyne as a contrary concept to his own understanding of the reality of God. Heyne's concept of myth allowed him to reject any being other than the wholly other God of dialectic theology, any link between the divine and the world of man, as an expression of a survival of a pre-scientific form of thought. Here Bultmann agrees completely with Heyne that the concept of myth refers in the first instance not to certain individual myths, but to the mode of conception which underlies them, the structure of

[25] Cf. Hartlich and Sachs, *op. cit.*, pp. 61f.
[26] *Ibid.*, p. 55.   [27] *Ibid.*, pp. 169ff.
[28] *Kerygma und Mythos* I, p. 23; ET p. 10. See also Bultmann's remark in his reply to J. Schniewind, *ibid.*, p. 135; ET p. 102.

consciousness of a humanity as yet untouched by modern science. For Bultmann as for Heyne this structural consciousness is characterized by the negative features of a deficient knowledge of the forces and laws of nature. The corresponding positive aspect was a belief in the direct intervention of supernatural powers in the course of events, and particularly a belief in miracles and demons.[29] Bultmann, like Heyne before him, regarded mythical conceptions as made "obsolete" by modern science.

Thus Bultmann and the debate about demythologization which he initiated followed Heyne's concept of myth, which Schelling classified as "allegorical". The more modern conception of comparative religion, which takes into account the function of myth as finding a basis for the world order and the social order in the primal age, is ignored. This distinctive phenomenon of myth, which was not observed until the category of the basis of the world order in the primal age was developed away from romantic associations, was never taken into account in the dispute about "demythologization". This statement is not meant to cast doubt on the importance of the arguments conducted under this heading. But it must be stressed that they are not disputes about the validity or non-validity of what modern comparative religion has come to know as myth. Rather, it is a question of the validity or non-validity of certain forms of thought and conceptualization from the pre-modern and pre-scientific age. These arguments may also concern themselves with myth as a phenomenon of comparative religion, in so far as it can be shown to be associated with such con-

---

[29] *Kerygma und Mythos* I, pp. 15ff.; ET pp. 1ff. Bultmann differs from Heyne, however, in seeing the main characteristic of myth as a particular world view underlying mythical conceptions. K. H. Bernhardt has rightly objected that a "three-storey" world view need not always be mythical (as does Bultmann in *Kerygma und Mythos* II, 1952, p. 183 n. 2.), nor on the other hand is the world view of myth always three-storied. "Thus, for example, according to the oldest Egyptian conception of the other world, the kingdom of the dead lay in the west and not in the underworld" ("Bemerkungen zum Problem der 'Entmythologisierung' aus alttestament-licher Sicht", *Kerygma und Dogma* 15, 1969, pp. 193–209; quotation from p. 197).

ceptual forms. But this is a theme which has hardly been discussed as yet. But the theme of the task misleadingly described as "demythologization" is much wider. The hermeneutic task of translating traditional matter from a prescientific world view into an understanding of reality based on modern science involves a number of themes which have nothing to do with myth in the sense in which the term is used in comparative religion. The stereotyped contrast made between the structure of conceptions which are supposed to be "mythical" and the true causes, forces and laws of nature, from Heyne right down to Bultmann, show that what is at issue here is a concept which is contrary to the understanding of the world in the modern natural science which was founded by Galileo and Newton, and is now known as "classical" science. But this contrary concept to that of a mythical structure of consciousness was originally meant to have not a polemic function, but a hermeneutic function. It was meant to bring about an understanding of the view of reality found in the earliest religious and literary traditions of mankind. But in practice the use that was made, and still is made, of this concept of myth was less that of making the present, scientifically enlightened age more open to the distinctive features of this long vanished experience of reality, but rather that of ridding man, on his final achievement of a true knowledge of nature, of the claims of traditions which were categorized as "mythical" and therefore as obsolete. By being described as mythical in Heyne's sense, they immediately ceased to disturb enlightened humanity by their strange assertions. Their oddities could be treated as no more than the expression of an inadequate stage of the understanding of nature which had now fortunately been left behind. In Bultmann's work, the concept of myth retained this function of ridding man of the ideas it contained. In spite of his emphatic assertion that he is concerned not to eliminate myth but to interpret it,[30] we find in Bultmann an interpretation which does away with the "mythical" form by regarding it as the expression of a self-understanding which must be

[30] *Kerygma und Mythos* I, p. 25; ET p. 12.

presented in a non-mythological form. Here the concept of myth is used to free the Christian tradition from the features which seem to be irreconcilable with an understanding of the world and man's own self which is based on modern science.

The effective elimination of "myth" by such an interpretation is connected with the structural feature of this view which Schelling has described as "allegorical". It treats the form of thought which it describes as "mythical", not as something irreducibly distinct and unique, but as the expression of something else, e.g. natural processes. To this extent it is allegory.[31] By so doing, it replaces the supposedly "mythical" conception by something else. What is wrong in this procedure is that it no longer looks at the conceptions and phenomena described as "mythical" to see what their own distinctive importance is, their own characteristic truth. This is all the worse, in that, as we saw, this concept of myth incorporates under the heading of "mythical" things which cannot be regarded as myth or mythical in the sense of comparative religion; but because they have been so classified, their own distinctive features are no longer discussed. In particular, there is reason to suspect that basic features of religious thought are labelled as "mythical" and therefore dismissed as irreconcilable with modern science, without this ever being discussed in each particular case. This is true above all of the acceptance of divine intervention in the course of events. Such an acceptance is fundamental to every religious understanding of the world, including one which is not mythical in the sense in which comparative religion uses the term. It is fundamental even to the understanding of God in dialectic theology itself, in so far as it sees God not only as opposed to the world, but also as revealing himself to the world as its salvation. By no means every form of this assertion is in conflict with the modern postulate that the laws of nature cannot be broken.[32] Can the other-worldly make its reality

[31] Of course Heyne defended himself against the charge of interpreting myth as (conscious) allegory, and opposed to this his concept of a mode of conception which worked involuntarily. But in a deeper sense this too is allegorical, in so far as it conceives of things otherwise than as they appear.

[32] To attribute all phenomena, and especially particularly striking and

known in any other way than by manifesting itself within the world? Is not the assertion of the pure transcendence of the divine a questionable one? But if religious thinking cannot simply be dismissed as antiquated in the name of modern science, ought not true myth be given the right and the opportunity to have its own proper importance evaluated, instead of being condemned as obsolete simultaneously with all kinds of other patterns of thought?

III

Unlike the theories which dismissed myth as a pre-modern mode of conception for ideas which are nowadays accessible in a non-mythical way, the interpretation of myth as poetry was able to do justice to its distinctive nature and to accord to it at least the possibility of a permanent value of its own, and a relevance of some kind to the present time. The view, based on the Greek association of myths with poets, and particularly with Homer and Hesiod, which regarded them as the creations of the poetic imagination, saw myth as belonging to a sphere in which it is judged by other standards than that of its understanding of the world. The liberating and elevating effect of artistic inspiration remains largely untouched by the change in man's understanding of the world. K. P. Moritz, whose work is typical of the view of myth held in German classicism and early romanticism, emphasized that mythological poems are "a world of their own . . . above the circumstances of all real things".[33] According to this view, the ideal truth of myths

extraordinary events, to the intervention of gods, neither presupposes ignorance, in every case, of the true relationship between cause and effect, nor is it comprehensible as the consequence of such ignorance. Rather, such a way of looking at things expresses the basic religious experience which apprehends the individual phenomenon not only in its association with other finite events and circumstances, but with reference to the "powers" which determine reality as a whole. Without this specifically religious element even an ignorance of true causes would not explain why any event was attributed to a divine power.

[33] *Götterlehre oder mythologische Dichtungen der Alten*, 2nd ed., 1795, p. xciii. The young Schelling praised Moritz for being the first German to

is above all historical limitations. This means that myth is not restricted to being an obsolete mode of conception from the "childhood of the human race".[34] Thus when myth is inter-

---

undertake the task "of presenting mythology in its distinctive nature as poetry" (*Philosophie der Kunst*, 1802, [see n. 1], Vol. 5, p. 412).

[34] Herder adopted an instructive middle position on this issue. Like his friend Heyne he wished to link mythical thought with history, and in particular with the primal age of mankind. In this point both Herder and Heyne are precursors of the later romantic view of myth as a tradition from the primal age of the human race. Creuzer, too, remained Heyne's disciple in this respect. But while Heyne associated this attribution of myth to the beginnings of human history with the view that mythical thought was superseded and obsolete at the present day, Herder was interested in the present day relevance of mythical tradition. This explains lack of interest in the critical question of the factual historicity of what was contained in myth (cf. Hartlich and Sachs, *op. cit.*, pp. 48ff.). He was interested in the relationship between myth and history only with regard to its origin in the particular tradition with which he was concerned with regard to its present day relevance. The best example of this specifically theological approach is Herder's attitude to the sagas of the Old Testament. But the present day relevance of "myths" was assured by their poetic quality. This was why Herder insisted "that poets and no others invented and determined mythology" (*Kritische Wälder* I, 11, in *Herders Werke*, ed. H. Düntzer and G. Hempel, Berlin, n.d., Vol. 20, p. 70). The *Ideen zur Philosophie der Geschichte der Menschheit* represents mythology as a product of the power of imagination, in which the mythology of every people is seen as "a reflection of the way in which they actually looked at nature" (*Ideen zur Philosophie der Geschichte der Menschheit* 8, 2, 4, in Herder *Ausgewählte Werke in Einzelausgaben*, ed. H. Stolpe, 1965, Vol. I, p. 298). The imagination explains "the enigma of what is seen by what is not seen" (*ibid.*, p. 296). Here Herder comes close to Heyne's idea: "Where there is any movement in nature, where a thing seems to live and changes, without the eye being aware of the laws (!) of the change, the ear hears voices and words which explain to it the enigma of what is seen by the unseen." But even here such products of the power of the imagination are not simply explained as obsolete conceptions. Rather, the imagination shares in the perception of the invisible in the visible, in which Herder recognizes "a kind of religious feeling for invisible, effective forces" (p. 374), which must precede every formation of rational ideas. Thus civilization and science were "originally nothing but a kind of religious tradition" (p. 373). With such ideas Herder is already approaching the romantic, religious conception of myth, especially in his emphasis on the role of tradition in human skills, and on religious tradition as the oldest and most sacred, the language of which "mostly derives from the sagas of the primeval world, and which is also the only thing which these [savage] people have retained by way of information about the past, of recollection of the early world or of the

preted as poetry rather than allegory, its modern interpreters
are not forced into opposing what it contains, but are as it
were in alliance with it. The same is true of the later version of
this view put forward by H. Blumenberg,[35] as much as of
Moritz, Friedrich Schlegel or the young Schelling. What is
new is the emphasis in Blumenberg on the poetic interpretation
of myth, which is not so immediately prominent as in Moritz
or Schelling, but represents a return to it, going back behind
another view of myth which had appeared in the meantime, a
view which in modern comparative religion and cultural anthropology has replaced the poetic interpretation of it. This
view is the religious interpretation of myth as the expression of
the consciousness of the continuing actuality of the primal age
on which the present world order is based. Blumenberg scarcely
discusses this empirically based phenomenology of the mythical
consciousness,[36] and the aim of his exposition, which is in the

---

glimmerings of science". (p. 373). But Herder's language about mythology
and saga fluctuates somewhat – between Heyne's "mode of conception",
the poetic and the religious concepts of myth – because Herder was not
concerned here to be precise.

[35] Cf. H. Blumenberg, "Wirklichkeitsbegriff und Wirkungspotential des
Mythos", in *Terror und Spiel: Probleme der Mythenrezeption*, ed. Manfred
Fuhrmann, 1971, pp. 15ff.

[36] He mentions only the interpretation of myth as terror, put forward
by Cassirer and Freud. Blumenberg sees in this (p. 14) the alternative to
the poetic interpretation. We may leave aside the question whether the
characterization of myth as terror, which is often true of Freud, does justice
to Cassirer's view. In both writers the empirical study of myth represented
by Malinowski and the discussion he provoked is noted to only a very
limited degree, on the occasions when it fits into the construction of a
system determined by a different approach, that of philosophy, or again of
psychology. Blumenberg does not take into account the study of myth in
comparative religion or cultural anthropology. This would quickly have
shown that the self-understanding of the mythical consciousness, based
upon and directed towards the archetypes of the primal age, is neither
solely nor mainly determined by an experience of "terror", least of all with
regard to what is uttered in the myth. For the myth is concerned with the
order which overcomes the terrifying chaos, an order which is thought
of as rooted in the events of the primal age. Nor are the events which
underlie this attitude assigned to the "free ranging imagination" (Blumenberg, p. 14) of poetry; by contrast to fairy tales and legends they are
regarded as the truth (B. Malinowski, *Myth in Primitive Psychology*, 1926,
p. 28;) cf. H. Baumann in *Studium Generale* 12, 1959, pp. 1ff.

opposite direction, is expressed in his attribution to myth of the
overcoming of the consciousness which looks back to the primal
age. Myth, he states, is an account "not of the first things, but
of the liberation from them".[37] It is characteristic of this
complete reversal of the passage from the poetic to the religious
interpretation of myth that Blumenberg should take up a
statement by F. Creuzer and use it in the contrary sense to
which it was intended. Creuzer demanded that there should be
a return from the poetic interpretation of myth by classicism and
early romanticism to a consideration of the original religious
nature of myths. He consequently complained "that the poetic
myth of the Greeks distorted the high seriousness of the distant
primal age into the free play of the imagination". But Blumenberg, casting no more than a glance at Creuzer's "religious
approach", makes use of this formula to claim that the nature
of myth is the transformation of a serious concern with the
primal age into the free play of the imagination.[38] Of course he
is considering as myth here only the "later dimensions" of myth,
such as the Homeric epic, while the roots of this kind of poetry
in "stories of the gods" are no more than the "material" which
has long ago been transformed into narratives. But from this
point of view it is surely the later literary dimensions of the
mythical tradition which become incomprehensible, because
the theory loses sight of the problem of how myth could
become literature at all. As long as the discovery of a mythical
and cultic background behind a poetry which is impregnated
with myth cannot simply be forgotten, there is no point in
restricting the concept of myth to the latter, in order to restore
the classical interpretation of myth as poetry.[39] To do so may

[37] *Op. cit.*, p. 15.

[38] *Ibid.*, referring to F. Creuzer, *Symbolik und Mythologie der alten Völker*,
1836–43.

[39] Nor does this offer the ideal and typical contrast to the "dogmatic"
character of Christian orthodoxy, which is supposedly to be attributed to
the "prohibition of names and images" in the Old Testament, as we find
in Blumenberg (esp. pp. 11ff.). The rich variety of the biblical saga tradition
is noted in every modern commentary on Genesis. And the luxurious
freedom of the primitive Christian tradition about Jesus is a long way from
the "inviolability of formulae" (p. 13). The history of the church too, which

have the advantage over the antiquarian tendency of the modern study of myth, in that it gives myth an immediate literary relevance. But interest in the continuing literary effectiveness and the renewal of mythical themes must not be satisfied at the expense of historical and ethnological fact. What matters is to understand the transition from a myth rooted in the cult to the free availability of its themes for literary use, and on the other hand the many kinds of imperfect link between free poetic creations and mythical origins. The ambiguity of

---

really originated the "inviolability of formulae", shows in fact a never-ending variety of theological constructions. The purpose, however, is no longer that of the free play of the imagination, but a struggle for the one truth. In spite of this we find at the climax of the poetic interpretation of myth, in earlier romanticism, an attempt to interpret theology in the same way: W. M. L. de Wette, in his *Beiträgen zur Einleitung in das AT*, 1807, made an attempt to interpret the Pentateuch along the lines of Herder's ideas as a religious epic, and ten years later, in his work *Über Religion und Theologie*, 2nd ed. 1821, he used the concept of myth as the starting point for a new version of the ancient theme that all religious conceptions are of the nature of images (p. 199). In this sense, the whole tradition of dogma was interpreted by de Wette as mythical. Hartlich and Sachs have rightly emphasized the importance of this view of myth for D. F. Strauss's criticism of the gospels (*op. cit.*, pp. 91–120, cf. p. 135). It was de Wette's view of myth as free poetic composition which made it possible to treat whole complexes of narratives as the product of the myth-making imagination, whereas the "mythical school" of Heyne, in the presence of a "historical" myth, always had to look for the historical facts which had come to be represented in the form of ancient mythical conceptions. Hartlich and Sachs failed to recognize that de Wette is to be understood on the basis not of Heyne, but on that of the poetic interpretation of myth. Yet it is instructive that in his work *Über Religion und Theologie* de Wette does not mention Heyne at all, but appeals to Herder (2nd ed. 1821, pp. 68 and 77). In complete contrast to Heyne's explanation of mythical conceptualizing by the weakness of minds still ensnared in sense impressions, de Wette states: "But where faith itself is still rooted in sense impressions, mythology cannot assert its independence and finds its free play restricted, for by its freedom of treatment the sacred would seem to be profaned" (pp. 90ff.). The steps Strauss took towards a "total mythical" interpretation of the New Testament would not have been possible on the presuppositions of Heyne and the mythical school. However, Strauss united de Wette's idea of the poetic productivity of the myth-making imagination with Heyne's condemnation of myth as an obsolete mode of conception. The disruptive force of this amalgamation is the driving impulse behind his radical criticism of the gospels.

mythological allusions, which may also be used in antithesis to the meaning of the original form of the myth,[40] would then provide a field for the discussion of the "new myth" which is created under conditions of literary freedom. The awareness of the pre-literary nature of the original myth would in this case form a background against which the distinctive features of the "new myth", which now appears as a poetic creation, and the problems it raises can more clearly be seen.

In his later *Philosophie der Mythologie* Schelling criticized both the "allegorical" interpretation of myth, and also its interpretation as poetry, which he had previously advanced himself, on the grounds that they did not leave room for the truth of myth itself.[41] The "allegorical" view which Schelling found in Heyne and Hermann took myth as the expression of something quite different from what it set out to express, such as natural processes. Myth had no truth of its own. The language of myth was treated as an unauthentic language. The view of myth as poetry worked in a different way. It left mythology untouched in its universality[42] and did not deprive the mythical language of its real meaning. But it dealt with myth as *invention*, either as the invention of individual poets or of the anonymous popular mind.[43] Schelling's main argument against this view – which he shared with Heyne (cf. n. 43) – was that poetic invention could be shown to be dependent on the already existing material of which it made use. It varied this material,[44] which in any case was incomprehensible as the creation of popular poetry. For in fact the reverse is true: an individual

[40] This is found in comparative religion wherever the attributes in myths of the deity are usurped by another.

[41] *Werke*, Vol. 6, pp. 68ff.; cf. pp. 12, 28f.   [42] *Ibid.*, p. 28.

[43] According to Schelling the poetic interpretation and the "allegorical" agree in this. But Heyne explicitly opposed the view that the mythical expression derived from poetic invention. Rather, it was already assumed as the *fundus* of poetic composition (*Sermonis mythici sive symbolici interpretatio*, etc. *Commendationes Societatis Regiae Scientiarum Göttingensis*, Vol. 16, 1807, p. 294). Only in a broader sense is it possible to speak here of invention, and that is with regard to the fact that according to Heyne mythical expression does not in fact correspond to the subjects of which it treats.

[44] Vol. 6, p. 27, cf. pp. 19f., 58f.

people is inconceivable without its own characteristic mytho-logy.[45] Thus even if its creation is attributed to the anonymous popular mind, the thesis of the poetic origin of mythology cannot be maintained. Going beyond Schelling's argument, one may suspect that the reverse is true; that the continuing significance of mythical material for poetry may also be related to the fact that it represents an intellectual dimension which precedes the subjective creation of the poet, and both pro-vides a stimulus to its creative interpretation and at the same time makes room for it. When they are compared with this process, the distinctive peculiarity of modern attempts to create a "new myth" by poets is clearly seen for the first time. The interpretation of myth as poetry could only regard this as an example of the way myths come into being in general. But the characteristic emotional force with which someone like Maya-kovsky makes himself the spokesman of a higher reality above and beyond his own subjectivity is inexplicable by this inter-pretation. So too is the problem that lies in the fact that this higher reality can at the same time be seen as the creation of the poet's subjectivity, so that the emotional force of the "new myth" can be maintained only by the poet's regarding himself as a prophet, speaking as one inspired. The specific problem raised by the "new myth" is an argument against the thesis that the normal origin of myth is to be sought in free poetic invention. The "new myth" can hardly be used as an example of the way myths in general derive from the poetic imagination. On the contrary, it is the most acute expression of the modern problem of subjectivity: the contradiction involved in the need for basing the individual subjectivity and its freedom in a truth above and beyond it, in order to overcome the arbitrariness and insignificance of mere subjectivity. In view of the decline of the traditions by which man's self-consciousness was pre-viously motivated, this need can now take the form only of an assumption on the part of a subjectivity seeking to transcend itself, and this leads to the collapse of the attempt to find a truth which lies above and beyond subjectivity and so provides

[45] *Ibid.*, pp. 66f.

a basis for it. It is forced back upon the pure subjectivity of the poet, which it was intended to overcome and give content to. The poet creating a new myth steps into the vacuum set up by the collapse of mythical and religious traditions. But can he replace from the creative power of his imagination the substance which in the past underwent modification in the mind of poets? Schelling's objection, that the interpretation of myth as poetry robs it of its truth by representing it as the mere invention of the poet, has received a confirmation which Schelling could not foresee in the fact that poets seek in vain to restore the truth of myth. Does not the last word of this subject lie in the futility of attempting to carry out a programme planned in advance in this field? Does the experience of inspiration contain a truth which goes beyond the status of philosophical reflection upon the problem of subjectivity? But any such possible truth in poetic experience would be obscured once again if the "myth" which takes form in the poet's words, were regarded only as the creation of his subjectivity.

Thus the poetic interpretation of myth can be suspected of distorting the truth of poetry itself. The religious understanding of myth seems to do better justice not only to myth but to poetry as well.

IV

The contemporary literary relevance of mythical material and categories raises the question of the relationship between Christianity and myth in a new form. It can no longer be limited to the conditions under which Christian traditions came into being, in a world in which human consciousness was characterized by outdated forms of conception. The question that arises is rather how, when the form in which tradition is handed down has been determined by Christianity, mythical material and categories can continue to be used. Is the use of mythical material and forms of expression, particularly from Greek and Roman mythology, in outright contradiction to the dogmatic spirit of Christianity? Or alternatively, is Christianity itself mythological, so that both Christian and non-Christian material, so long as it takes the form of sagas, or is religious in nature, can be regarded in general as the "mythological" stock in trade of literature? It might seem that to so regard it implies such a wide and unspecific use of the term myth that however well established it may be, it is meaningless. But the more precisely defined religious conception of myth set out above raises in an even more urgent form the question whether Christianity itself must be regarded as mythical, and if not, how the persistence and continuing creation of mythical themes within the domain of the Christian tradition is to be explained. The considerations that follow cannot pretend to cover the whole range of problems involved. In particular, there are detailed questions in the field of the history of literature which are not discussed. What follows will be limited to the basic outlines of the question of the relationship between Christianity and myth, and will give examples of them at the point where they have been subject, relatively speaking, to the most intensive process of interpretation, that is, in biblical literature.

While New Testament scholars admit the existence on a considerable scale of mythical modes of thought in primitive Christian literature, Old Testament exegesis presents a different picture. "The true tendency of the religion of Yahweh is unfavourable to myths" was the judgment of Hermann Gunkel,[46] and his view has remained the dominant one in this field of scholarship down to the present day. Myth has largely been treated from the point of view of outside influences on the history of Israelite religion. In Gunkel's case, this outlook is explained by the fact that he regards myth as the "history of the gods"; "but for a history of the gods there must be at least two gods". Consequently the monotheism of Israelite religion "did not tolerate authentic and unaltered myths".[47] But in

[46] *Genesis*, 3rd ed., 1910, p. xiv. The effects of this view on subsequent Old Testament study are discussed in K. H. Bernhardt, "Bemerkungen zum Problem der 'Entymythologisierung' in alttestamentlicher Sicht", in *Kerygma und Dogma* 15 (1969), pp. 193ff.

[47] *Ibid.* In Gunkel's work this view does not exclude the description of myth as a visible and tangible conception of the spiritual and the divine,

recent years this concept of myth as the history of the gods has been rejected as too narrow. It does not make it possible to understand the function and part played by myth in forming the spirit of a culture. Its main effect has been to make it very much easier to distinguish genuine Israelite tradition from everything mythical, and the possibility has been ignored that in spite of the struggle against polytheism a mythical understanding of reality might have been at work in the Old Testament.[48] B. S. Childs, in his attempt on this basis to establish a wider concept of myth, was in agreement with the modern study of myth in comparative religion, which proceeds from the formal characteristic of a primal age as the basis of the present world order, seen as essential to the concept of myth, and regards it as a matter of indifference whether the acts in the primal age on which the present world order is based are attributed to tribal ancestors, heroes of the primal age or divine beings. However, gods can be regarded as in reality the typical actors in the mythical drama, because in the end the function of laying, in the primal age, an absolutely valid foundation for the present order is a divine function. But the priority of the understanding of reality must also be acknowledged as a matter of fact, in so far as reality is thought of in the myth as determined by what happened in the primal age.[49] But the mythical understanding of reality in this sense must not be confused with the much more general concept of a

---

a view reminiscent of Heyne and the mythical school (cf. n. 20). But in spite of Gunkel's occasionally loose terminology, this mode of conception, described as "mythical", is still associated with the idea of the "history of the gods", whereas later, in Bultmann, the concept of myth is defined by the mode of conception, regardless of the themes in connection with which it is found.

[48] B. S. Childs, *Myth and Reality in the Old Testament*, London 1960, pp. 15ff. Childs has rightly pointed to the difference between Gunkel's narrower view and Bultmann's conception of myth as a mode of conception (pp. 13ff.) but overlooks the loose terminology which already exists in Gunkel. The fact that in a mythical action it is by no means necessary for the agent to be a god is emphasized in L. Radermacher, *Mythos und Sage bei den Griechen*, 3rd ed., 1968, p. 71.

[49] In this sense Childs also speaks of the "understanding of reality", cf. *op. cit.*, pp. 17ff., esp. p. 19.

mythological mode of conception in Bultmann's sense (see above).

The study of the links between the Old Testament and the mythology of the ancient Near East, as found in Babylon and Egypt, has repeatedly shown that Israel everywhere took up mythical material into its traditions, but changed its mythical structure in such a way that this adaptation gives a marked impression of a "demythologization". Thus Gunkel affirmed that the elimination of the polytheistic features of the Babylonian myth in the biblical creation narrative amounted to the "retreat, step by step, of the mythological element".[50] And even Childs, who included in his concept of myth not only the "histories of the gods" of the ancient Near East, but also the understanding of reality which underlay them, came to the conclusion that there was clear evidence in the Old Testament of an understanding of reality opposed to the mythical understanding, and directed towards an eschatological future rather than a primal and archetypal period in the past.[51] This seems to be true to the extent that the Old Testament no longer contains the expression of a self-contained mythical consciousness, but instead what can be called the "later dimension" of myth. One can speak of an unfragmented mythical understanding of reality in the Old Testament only if one's starting point is not a comparison with the concrete forms of ancient Near Eastern mythology and the understanding of reality which underlay it, but instead a more general conception of a mythical world view which, in the sense found in Bultmann and the view of myth which originated with Heyne, describes as mythical every intervention of divine powers in earthly reality.[52] But in this case the concept of myth loses, as we have

[50] Gunkel, *Schöpfung und Chaos in Urzeit und Endzeit*, p. 120.

[51] Childs, *op. cit.*, p. 83 and 93. Cf. also M. Eliade's argument that the concentration and dependence upon archetypes in Israel, especially through the effects of prophecy, was broken down by a positive evaluation of the future, and a corresponding historical understanding of reality (*The Myth of the Eternal Return*, ET 1955, pp. 102ff., esp. pp. 106ff.).

[52] In this respect Bernhardt approaches the matter from the same point of view as Bultmann (*op. cit.*, pp. 197ff.), although he rightly rejects this concept of a mythical world view, for a religious belief in miracles is not

shown, the specific outlines which can be demonstrated in historical and ethnological material,[53] and serves instead to legitimize a modern consciousness which is increasingly excluding religious topics altogether. Thus it would be more appropriate to speak here of a religious world view rather than a mythical one; for the latter has much more specific characteristics. It is a world view which is religious in the sense that people constantly looked behind what they perceived for divine powers, and powers hostile to divinity, and assumed the possibility of their intervention in some form or another in the course of earthly events. And such a world view of course is to be found everywhere in the biblical writings.[54] It must be

---

always associated with a three-storey world view, nor is such a world view always associated with belief in miracles (see also n. 29).

[53] Cf. above, pp. 11ff. Bernhardt is also aware of the narrower concept of myth as "history of origins" (pp. 194ff.). But he regards this as entirely aetiological. In his view myths served "to provide an interpretation on the basis of earthly processes and situations in the sphere of nature or history by means of events in the world of the gods, or by divine intervention in the earthly sphere" (p. 194). Malinowski's important objections to the procedure of attributing an explanatory and aetiological purpose to myth (cf. above, n. 6) are ignored. The aetiological view of the explanation of secular situations in nature or history leads logically to the idea of a mythical world view, because the mythical "explanation" must inevitably appear to be a "primitive" interpretation of phenomena which with our knowledge we would explain differently. Yet even in this perspective there is doubtful justification for including belief in miracles in general in the mythical world view, or even for claiming that it is particularly characteristic of it. It is perfectly possible for a belief in miracles to be neither indispensable as a typical structural element of an allegedly mythical aetiology, nor to be conditioned by it in its turn.

[54] In this we agree with Bernhardt's account (pp. 200ff.) of the religious world view of the Old Testament and the New Testament (which he consistently refers to as mythical). Here his arguments display the confusion brought about by the use of the concept of myth in dealing with the religious themes under discussion, on account of the idea associated with it that it is historically obsolete. We find on the one hand an attempt made for apologetic purposes to dismiss the significance of mythical conceptions for people in antiquity as trivial. For example, he states "that mythical conceptions, even for the people of antiquity, had at best only a relative reality" (p. 199). We then read that "it is not possible for us to attribute" to certain traditions, such as the story of the resurrection of Jesus, "the same degree of reality as did early Christianity, because of its mythical

distinguished from the effective presence of a mythical world view, a mythical understanding of reality, in the thought of ancient Israel and of primitive Christianity; and it must also be distinguished from the function of individual mythical themes and conceptions in the Bible. One must of course always take into account the possibility of the creation of specifically Israelite myths. The view accepted almost everywhere, that in Israelite tradition myth can occur only as an alien influence and not as an indigenous creation,[55] is very convenient for a theology concerned to establish that the heart of the religion of

world view" (p. 202). But he then goes on to say that faith "cannot do without the mythical world view . . . as an assumption". Rather, it is the "foundation of every religion. This basis cannot be rejected" (p. 209). Better justice would be done here to a true understanding of the fundamental significance for religion of what is here called a "mythical world view", if it were distinguished as the religious world view from the more specific phenomenon of myth. There is no agreement in the works of those who have tackled this intellectual problem as to whether or not this is an obsolete world view, even though some of the historical forms it has taken, such as the idea of a divine "breaking" of natural laws, are no longer taken seriously. A decision about the possibility of any religious world view at all is prejudiced on insufficient grounds if it is labelled "mythical" and at the same time described as a world view which in fact is obsolete – the fatal division into three storeys, heaven, earth and the underworld.

[55] On Gunkel see above, pp. 23ff. See also A. Weiser, *Einleitung in das AT* 2nd ed., 1949ff.; ET *Introduction to the Old Testament*, 1961, pp. 57ff.; and Sellin and Rost, *Einleitung in das AT*, 8th ed., 1950, p. 15. In Gerhardt von Rad's commentary on Genesis the concept of "saga" is very prominent (*Das erste Buch Mose*, ATD 2, 1949, pp. 22ff.; ET *Genesis: a Commentary*, 1961, pp. 57ff.) and mythological themes are only discussed in the context of the statement that they have long lost their true mythical sense in the Old Testament (p. 38; cf. pp. 51, 56, 65, 70, 79f., 94, 120f.; ET pp. 47, 61, 63f., 76, 79, 95ff., 111, 139ff.). W. M. Schmidt emphasizes that myth and faith are "foreign" to each other (*Die Schöpfungsgeschichte der Priesterschrift*, 1964, p. 180), and will not even allow that myth may be a possible "form of expression of faith", as J. Hempel suggested ("Glaube, Mythos und Geschichte im AT", *ZAW* 65, 1953, p. 110). In his article "Mythos in Alten Testament", *EvTh* 27, 1967, pp. 237–54, Schmidt admits that Old Testament traditions were "mythical in form" (p. 247), but describes it as characteristic that Israel itself did not create mythical narratives, but only "took over foreign . . . myths in fragmentary form and changed them" (p. 246). It is clear that even Childs regards Gunkel's thesis on this point as so obvious that he does not even discuss it but assumes it throughout his exposition.

revelation is uncontaminated by myth. If myths cannot occur in Israel in the polytheistic form found elsewhere in the ancient Near East, this does not mean that the idea of a primal age on which the present world order is based is not a living element in Israel, and is not represented in certain traditions.

V

Indications that a mythical world view is either actively present or has left traces of its earlier presence can be found in basic features of the understanding of time and space in ancient Israel.[56] A mythical basis of the understanding of time can be seen in the fact that the Hebrew language always describes the future as lying behind the observer, while people have the past "before" them, and look towards the previous era.[57] This previous era of course does not always possess as such the character of a mythical primal age. Whether anything of this kind plays a role in the Israelite understanding of reality cannot be decided by formal observations of linguistic usage, but only be examining the actual content of the tradition. Here it is evident that the attention was directed towards the figures of the patriarchs and towards the events of the entry into the Promised Land, which were fundamental to the existence of the nation, and in many of their features are comparable with the function of the events of the primal age for the mythical understanding of reality. In the case of the stories of the fathers, the main feature is that of the transposing of later experiences

[56] For these two themes, and particularly the latter, cf. Childs, *The Old Testament Categories of Reality*, pp. 72–93. In Childs the discussions of the understanding of time are too exclusively restricted to the correspondence between the primal age and the final age. For the understanding of time in the Old Testament see also G. von Rad, *Theologie des AT* II, 1960, pp. 112ff.; ET *Old Testament Theology* II, 1965, pp. 99ff.

[57] T. Boman, *Das hebräische Denken im Vergleich mit dem griechischen* 3rd ed., 1959, pp. 128f.; ET *Hebrew Thought Compared with Greek*, 1960, pp. 149f. The analogies given by Boman in the non-Israelite, modern experience of time with the possibility implicit in them of using different perspectives to describe the relationship of the future to us, in fact testify how different the Old Testament understanding of time was.

back into the traditions concerning them, beginning with the genealogical link made between the patriarchs Abraham, Isaac and Jacob. Secondly, there is the question of the relationship of the traditions of the fathers to the worship of the gods of the fathers in the pre-Yahwist period of Israel's origins.[58] That the function of some at least of the traditions of the patriarchs was to provide a basis for the cult can be seen from the story of Jacob's dream in Bethel, which provides the basis for the setting up (or adaptation) of a cult for the god of Jacob in Bethel (Gen. 28.18ff). We also hear elsewhere of the patriarchs setting up cults in particular places (Gen. 13.18, etc.). A secondary link between cultic rituals and a patriarchal figure can be found in the tracing back of circumcision to Abraham (Gen. 17). For the Israel of the covenant with Yahweh, however, the traditions of the fathers no longer possessed the mythical function of a primal age which provided the basis for the whole of the present order of life. This function was exercised rather by the traditions of the exodus and the entry into the Promised Land, associated with Moses and Joshua.[59] Here again, particularly in the Sinai passages, we can observe the transposing of later traditions: legal formulae which cannot have come into being until Israel was settled in the Promised Land were transposed back into the situation of the first proclamation of the divine law to Moses, and through Moses, on Sinai. Thus in Israelite legal conceptions what took place at Sinai played the part of a primal age, and fulfilled the function of an event which provided the basis of all later legal practice. In the course of the process of tradition the Sinai narrative grew in an unwieldy fashion, and part of it probably also had a cultic function, particularly in the context of the renewal of the covenant.[60] This seems to have been a repetition of the

[58] For the cult of the gods of the fathers, cf. A.Alt, *Kleine Schriften zur Geschichte des Volkes Israel* I, 1953, pp. 1ff.; ET "The God of the Fathers", *Essays on Old Testament History and Religion*, 1966, pp. 3ff.

[59] The concept of the previous age or primal age is explicitly found in such a sense in Micah. 7.20; Isa. 51.9; Pss. 44.2; 74.2; 77.12; 78.2.

[60] Further details in R. Rendtorff, "Der Kultus im Alten Israel", in *Jahrbuch für Liturgik und Hymnologie* 2 (1956), pp. 1–21, esp. pp. 7f., and also

making of the covenant between Yahweh and Israel at the beginning, *in illo tempore* (Josh. 24). But the time when this covenant was made was not regarded in Israel as the beginning of everything that happened, nor as the beginning of the present order of nature (like the covenant with Noah, Gen. 8.22), but was thought of as an event which took place within history, not at the very beginning, but at the end of a series of events which laid the basis of the nation, and by which they came into possession of their land.[61] Every one of the feasts and the cults of Israel seem either to have consisted from the first of such "memorials", which repeated the fundamental events of the period of the exodus and the entry into the Promised Land, or else to have been later associated with them. The latter case, the "historicization" of rites which existed previously, can be demonstrated in the case of the passover and the harvest festivals.[62] But a "historicization" of this kind is an equivocal argument against a mythical understanding of Israelite cults. Of course it shows that the non-Israelite mythology, originally associated with many rites, was defeated, and these rites appropriated by being traced back to some event

---

in K. Baltzer, *Das Bundesformular*, Neukirchen, 1960, pp. 68f. Baltzer believes that at the early period the renewal of the covenant, understood as a penitential act, could take place at irregular intervals when required, and was not tied to a fixed festival.

[61] Compare what M. Eliade, *The Myth of the Eternal Return*, p. 76, says about the non-historical character of cult associated with myth. Von Rad, *Theologie des AT* II, p. 121; ET, pp. 110f., also referred to this distinction. We must note, however, that even the role of the Egyptian king, which was powerfully influenced by myth and ritual and expressed his function of "creating, maintaining and renewing the ordered world of creation" (E. Hornung, *Geschichte als Fest* 1966, p. 26), left room at least in Egyptian thought for the recognition of events which had "never yet happened since the primal age", and could themselves form the bases of new rituals (*ibid.*, p. 20).

[62] R. Rendtorff, "Kult, Mythos und Geschichte in Alten Israel", in *Sammlung und Sendung* (H. Rendtorff *Festschrift*), 1958, pp. 121ff., sharply distinguished this "historicization" of foreign cult traditions (pp. 127ff.) from the widespread assertion that – particularly in the feast of Tabernacles – Babylonian myths, and especially the myth of creation, were of constitutive importance and were "historicized" in the process (pp. 123ff.). For the passover see the article by Rendtorff quoted in n. 60 above, p. 3.

in the salvation history which legitimized the possession of the land. But this meant that this history itself took on the mythical function of a primal age which provided the basis of the present age.[63] The passage through the Red Sea, the time spent in the wilderness, and the making of the covenant itself, as well as the disobedience and idolatry of the people in the wilderness, became archetypes in the light of which Israel interpreted the experiences of its later history. And yet this history of the nation's origins never lost its contingent, once for all character. The God who had carried out the historical saving acts was also thought of as the creator of the world and man, but in only a few hymns and prophetic poems are these two groups of themes drawn into one. Thus the saving acts of God remained the expression of his choice and his desire to make a covenant with men; they did not become a constituent part of the unchangeable establishment of the world as a whole, and it was possible to believe that in the future course of history their outcome remained at stake. This is the assumption on which the prophetic proclamations of judgment were possible; they created an awareness that the salvation which the nation possessed was historical in nature and could therefore be lost. There were tendencies opposed to the prophets which can be perceived only indirectly in the texts which have come down to us, because they were excluded from later tradition as a result of the political catastrophes that overcame the two Israelite states; they regarded the salvation which the people possessed – the possession of the land in particular, but also the existence of the kingdom – as something final which they could never lose. It is not impossible that in these traditions the facts of the history of salvation were more closely associated with the mythical creation of the world. There are indications of this in the specific cult traditions of Jerusalem.[64] It would be par-

[63] J. Hempel, "Glaube, Mythos und Geschichte im Alten Testament" *ZAW* 65, 1953, pp. 113ff., speaks of a mythologizing of history in a different sense, with reference to the interpretation of the event of the exodus in the language of the creation myth.

[64] See H. Schmid, "Jahwe und die Kulttradition von Jerusalem", *ZAW* 67 (1955), pp. 168–97.

ticularly interesting if in fact the Jewish New Year feast could be understood on the analogy of the Babylonian, as a renewal of time, and therefore of the creation, in the form of the annual renewal of the enthronement of Yahweh himself. But conjectures in this direction have remained subject to dispute.[65] The distinction between the creation of man and the world at the beginning and the saving historical acts of Yahweh's election in the events of the patriarchal age, the exodus from Egypt and the entry of the Israelite tribes into the Promised Land, remains fundamental to the Israelite understanding of time. The continual awareness of the historical contingency of these events means that there are limits upon the extent to which they can be taken as a mythical primal age. This explains why the devout in ancient Israel, particularly in the prophetic period, did not regard the final age simply as a return to the primal age, either to the age of the creation with its life in paradise, or to the age of the divine ordinances of salvation in history, but rather as the excelling and bringing to surpassing perfection of all that had previously existed, as the period of a *new* exodus (Isa. 43.16ff.), and a new covenant (Jer. 31.31ff.), a new David (Jer. 30.9, cf. Hosea 3.5, Ezek. 34.23) and a new paradise which he would introduce (Isa. 11.6ff.), and ultimately a new creation, in which "the former things shall not be remembered" because they are superseded (Isa. 65.17).[66]

[65] This thesis was developed above all by S. Mowinckel in his *Psalmen-studien* II, 1922 (cf. also *Religion und Kultus* (German trans.), 1953, pp. 73ff.). A summary of the discussion and a criticism of this thesis can be found in W. H. Schmidt, *Konigtum Gottes in Ugarit und Israel*, 2nd ed., 1966, pp. 74ff.

[66] B. S. Childs discusses at length the question whether the correspondence between the final age and the primal age, to which ancient Israel looked forward, was the expression of a cyclical understanding of reality based on myth, as has often been asserted since Gunkel (*Schöpfung und Chaos in Urzeit und Endzeit*). In addition to the fact that the historicity of the event of salvation in the Israelite consciousness is only adequate in a qualified sense for the function of a primal age, he also points out that "the relationship of *Urzeit* to *Endzeit* is not one of simply identity" (*Myth and Reality in the Old Testament*, pp. 77ff.). Besides statements which imply an eschatological exaggeration of everything that has previously existed, and which are particularly characterized by the occasional explicit affirma-

Like the understanding of time, the conception of space in the Old Testament is still close to mythical thought. For the mythical consciousness the homogeneity of time is not possible because a "primal age" is specially distinguished, and because there is a constant possibility of making it a present reality in the cult. In the same way, space is not homogeneous, because a sacred revelation has made one place the "centre" of the world, by which secular reality is linked with the divine sphere, and where therefore gives this reality the structure of a "world" or cosmos.[67] In ancient Jewish thought the city of Jerusalem, Mount Zion and the house of Yahweh there, the temple, had had this function since the time of the kings. In Isaiah in particular, as well as elsewhere (e.g. Ps. 46.5; 48.3ff.; 50.2) a tradition can be seen at work that Jerusalem with Mount Zion, Yahweh's dwelling place (Isa. 8.18) is his people's impregnable place of refuge: "Yahweh has founded Zion, and in her the afflicted of his people find refuge"[68] (14.32). Yahweh protects his holy mountain against the attacks of the nations (Isa. 17.12ff.; cf. 10.12,32; 29.7f.; 31.5). In these traditions, and especially in the conception of the mountain of God *in the extreme north*, a conception associated with Zion, although not very appropriate to it within the framework of the geography of Israel (Ps. 48.3; cf. Isa. 14.13), we can see traces of pre-Israelite conceptions originally deriving from northern Syria.[69] A high mountain as the dwelling of the gods, as the place where

---

tion that people will no longer remember what has gone before (Isa. 65.17; cf. Isa. 48.6; 43.18, as well as Jer. 23.7f. and 3.16ff.), there are others which merely announce the return of the circumstances of the past (Jer. 30.20; 33.7; Amos. 9, 11, 14).

[67] An idealizing and generalizing account of this view is given by Mircea Eliade in *The Sacred and the Profane*, pp. 36ff.

[68] Von Rad devoted a separate section to the Zion tradition in Isaiah in his *Theologie des AT* II, pp. 166–79; ET pp. 155–69. For the general background in the tradition see Vol. I, 1957, pp. 54ff., ET Vol. I, 1962, pp. 46ff. The analogy to the mythical understanding of space is discussed in Childs, *op. cit.*, pp. 84f.

[69] As shown by O. Eissfeldt, *Baal Zaphon*, 1932, pp. 5f. See also W. H. Schmidt, *Königtum Gottes in Ugarit und Israel*, pp. 32ff: "Der Gottesberg im Norden".

the earth comes into contact with the world of heaven, is a theme widely found in mythology. Paradise too, the Garden of Eden, seems to have been thought of in Israel as a mountain of the gods in the middle of the world, from which the streams of water which fructifed the whole earth went out.[70] But in the pre-exilic period Israel did not regard the distinctive function of Zion as something established in the primal age, but as the expression of an historical act of choice by Yahweh (cf. Pss. 78.68; 132.13ff.). This again is an expression of Israel's specific awareness of history. Isaiah anticipates that Zion will not be the "highest of the mountains" and "raised above the hills" (Isa. 2.2.), so that the nations come in pilgrimage to it, until the future age of salvation comes.[71] In Ezekiel, too, Jerusalem is addressed as the world navel, the centre of the earth (38.12), only in the context of eschatological prophecies.[72] The mythical interpretation goes a step further when Mount Zion is identified with the Garden of Eden, the site of paradise.[73] Here again the context is usually that of the imaginative portrayal of eschatological expectations, but they are represented here as the return of the primal age. A similar tendency can be observed in the history of the Chronicler, where Zion is linked with the patriarchal history and identified as the place where Abraham set out to sacrifice Isaac (II Chron. 31.1).[74] This tendency,

[70] W. Zimmerli, *Ezechiel*, 1969, pp. 1192ff., cf. p. 997.

[71] For the subsequent history of the eschatological theme of the pilgrimage of the nations to Zion in Deutero- and Trito-Isaiah, Haggai, Zechariah, Zephaniah and Revelation, cf. von Rad., *op. cit.*, Vol. II, pp. 307ff.; ET Vol. II, pp. 294ff.

[72] For the mythical background of this formula see Zimmerli, *Ezechiel*, pp. 955ff. The theme is also found in Judg. 9.37, when it likewise refers to a mountain, perhaps to Gerizim. The range of this theme in comparative religion has been described by W. H. Roscher, *Omphalos*, 1913, and *Der Omphalosgedanke bei verschiedenen Völkern*, 1918. The influence of the mythical interpretation of the hill of Golgotha in Christian tradition by this idea has been studied by J. Jeremias, *Golgotha*, 1926. Cf. Childs, *op. cit.*, pp. 85ff.

[73] References in Childs, *op. cit.*, pp. 86ff.

[74] Referring to other similar statements in Chronicles, Childs affirms: "The mythical tendency within later Judaism to project Zion back into the *Urzeit* and reinterpret history to reflect its central role only goes to emphasize the non-mythological character of the original Zion tradition" (p. 90).

however, reaches its ultimate conclusion, the linking of Zion
with creation itself, as its beginning and starting point,
only in later Jewish literature. Thus we read in the tractate
Yoma that the creation of the world began with Zion.[75] The
theme occurs again in Christian literature. Here the hill of
Golgotha replaced Zion as the central point of the earth.[76] The
cross of Christ, it was said, was set up at the very place where
Adam lay buried, so that the redeeming blood of Christ would
sprinkle his skull.[77] Here we have a "remythologization",
though no doubt meant in only a symbolic sense, and also, as
we shall show, fragmented by the comparison of type and
antitype. It can be explained by the fact that the mythical
conceptions of the mountain of God and the centre of the world
were in some way understood as of value, and used, for the
exposition of faith in the salvation history of the choosing of
Zion by Yahweh, and in the cosmic significance of the event
of the crucifixion of Christ. But in earlier Jewish literature the
inner logic of the mythical conception of space was broken
down by the abandonment of the essential connection with the
primal age. Instead of this, the historical choosing of Zion by
Yahweh is the point of reference for all other statements, and its
function as the centre of the world and the place of salvation is
reserved for the eschatological future. At the present time the
setting apart of Jerusalem and Zion as the dwelling place of
Yahweh protects both against the arrogance of human enemies,
but not against a visitation from Yahweh himself, who can
make use of the enemy's weapons. Thus even Isaiah was able
to proclaim Yahweh's anger against Zion (Isa. 29.1ff.), although for Isaiah this could not be the last word (cf. v.8). On

---

[75] J. Jeremias, *Golgotha*, p. 54; cf. also W. Roscher, *Neue Omphalosstudien*,
1915, pp. 16f., 73f., and A. J. Wensinck, *The Ideas of the Western Semites
concerning the Navel of the Earth*, Amsterdam, 1916, p. 15.

[76] Ps.-Cyprian, *Carmen de Pascha vel de ligno vitae*, ed. G. Hartel (CSEL 3),
1968, pp. 305–8, quoted in H. Rahner, *Griechische Mythen in christlicher
Deutung* (1957), 3rd ed., 1966, p. 69; ET *Greek Myths and Christian Mystery*,
1963, p. 62. Further references there.

[77] This theme, which is found in representations of the crucifixion, has
been found by H. Rahner in the Ethiopian Book of Adam, *op. cit.*, p. 70.

the other hand, Micah (3.12) and later Jeremiah (21.4ff.) were able to prophesy the fall of Jerusalem and even of the temple (Jer. 26.6). Later still, the association of Zion with the patriarchal history and paradise gave an unbroken continuity with the mythical events of the primal age. The Christian replacement of Zion by the hill of Golgotha differs from this because it relates Christ as antitype to Adam, whose sin was overcome by the sacrificial death of Christ.

Seen as a whole, the mythical experience of space does not seem to have had any more fundamental a power over the consciousness of Israel than the mythical relationship to time. Statements about the significance of Jerusalem which used mythical forms of thought always assume a non-mythical starting point in the consciousness of the choice of Jerusalem by Yahweh for his dwelling which took place in history, in the time of David. On the other hand, it was only in the course of Israel's history that Israelite thought became liberated from the formal pattern of a primal age which determined everything; and this liberation was never complete. Only the prophets succeeded in disassociating belief in Yahweh from the primal age, the exodus and the entry into the Promised Land, which provided the basis for the life of the people and the way it was ordered. In so doing, they directed it towards a future action of Yahweh in history. But this in its turn could only be interpreted in the images handed down by tradition, so that eschatological language is exposed to the misunderstanding that there is a qualitative identification of the primal age and the final age, an identification guaranteed in genuine myth.

VI

A distinction similar to that between the effective presence of the mythical experience of time and of the mythical conception of space, can perhaps also be seen in a comparison between the two institutional spheres in which mythical thought forms were particularly persistent, the cult and the monarchy; and it is no accident that this should be so. We can ignore here the kings of the northern kingdom. They seem to have required charismatic authentication by prophets to a considerable degree, whereas the continuity of the dynasty of David was a characteristic of the Jerusalem monarchy. There are very interesting indications of the theological understanding of this monarchy in the Old Testament texts. The kings of Jerusalem regarded themselves as representatives of the rule of God not only over Israel, but over the world of the nations as a whole. In this sense they were solemnly addressed as the "son" of Yahweh at their coronation (Ps. 2.7; cf. II Sam. 7.14), and on this they based at least in theory a claim to be rulers over the whole world (Ps. 2.8f.; cf. Ps. 110.1f.). "The throne of Yahweh and of his anointed were inseparable – indeed, in the light of Ps. cx. 1f, they were really one."[78] But the view of many scholars, that the Jerusalem monarchy and "the" divine kingship of the ancient Near East are similar, has been rejected for convincing reasons.[79] The historical memory of the late origin of the monarchy, and the requirement that every change in the monarch, even if it took place according to dynastic rules, had to be approved by the people,[80] make this view unlikely. In these circumstances it would be difficult for the king to be understood as a divine king in the sense of the Egyptian monarchy, where the ruling monarch was regarded as the living Horus and the son in the bodily sense of Re. But even the less advanced conception of the king as the son of God in the Mesopotamian region[81] cannot be applied without reservation to the circumstances of Judaea. Here the monarchy represented a relatively short historical episode, and the circumstances in which it came into being and its dependence upon the popular will were still alive in the tradition, and in addition a more or less vigorous critical judgment upon the kings

---

[78] G. von Rad, *Theologie des AT* I, p. 54; ET Vol. I, p. 46.

[79] M. Noth, "Gott, König und Volk im AT" *Gesammelte Studien zum AT*, 1957, pp. 188–229; ET "God, King and Nation in the Old Testament", *The Laws in the Pentateuch and Other Essays*, 1966, pp. 145–78.

[80] Noth, *op. cit.*, p. 217; ET p. 168.

[81] The difference between this and the Egyptian monarchy has been described by H. Frankfort, *Kingship and the Gods*, Chicago, 1948.

remained possible and was in fact effective throughout the period of the monarchy. As a consequence, the mythical elements in the conception of the kingship which are found in the Old Testament cannot be taken as indications of a genuinely mythical understanding of the monarchy, but merely as attempts to interpret in different terms an institution the roots of which lay not in myth, but in the idea of divine election.[82] This, however, inevitably raises the question of the function that the mythical elements could have had with regard to a monarchy which was legitimized in this way. The necessary attention has not always been paid by Old Testament scholars to questions of this kind. Their concern has often been too limited to the questions whether Old Testament conceptions are to be derived from mythical themes, or whether instead the mythical material has been adapted to the Israelite traditions of the history of salvation. But a methodical approach requires in addition a study of the positive function which makes plausible the retention or even the introduction of mythical conceptions into the complex of ideas which provided the motivation for Israel's tradition of the history of salvation. The idea of adaptation to the existing views of the age is insufficient, for it cannot explain why such an adaptation took place in one case but not in another. Whenever a conception cannot be explained as the expression of a dependence upon a mythical understanding of the world that is still taken for granted, we must ask what it contributes to the particular concern, motivated by the whole complex of Israelite tradition, which is found in each particular text. With regard to the Jewish monarchy it is very likely that the conception of the king as the "son" of God who represents the world dominion of Yahweh himself upon earth is an expression of a concrete claim to

---

[82] Noth's view (*op. cit.*, p. 222; ET p. 172), that the declaration that the sons of David are "sons of God", at their enthronement provides, because of its peculiar nature as a formula of *adoption*, the basis of a fundamental distinction by comparison with the Egyptian and Mesopotamian understanding of the king, seems less certain, since the idea of an adoption and of "divine origin and nature" are not as mutually exclusive as a modern understanding might suppose.

empire which for a single moment in the history of the world, in the situation in which the empire of David came into being, could have seemed meaningful, and was maintained by David's successors as a memory and an obligation.[83] As in the case of the tradition concerning Zion, the substance of which is closely related, the mythical conception – in this case that of divine sonship, as of the mountain of God in the other case – was used to formulate a claim which had its basis in the idea of the historical choosing of David by Yahweh, but was raised by the language of the myth to an ideal and universal level, with an intensity which could not be achieved in any other way. This was particularly so in that the claim of the descendants of David could be put forward as a reality which already existed in the ordering of the world, and this was expressed in the same conceptual form as was used in the thinking of the neighbouring peoples, against whom this claim was directed. The one isolated instance in the Old Testament in which the king is addressed as God (*'elōhīm*), Ps. 45.7, which is the main piece of evidence for the acceptance of an ideology of divine kingship in Israel, can be understood as an expression of panegyric courtly language.

In the cult we find a quite different picture. Here mythical forms of thought are clearly not only used to interpret institutions and traditions which have a historical basis, but have a constitutive function. This is true above all of the conception of the events of the primal age, which are celebrated in the cult. This state of affairs has been already discussed with regard to the understanding of time. It is characteristic of the Israelite understanding of the cult that its festivals and rites are rooted in the history of salvation. But this is not of itself an argument against the mythical meaning of such cultic actions, in so far as in them historical or allegedly historical events took over the function of events in the primal age which provided the basis of the present order. Where this function is not based upon the

---

[83] A. Alt, "Die Deutung der Weltgeschichte im AT", *ZThK* 56, 1959, pp. 129ff., similarly described David's empire as the historical origin of Israel's awareness of world history.

historical significance of the events concerned, but appears directly as their essential content, the mythical view is no longer a device to interpret the historical event, but has replaced its historical meaning. Of course in any given case it is not easy to tell whether such a replacement has come about. Thus for example the eating of unleavened bread in the originally Canaanite *mazzōth* feast, at which originally "the first produce of the land was offered for the cultic consecration of the harvest and eaten still uncontaminated by the addition of leaven" at the beginning of the corn harvest,[84] was related by the Yahwist to the hasty exodus of the Israelites from Egypt, and in this way incorporated into Israel's tradition of the history of salvation (Ex. 12.34–39). This raises the question whether its celebration in Israel had the significance of a cultic repetition and a making present of the events of the exodus, so that its rooting in the history of salvation had the function of a cultic myth, or whether it is no more than a secondary explanatory, a cult-aetiological narrative, which had replaced the original cult myth, but without taking over its function in the ritual itself. Similar questions can be asked about the passover, which was originally an apotropaic rite, perhaps of nomadic origin, which in Israel was related to the situation of the exodus from Egypt, and particularly to the tradition that as Yahweh went about Egypt on the night of the exodus as a death-dealing demon and killed the first born of men and animals, he spared the Israelites, whose houses he passed over because they were protected by the passover blood on the lintels and posts of their doors (Ex. 12.12f., 23ff.). Here it is in fact probable that the passover – perhaps celebrated in its original nomadic form particularly when wandering shepherds moved territory to protect their family and their herds – was celebrated in Israel "as a constantly repeated cultic representation of the one great 'departure', namely the departure from Egypt". This will explain why the "preparedness of the participants for the march which was maintained even when

[84] M. Noth, *Das zweite Buch Mose* (ATD 5), 1958, p. 76; ET *Exodus: a Commentary*, 1962, p. 97.

Israel had become a settled nation",[85] is a notable feature of it:

In this manner you shall eat it: your loins girded, your sandals on your feet, and your staff in your hand; and you shall eat it in haste. It is Yahweh's passover. (Ex. 12.11).

It is clear here that the legitimation in the history of salvation has not merely the significance of a cult-aetiology, but is functioning as a regular cult myth. This may have changed at a later period, when the rite was no longer carried out as a repetition of the original situation, but merely as an act of obedience to a divine command to remember the historical occasion.

The (annual?) repetition of the conclusion of Yahweh's covenant with the people at the renewal of the covenant may also have had a mythical significance,[86] although the tradition of the making of the covenant at the time of Joshua (Josh. 24) was not mythical in nature, but rather possesses the character of an historical narrative, and although the repeated affirmation of an historical origin can be non-mythical in meaning, if this repeated affirmation is not meant to have any identity with the original event. But it seems that the intention in Israel was that at the renewal of the covenant later generations should enter into the original situation of the covenant with Yahweh (Deut. 27.9).[87] The mythical form of an identical repetition is probably in general the most obvious and most powerful form available for the consciousness of historical continuity. But when it is used, this continuity is in fact no longer thought of as historical, but is maintained in spite of the march of history, bridging over the historical gap which divides the present time more and more from the origin which has made it what it is.

Whereas in the previous examples we have looked at traditions which in their content cannot be identified as mythical at all, but take on mythical significance only with regard to the

---

[85] *Ibid.*, p. 71; cf. the whole passage, pp. 68 ff.; ET pp. 91, 87ff.

[86] Rendtorff, "Der Kultus im Alten Israel" (see n. 60 above), pp. 7f.

[87] Also Deut. 26.16–19; cf. G. von Rad. *Deuteronomiumstudien*, 1947, p. 49; ET *Studies in Deuteronomy*, 1953, p. 70; *Das fünfte Buch Mose* (ATD 8), 1964, pp. 118f. and 114; ET *Deuteronomy: a Commentary*, 1966, pp. 165f. and 161.

function which they perform in cultic life, the situation is otherwise with the institution of the sabbath. One of the Old Testament texts which gives a basis of the commandment to keep the sabbath refers only to the significance of the seventh day as a day of rest (Ex. 23.12). But the second goes further, and links it with the history of salvation by recalling that in Egypt the Israelites themselves had to work as slaves and should therefore understand that even the members of their household and their slaves need rest. (Deut. 5.14f.). But the third text gives an explicitly mythological basis for the commandment of sabbath rest:

In six days Yahweh made heaven and earth, the sea, and all that is in them, and rested the seventh day; therefore Yahweh blessed the sabbath day and hallowed it. (Ex. 20.11)

Man ought to do what God himself did at the beginning: a basic theme of mythological thought which is all the more significant here in that it is concerned with the basis for the rhythm of time represented in the week. This secondary expansion of the commandment concerning the sabbath in the decalogue[88] assumes the existence of the relatively late creation narrative of the priestly document, which in its turn, by its representation of the creation as the work of seven days, conceived of the divine creation as the underlying pattern of the rhythm of time represented by the week. Since the seven-day week originated in Babylon and corresponds to the seven planet gods which in turn rule the days of the week, the tracing back of the week to Yahweh's act of creation must be regarded as a statement of opposition to Babylonian astral mythology,[89] an opposition which is also expressed in the reduction of the stars to a subordinate function as creatures in Gen. 1.14ff. But the result is merely the replacement of the foreign myth by a different but equally mythical basis for the week and the

[88] Cf. M. Noth, *Das zweite Buch Mose*, p. 132; ET *Exodus*, p. 164.

[89] The seven-day pattern was not imposed upon the creation narrative of the priestly writing until later (W. H. Schmidt, *Die Schöpfungsgeschichte der Priesterschrift*, 1964, pp. 67f.), probably not until the period of the exile (p. 72), which provided a direct opportunity for a reaction against the basing of the week upon astral mythology.

sabbath.[90] That the mythical idea of a periodical renewal of
time to be carried out in the cult was not unknown to Israel is
implied not only by the New Year feast, although we have
little firm evidence for the form this took in Israel,[91] but also
by the distinctive practice of the sabbath year, a fallow kept
every seven years. M. Noth suspected that this ordinance –
and also the sabbath, because of its close connection with it –
contained the idea of "a 'return to the original state', a *restitutio
in integrum* which is to be effected at certain intervals".[92]

Another form of mythical thought was retained in Israel in
connection with the cult, and this was the basing of cultic
institutions on a heavenly pattern. Just as King Gudea of
Lagash was given instructions for the building of a temple in a
dream by the goddess Nidaba[93] and carried out the building of
his temple according to divine guidance,[94] so, according to
Ex. 24.9, Yahweh showed Moses on Sinai a model of the
tabernacle and its sacred furnishings, according to which they
were all constructed (cf. also Ex. 25.40). According to the
Chronicler's history David showed his son Solomon a model of
the temple, which he was to build in accordance with "the
writing from the hand of Yahweh" (I Chron. 28.19), and the
prophet Ezekiel received in exile in Babylon, through a vision,
an exact picture of the new temple which was to be built,
including every detail (Ezek. 40ff.), and Yahweh himself
commanded him to make known this model to the people

[90] Schmidt, *op. cit.*, pp. 185ff., considers that myth has been "abandoned"
here. This view is possible only because he assumes a one-sided conception
of the timelessness of myth (*ibid.*) and overlooks the fact that this timelessness implies that the events of the primal age effectively exist at any and
every time.

[91] Cf. also n. 65. For the New Year feast compare the discussion by
Noth, *Das dritte Buch Mose* (ATD 6), 1962, pp. 150f.; ET *Leviticus: a Commentary*, 1965, pp. 172ff. According to Noth the "Great Day of Atonement"
in Lev. 16 was originally associated with the turn of the year, "for a great
atonement was peculiarly fitting at this particular season" (p. 151; ET
p. 173).

[92] M. Noth, *Das zweite Buch Mose*, pp. 153f.; ET *Exodus*, pp. 153f.

[93] E. Burrows, in *The Labyrinth*, ed. S. Hooke, London, 1935, pp.
65ff.

[94] *ANET*, p. 268.

(43.10ff.).[95] Not only the origin of the temple but also its furnishings show mythical characteristics in important details. This is certainly true of the bronze sea set up in the courtyard (I Kings 7.22ff.), which in spite of its later innocent interpretation as a wash basin (II Chron. 4.6), must originally have represented the primeval sea, and has repeatedly aroused speculation concerning the role of the Babylonian creation myth in the cult of the Jerusalem temple. Even the seven-branched lampstand would have been mythological in significance, as the world tree rising out of chaos (cf. the sea monster carved on its base) and bearing the lights of the seven planets, the "eyes of Yahweh, which range through the whole earth" (Zech. 4.10).[96] The mythological connections of other parts of the temple furnishing, such as the two pillars at the entrance of the temple, and the twelve oxen on which the bronze sea stood, and the cherubim (I Kings 6.23ff.; 7.15ff.,25.) is less certain. Apart from the Jerusalem temple and its furnishings, the mythical themes in the cultic sphere do not represent in the first instance the adoption of foreign mythical material, but an attitude to the content of authentic Israelite tradition which takes a mythological form. The result of this is that in the cultic sector mythical themes have a constitutive function, in contrast to the role of myth as an interpretative vehicle for traditions of non-mythical origin which we saw in the sphere of the monarchy. However, the mythical sub-structures of cultic life came to be overlaid by the later tendency to legalist observance, in so far as cultic actions

[95] For the symbolical significance of these steps, particularly the disposition of the temple as the seventh building after a passage through twice three gates (corresponding to the seventh day of the week of creation) and for the number twenty-five as half the period of seven times seven years which had expired in the exile in Babylon at the time of the prophet's vision, and which according to Israelite law (Lev. 25) were to be followed by a year of liberation and a remission of debts, and the restoration of the original conditions, something which had clearly become for the prophet the starting point of the hope of salvation for the exiles, see Zimmerli, *Ezechiel*, pp. 992ff., 1020.

[96] Further details in the article "Menora" in *RGG* 4, 3rd ed., 1960, col. 859, and in the bibliography there. See also Gunkel, *Schöpfung und Chaos*, pp. 124f.

continued to be carried out for the sake of obedience to commandments of Yahweh for which a reason could no longer be given. This happened even when their original mythical meaning had been forgotten.

VII

This essay can give no more than a superficial impression of the use of mythical material in the literature of ancient Israel. The study of comparative religion in the late nineteenth and early twentieth centuries first recognized the extent to which Babylonian mythology in particular supplied the imagery even of ancient Israel and found its way into traditional sagas as well as into the language of hymns and poetry.[97] This material consists in particular of conceptions associated with creation, with paradise and the flood, with the building of the tower of Babel and the dispersal of the nations – that is, materials from the primeval history which the Yahwist, and the priestly document after him, used to precede the account of the history of salvation in the proper sense, which began with the choosing of Abraham.[98] However, the two versions of the creation narrative themselves show great reserve with regard to the mythical elements in their material. Thus in the priestly creation narrative (Gen. 1) all dualistic conceptions of the battle of the gods against the chaos dragon from whose body the cosmos was formed are carefully excluded.[99] Besides the

[97] Gunkel above all, in his book *Schöpfung und Chaos in Urzeit and Endzeit*, and in his commentaries on Genesis and Psalms, drew attention to the overwhelming amount of mythical quotations and allusions of every possible kind in the saga material, and in the prophetic poems and hymns of Israel, although he placed too much emphasis on the influence of Babylonian mythology.

[98] For the significance of the Yahwist primeval history cf. von Rad, *Das erste Buch Mose*, pp. 15f.; ET pp. 22f.; and R. Rendtorff, "Genesis 8.21 und die Urgeschichte des Jahwisten", *Kerygma und Dogma* 7, 1961, pp. 69–78.

[99] Von Rad, *op. cit.*, p. 62; ET p. 48. Childs, *op. cit.*, pp. 42–6 very elegantly demonstrates how the Yahwist "retained the demonic character of the snake, arising out of the myth, but affirmed that he was a mere creature under God's power" (p. 48), so that he can speak of "broken myth".

conception of the divine word working magically, the idea of a primal age of the foundation of the world, with the world coming into being completely at the beginning, is also mythical. But by being incorporated into the chronology of the priestly document, the character of the creation narrative as the account of a primal age lost the possibility of being repeated in the cult; it became an event which was definitively in the past, and in precisely this way provided the basis of the later history of the world. It thus lost the essential feature of myth, the ability, as the events of the primal age, at the same time to be present in any age through the events of the cult.[100] What we have here, then, is a historicization of myth.[101] The same is true of the Yahwist story of paradise (Gen. 2–3). Here again the myth has been "broken".[102] The conceptions of the golden age and of

[100] I am grateful to my colleague O.H. Steck for this suggestion.

[101] Whether any such historicization in present in Gen. 6.1–4 is very doubtful, because there are objections in general against classifying as myth the explanation of the origin of heroes from the union of gods with human wives. Although this tradition, which lies behind Gen. 6, is repeatedly taken as a typical example of the existence of myth and its adaptation in the Old Testament (especially in W. A. Schmidt, "Mythos im Alten Testament", 27, 1967, pp. 237–54, esp. pp. 243ff.; cf. also Childs, *op. cit.*, pp. 49f.), and although it shows particularly clearly the way this material is transformed when it is incorporated into Israelite thought, the tradition it assumes lacks the characteristics of a myth providing the original pattern and basis of the present order and celebrated in the cult. Although in other contexts the divine origin of a particular hero may have a mythical significance – that is, if the hero himself is understood as the mythical originator of present ordinances – the tradition assumed in Gen. 6 has itself an aetiological starting point in the question of the origin of the heroes themselves – and consequently it cannot be a myth, but only an aetiological saga (cf. above n. 66). That myth and stories of the gods are not identical means that a myth is not always present where there are stories about gods.

[102] The discussions of the relationship of the act of creation to chaos in Childs, *Myth and Reality*, pp. 30–42, confirm in their conclusion (p. 42) von Rad's affirmation on Gen. 1.1ff. that the relationship to chaos (*tehōm*) reflects "what man has always suspected, that behind all creation lies the abyss of formlessness, further that all creation is always ready to sink into the abyss of the formless, that the chaos, therefore, signifies simply the threat to everything created" (*Das erste Buch Mose*, p. 38; ET *Genesis*, p. 49). But against von Rad's view that "the actual mythical meaning . . . has long been lost" (*ibid.*), we must stress that what "man has always sus-

paradise as the dwelling of God in the centre of the world and the place where all earthly fertility continues to originate lie in the background, but do not form the theme. In the account of paradise the mythical elements serve the purpose of an aetiological narrative which is intended to explain the origin of the desire of man and woman for each other, and the reason for the pains of childbirth, the weariness of work and the meagre products of agriculture. Here the case which provides the example underlies an aetiological narrative which must be distinguished from true myth, for its explanatory purpose is alien to myth (cf. above p. 5). The mythical themes are drawn into the framework provided by the aetiological intention merely as vehicles of expression, and in this case largely as a foil to offset against the present reality of existence. In order to explain the present arduous situation of man the contrasting picture of a different and better form of life is drawn; it is conceived of in a mythical fashion as the original form, and portrayed as a paradise, the continued enjoyment of which man forfeited by his behaviour. It would not be possible to represent this lost perfection without the mythical features. But they were regarded as belonging definitively to the past. The events narrated are not mythical as far as the narrator is concerned – it was later Jewish exegesis and the church's doctrine of the state of primal innocence and the fall which first took the aetiological saga as a myth. However, it is impossible to deny that the figure of Adam, man himself, who together with Eve, "the mother of all living" (Gen. 3.20) is the representative of all men, possesses mythical features. But within the framework of the Yahwist history, Adam is now no more than the historical first man, and no longer a representative example of all later humanity. For this goes beyond its beginnings in Adam by way

---

pected" in this way is a basic mythical theme, although here it only in fact provides a foil for the divine action and receives no dramatic development (p. 37; ET p. 48). Its mythical sense has fallen into the background only in so far as the priestly source limits this fundamental experience exclusively to the situation at the beginning of creation, and has therefore deprived it of its relevance to the present day.

of the figures of Noah, Abraham, the other patriarchs and Moses.

The conception of the golden age and the pattern of life in paradise is also found in other biblical texts. Thus the prophecy of salvation in Isaiah 11 (it is doubtful whether it derives from Isaiah himself) describes the future age of the Messiah in the idyllic colours of paradise:

> The wolf shall dwell with the lamb,
> and the leopard shall lie down with the kid,
> and the calf and the lion and the fatling together,
> and a little child shall lead them. (Isa. 11.6)

The deadly conflict in the animal world, as well as that between animals and man, will be overcome. This theme from the picture of the primal age in paradise has here become the content of the eschatological hope of future perfection.[103] Underlying this is not the conception of a necessary correspondence between the final age and the primal age in accordance with the cosmic order (cf. n.66). Instead, the mythical theme is used to elaborate the significance for salvation of the historical hope of the restoration of the temple or of a true descendant of David on the throne of Jerusalem. Once again we have an example of the way in which the mythical images are used to express the universal significance of a historical phenomenon – in this case, a phenomenon expected in the future.

We find themes from the Babylonian creation myth in a large number of Old Testament texts as literary allusions, though

[103] Childs, *op. cit.*, pp. 63ff., emphasizes in Isa. 11.6ff. the untroubled incorporation of the originally mythical "fanciful description" into the thought of the prophet. "The material in its present state has lost its purpose within myth and assumed a new role" (p. 65). But this change of function must be understood as the result of the association of originally mythical themes with an historical future expectation. The same is true of texts which take up the theme in the description of paradise of luxurious vegetation, flourishing without cultivation, in the context of eschatological promises, such as Ezek. 47.12, Joel 4.18 and a later addition to the book of Amos (9.13). In Ezekiel and Joel this fruitfulness is the effect of a spring or stream which is to rise in the future in the temple hill (cf. Rev. 22.1f.), while in Amos 9.13, as in Isa. 11, it is related to the political hope of the renewal of the Davidic monarchy.

mostly through the medium of the Canaanite myth of Baal. In particular, the theme of the struggle with the sea-dragon, which in Babylon is attributed to the god Marduk and is celebrated as his act of creation, is associated with features of a theophany in a storm, but has no explicit link with the act of creation. This is explained by the Ugaritic variant of the Babylonian myth, which attributes to the storm and thunder god Baal the struggle with the sea, but not the creation of the world, which is reserved to the older god El.[104] Although in Israel this conflict with the dragon and the creation are once again attributed to a single god, Yahweh, features of the Baal myth are still recognizable in the mythical allusions of the Psalms. Here reminiscences of the myth serve to elaborate the historical events which were fundamental for Israel, particularly in the account of the passage through the sea at the exodus from Egypt:

> Thou didst with thy arm redeem thy people,
>> the sons of Jacob and Joseph.
> When the waters saw thee, O God,
>> when the waters saw thee, they were afraid,
>> yea, the deep trembled.
> The clouds poured out water;
>> the skies gave forth thunder;
>> thy arrows flashed on every side.
> The crash of thy thunder was in the whirlwind;
>> thy lightnings lighted up the world;
>> the earth trembled and shook.
> Thy way was through the sea,
>> thy path through the great waters;
>> yet thy footprints were unseen.
> Thou didst lead thy people like a flock
>> by the hand of Moses and Aaron. (Ps. 77.15–20)[105]

[104] Whereas Gunkel saw all reminiscences of a conflict with the dragon in the Old Testament as allusions to a Babylonian creation epic, the discovery of the Ugaritic texts from Ras Shamra has made a more varied interpretation possible. Thus W. H. Schmidt (*Königtum Gottes in Ugarit und Israel*, pp. 46ff.), following O. Kaiser (*Die mythische Bedeutung des Meeres in Ägypten, Ugarit und Israel*, 1959), emphasizes the distinctions between the Babylonian myth of Tiamat and the Ugaritic myth of the struggle of Baal against the sea (*yām*).

[105] See also Ex. 14.26ff. Clearer allusions to the creation, and incidentally to the Babylonian version of the myth, are to be found in Ps. 89.10ff.:

Deutero-Isaiah, looking forward to the imminent liberation of the exiles from Babylon, used the language of the myth of the conflict with the dragon to evoke in a particularly impressive way the memory of the ancient saving acts of Yahweh, and especially of the saving of Israel from the Egyptian pursuers as they passed through the Red Sea:

> Awake, as in days of old,
>   the generations of long ago.
> Was it not thou that didst cut Rahab in pieces,
>   that didst pierce the dragon?
> Was it not thou that didst dry up the sea,
>   the waters of the great deep;
>   that didst make the depths of the sea a way
>   for the redeemed to pass over? (Isa. 51.9f.)

In itself such a text hardly allows us to decide whether the mythical themes are being quoted simply in order to interpret the history of salvation, or whether they create salvation history for the first time by transposing historical facts into the light of a mythical primal age.[106] But a knowledge of the context of the message of Deutero-Isaiah, and particularly his emphasis on the unparalleled novelty of the future event which he proclaims (Isa. 42.9; 43.18ff.), shows that the mythical themes have here become a poetical interpretative device. What function do they have? The question is not answered simply by pointing out that the myth, like the historical narratives of the Old Testament, speaks of an act of God.[107] The question is, what does the mythical allusion contribute to the purpose of the prophetic text? Attention should be paid here to the distinctive link between belief in creation and historical action in Deutero-

---

here the creative power of Yahweh, who "didst crush Rahab like a carcass" (v.11) is called upon to be the constant protection of the successors of David against their enemies. The perhaps independent mythical theme of the rebellion of the nations against Yahweh and the battle of the nations (cf. Ps. 2.11f., etc., and Schmidt, *op. cit.*, p. 91ff.) is associated in Ps. 74.13ff. with the theme of the divine conflict at the creation. Cf. also 68.31, as well as Isa. 17.12ff.

[106] So Schmidt, *op. cit.*, p. 52.

[107] This is Schmidt's answer, *op. cit.*, pp. 52ff., to the more general question: "Why was the Old Testament able to assimilate myth?"

Isaiah.[108] The historical acts of Yahweh are removed from the contingency and purposelessness of ordinary events, by being presented as acts of creation, while the belief in creation which Deutero-Isaiah received from the cultic tradition of Jerusalem, was now renewed as a present historical experience, separate from its celebration in the cult, which had come to a stop with the destruction of the temple.

The myth of the conflict with the dragon is taken up and used in a different way by Ezekiel. In two announcements of the imminent destruction of Egypt by Nebuchadnezzar he portrays Pharaoh, conventionally represented under the image of the crocodile, in features which recall the chaos dragon of the primal age (Ezek. 29.3–6; 32.2–8). Of course one ought not to speak of an allegory here,[109] but we seem to have a mythical exaggeration of the image of the crocodile used to represent Pharaoh (and with him, Egypt).[110] As in the case of the image, likewise directed against Egypt, of the fall of the world tree whose roots reached down into the waters of chaos and whose top reaches the clouds (ch. 31), the present passage makes clear "with all the boldness of mythical statements, that in earthly concentrations of power there are fundamental and primeval forces involved as well".[111]

In Psalm 104 and the book of Job the chaos dragon Leviathan appears in a strangely powerless guise. He appears in the relatively innocent role of an astonishing fabulous creature.

[108] Cf. R. Rendtorff, "Die theologische Stellung der Schöpfungsglauben bei Jesaja", *ZThK* 51, 1954, pp. 3–13, esp. pp. 12f.

[109] Gunkel, *Schöpfung und Chaos*, pp. 73ff. The characteristic apportioning in an allegory of individual features of the image to details of the situation intended is absent here. On the question of allegory in Ezekiel cf. also Zimmerli, *Ezechiel*, pp. 343ff. For the sayings against Pharaoh, *ibid.*, pp. 707ff., 767ff.

[110] This is true also of the use of the name Rahab for Egypt, Isa. 30.7 and Ps. 87.4. The usage was clearly a common one.

[111] Zimmerli, *op. cit.*, p. 762. In the image of the world tree which towers over all other trees in the garden of paradise and is envied by them, while at the same time its mighty branches provide protection and shade, it is easy to find individual allegorizing themes, but not an allegory carried through consistently.

The features of the myth of the conflict with the dragon become
the themes of an aimless divine game: Yahweh draws out
Leviathan with a fish hook, pierces his jaw with a hook, puts
a rope through his nose (Job. 41.1ff.). For the chaos monster to
be portrayed as powerless is likely to have been an expression
of belief in creation, which could no longer tolerate the conception that Yahweh had first to strive for his power as creator
in a struggle against a serious opponent. This does not mean
that belief in the existence of the chaos monster had disappeared.
But it had ceased to have any function. A new meaning is given
to the existence of Leviathan by the explicit statement that
Yahweh created him as a toy (Ps. 104.26, cf. Jos. 41.5). This
seems still to assume a mythical knowledge of the terrifying
power of the primeval monster. The creative power of Yahweh
is shown in its proper light by the fact that he treats this monster
like a toy which he has made for himself.

The example of Ezekiel shows that the myth of the conflict
with the dragon can be used in the setting of prophetic threats
against foreign nations. Other mythical themes are used for
this purpose, like the myth of the world tree in paradise in
Ezekiel 31. In particular, the lament for the dead was a form
which clearly left room for mythical elaboration. An example
of this is the lament over the King of Tyre (Ezek. 28.11ff.),
which describes him as the primal man in paradise, who because
of his arrogance was cast out and given up to enemy kings. The
prophet here exaggerates the expected fate of Tyre, which
apart from Egypt was the only kingdom to resist the power of
Babylon; he does so by taking the King of Tyre as an example
of the ultimate tragedy of man as a whole. The description of
the descent of Egypt into the underworld, Ezek. 32.17–32,
likewise takes the form of a lament for the dead, though there
are hardly any allusions to the mythological features of the
descent into the underworld by the deities of the ancient Near
East. The theme of the descent into the underworld also
appears in the taunt concerning the fall of Babylon in Isa.
14.4ff. Here, the greatness of the fall is described not only in
terms of being cast down from the greatest heights into the

underworld, but also by the dishonourable denial of a proper burial. In addition, Isaiah 14 describes the fall of Babylon in the language of the astral beliefs which meant so much to the Babylonians, and also by means of features of Canaanite mythology. Gunkel's interpretation of the mythological background of the text is as follows:

> The fate of the morning star, the son of the dawn, is a strange one. Shining very brightly, he rises rapidly in the heavens, but does not reach the highest point, for the rays of the sun outshine him. The myth describes this natural process as the struggle of Elyon against Helal, who once tried to climb to the highest point in heaven, but was forced to go down to the underworld.[112]

The Canaanite background of the idea of a kingdom of God in the Old Testament is clearly recognizable here.[113] The origin of this idea is not connected in its themes with the Davidic kingdom, and may very well be older than the institution of the monarchy in Israel. In a period in which other gods were still assumed to exist, the idea of the kingdom of Yahweh is an expression of Yahweh's superiority over the gods: "Yahweh is a great God, and a great king above all gods" (Ps. 95.3, cf. 97.7). As a rule this superiority is presented as having existed from the very first. Yet some texts, particularly Psalm 82, show that it was won in a struggle with other gods. In this psalm Yahweh enters the assembly of the gods, which takes place under the presidency of the Ugaritic father of the gods El, and accuses the other gods of unjust judgment. A similar idea occurs in Psalm 58. The way Yahweh comes forward here recalls Baal, who likewise had to maintain his cause against the other gods and so became king; he had not always been king. But Baal's becoming king is linked to the vegetation cycle, whereas in Yahweh's case it is a matter of the rule of law. Above all, however, the kingdom of Yahweh in the Old Testament is never merely something which is coming into being.

[112] Gunkel, *Schöpfung und Chaos*, p. 133. Cf. also Childs, *op. cit.*, pp. 67ff.
[113] On what follows, see Schmidt, *Königtum Gottes in Ugarit and Israel*, pp. 85f. and *passim*. For the "enthronement psalms" 47, 93, 96–9, cf. *ibid.*, pp. 74ff.

The dynamic features of the kingly rule of Baal are in Yahweh's case amalgamated with those of the kingly rule of El, which had existed from the very first. The other gods at the same time fall into the background, as the object of the kingly rule of Yahweh, for "All the gods of the peoples are idols; but Yahweh made the heavens" (Ps. 96.5). Thus the object of his rule in the first instance is Israel, then the world of the nations. But it is characteristic that the kingdom of Yahweh is always marked as well by the dynamic features of a rule which still has to be made to prevail in history. This is the starting point of the hope which arose in late prophecy of the direct rule of God, which would do away with all human rule, and would bring an end to the succession of world empires. Here the myth, and above all the myth of Baal, helped in the formation of one of the central themes of the Bible, the idea of the future kingdom of God.

The prophet Hosea demonstrates the conflict between faith in Yahweh and the myth of Baal in a quite different way. His concern is not with the idea of the kingdom of Baal achieved in battle, and the possibility of taking it up into Israel's under-standing of God, but with the aspects of vegetation religion which had to be rejected, and which formed the essence of the kingdom of Baal. We also find here a use of mythical themes which is extremely skilful in its literary form, in that they are used against the original intention of the myth, and castigate Israel's lapse into the vegetation cults. Hosea uses the language of the myth of the sacred marriage of Baal with Anath, which took place in the rain which fertilized the land in the spring and autumn, and was conducted by means of cultic prostitution. He uses it in order to describe the relationship of Yahweh to his people as that of a divine lover to those he loves (Hosea 3.4–17). That the love of Yahweh is for the people and not for the land is the first departure from the ideas of the vegetation myth. The polemic application lies in the fact that the beloved of Yahweh is described as faithless, as a whore, for the very reason that Israel has taken part in the fertility cult with its cultic prostitution. The introduction of the idea of adultery

and divorce means that "a mythical theme is finally transformed into a parable, used for the most violent polemic against
the adoption of Canaanite myth by Israel".[114]

VIII

Many different examples have already shown that the literary
activities which were able to assimilate mythical themes in the
context of prophetic composition included the description of a
future age of salvation. This is seen in particular in the adoption
of the conceptions of the peace and fertility of paradise within
the framework of eschatological prophecies of salvation. But
the theme of the struggle with the chaos dragon was also
applied eschatologically. Whereas in older texts it usually
occurs as a reminiscence of the divine acts of creation and
salvation in the primal age, in Ezekiel's portrait in mythical
terms of Pharaoh, Ezek. 32.2; 29.3, it is projected on to historical conflicts in the future. A similar allusion, the application
of which, however, remains uncertain, is found in Ps. 68.31:
"Rebuke the beasts that dwell among the reeds, the herd of
bulls with the calves of the peoples." An application to the final
age is not found until the so-called "Apocalypse of Isaiah",
which comes from post-exilic times (Isa. 24–27):

In that day Yahweh with his hard and great and strong sword will punish
Leviathan the fleeing serpent, Leviathan the twisting serpent, and he will
slay the dragon that is in the sea. (Isa. 27.1)

This perhaps refers to three historical kingdoms, portrayed
under the image of the three mythical animals.[115] In this case
the prophecy is similar to the vision in the book of Daniel of
the four animals which rise up out of the primeval sea, which

---

[114] H. W. Wolff, *Dodekapropheton* I: *Hosea* (BKAT 14.1), 2nd ed., 1965,
p. 54. For the mythical background of the passage see especially p. 47.
Hosea 5.6 also alludes to the theme of the absence of Baal who has des-
cended into the underworld, and who is now sought for in vain, and applies
the latter idea to Yahweh, who will withdraw in anger from those who seek
him (p. 127).
[115] Gunkel, *Schöpfung und Chaos*, p. 47, cf. O. Plöger, *Theokratie und
Eschatologie*, 1959, p. 90; ET *Theocracy and Eschatology*, 1968, p. 71.

has been stirred up by the winds[116] from the four quarters of heaven (7.2ff.).[117] There, however, the image refers not to a future at the end of time, but to the succession of world empires since the destruction of Jerusalem: Babylonians, Medes, Persians, Greeks. In Enoch 60.7ff. (cf. v.24) the two chaos monsters Leviathan and Behemoth once again play an undefined role in the judgment and punishment of the final age, and similar mysterious allusions are found in IV Ezra (6.52) and the Apocalypse of Baruch (29.4).[118] In the Revelation of St John the "beast that ascends from the bottomless pit" (11.7, cf. 12.18) occurs in the description of the final age, where it represents the Roman world empire, and the final struggle with the beast which is announced (ch. 17–19, esp. 19.20f.), like the battle of Michael against the dragon which is described earlier (12.7ff.) and which takes place in heaven, is another late example of the continued vitality of the theme of the struggle with the chaos dragon.[119] In portraying the final struggle between the divine forces and the forces opposed to them, the Revelation also adopted the theme of the rising up of the nations, which is related to that of the struggle with the dragon, and is already associated with it in the Old Testament (19.19ff.; 20.7ff.). Here again we have an originally mythical theme (see above p. 55), which has been used eschatologically.

---

[116] Cf. Ezek. 37.9, and Zimmerli, *Ezekiel*, p. 895, especially the observation that in the Babylonian creation epic Marduk calls the four winds to help him, in order to blow from all sides upon Tiamat, "that nothing of her might escape" (*Enuma Elish* 4.42, in *ANET*, p. 66). This is also reminiscent of the "storm of God" over the primeval sea, Gen. 1.2.

[117] See Noth, *Gesammelte Studien zum AT*, 1957, pp. 266f.; ET "History in Old Testament Apocalyptic", in *The Laws in the Pentateuch and Other Essays*, pp. 208ff.; O. Plöger, *Das Buch Daniel*, 1965, pp. 108f.; K. Koch, in *Historische Zeitschrift* 193/1 (1961), pp. 9f. and 25f.

[118] Further references in Gunkel, *Schöpfung und Chaos*, pp. 314f.

[119] Gunkel, *op. cit.*, pp. 336ff., interpreted the dragon and the beast from the abyss as two expressions of the same theme (p. 338). But the one-sided derivation from the Babylonian conception of the struggle with the dragon runs into difficulties here. The narrative in ch. 12 of the birth of the child, his flight from the dragon and his later victorious battle against him seems to find its closest parallel in Egypt, cf. E. Lohse, *Die Offenbarung des Johannes* (NTD 11), 1960, pp. 6ff.

The point at which it was transformed into an eschatological vision of the future can actually be identified in this case: it occurs in Ezekiel, who takes up an as yet unfulfilled prophecy of an attack by a people "from the north country" (Jer. 6.22) and renews it with reference to an event at an indeterminate historical time, which Ezekiel regarded as the final battle of Yahweh himself on the mountains of Israel (Ezek. 39.4), the navel of the earth (38.12), against a prince called Gog from the land of Magog and the peoples who accompany him.[120] The recollection of this prophesy has left traces both in the description of the final battle of Yahweh against the powers of darkness under the leadership of Belial in the *War of the Sons of Light* from Qumran,[121] and also in the Revelation, according to which the last decisive battle will take place at Jerusalem against Gog and Magog (20.8) and will be decided by God's own miraculous intervention.[122]

Mythical themes undoubtedly underlie such conceptions. They play a large part in apocalyptic literature in general,[123] but here they form part of the events of the end. Gunkel, who

---

[120] For an analysis of Ezek. 38–9 in terms of tradition-history, see Zimmerli, *Ezechiel*, pp. 938ff.

[121] 1QM I 4 describes the enemies as "kings of the north"; the hymn 1QM XI, in its final verses, which are unfortunately largely destroyed, names Gog as the enemy (v. 16).

[122] On Rev. 20.1–20, cf. E. Lohse, *Die Offenbarung des Johannes*, pp. 95ff.

[123] The following examples of references to themes of astral mythology alone can be given: the seven stars mentioned in Rev. 1.16 and 20 are, as in the case of the seven eyes of God, Zech. 4.10, the seven planets which were identified with the principal gods of Babylon. In Judaism they were reduced in status to seven archangels (Tob. 12.15; cf. Enoch 20.1ff., where the Greek text gives seven archangels, while the Ethiopian text gives only six) and to these the "seven spirits", Rev. 1.4; 4.5; 5.6, correspond. The seven lampstands, 1.12, 20; 2.1, as well as the seven-branched lampstand of the Jewish temple (cf. also p. 44) go back to this origin. The twenty-four elders seated upon the throne (Rev. 4.4) are derived from the Babylonian reckoning of twenty-four stars, or alternatively gods, and the "four living creatures" which according to Rev. 4.6 stand round the throne of God are the star figures which according to Babylonian belief supported the vault of heaven: the bull, the lion, the scorpion (represented as a human being) and the eagle, which in Christian tradition became symbols of the evangelists.

was one of the first to point to this situation, thought it expressed the view "that the eschatological would be the same as the primeval": "in the final age what existed in the primal age will be repeated: the new creation will be preceded by a new chaos; the monsters of the primal age will appear on earth a second time."[124] This correspondence is then understood as an expression of the "cyclical" nature of myth itself.[125] The view that the final age corresponded with the primal age, as evidenced in the cyclical course of the years which expressed the characteristically mythical understanding of time, and that in these eschatological conceptions a similar correspondence or identification is to be found, is the basis of the revival of the opinion that the eschatological conceptions of Judaism and primitive Christianity should be regarded as mythical. Thus according to Bultmann Jewish eschatology arose from "the concept of *the periodicity of the course of worldly events*", which came into being by "conceiving the course of the world on the analogy of the annual periodicity of nature". This was done by limiting the periodicity to a single cycle, a single world year.[126] The assumption behind such a view of the origin of Jewish eschatology in earlier religious belief is that of the identity already maintained by Gunkel of the final age and the primal age. But if we look more closely, we see that the eschatological texts of Jewish and primitive Christian literature express the idea that the final age and the primal age *correspond*. There is not simply a "linear" understanding of the historical process,[127]

[124] Gunkel, *Schöpfung und Chaos*, pp. 369f.
[125] H. Gressmann, *Der Ursprung der israelitisch-jüdischen Eschatologie*, 1905, pp. 160ff.   [126] R. Bultmann, *History and Eschatology*, 1957, pp. 23ff.
[127] Thus A. Weiser (*Glaube und Geschichte im AT*, Stuttgart, 1931, pp. 23ff.) and W. Eichrodt (*Theologie des AT*, Vol. I, 3rd ed., pp. 244ff., 252ff.; ET *Theology of the Old Testament* I, 1961, pp. 461f., 469ff.), asserted that the cyclical understanding of time in the mythology of the ancient Near East was replaced by the linear thinking associated with salvation history. But this view does not take account of the characteristic phenomenon of the repetition of earlier events, which must be seen in connection with the rhythmical understanding of time of the Israelites (cf. T. Boman, *Das hebräische Denken im Vergleich mit dem Griechischen*, pp. 114ff.; ET *Hebrew Thought Compared with Greek*, pp. 133ff.)

but neither is there an *identity*, a return to the beginning.[128]
Rather, there is a correspondence of the kind which has long
been discussed under the heading of "typology".[129] From this
point of view the elaboration of the hope of the final age by
means of the primeval themes of creation and paradise fits into a
total picture of the use of tradition to portray the eschatological
hope, characterized by the return to historical saving ordinances
which, it is hoped, will be repeated, surpassed and brought to
perfection in the final age. Thus beside the theme of the struggle
with the chaos dragon, with which the description of the terrors
of the final age is associated, and besides the features of paradise
which are used to describe the time of salvation which will
follow, we also find the expectation of a new exodus, a new
covenant, a new temple, a new David (the Messiah), a new
Elijah and a new Moses. Some examples have already shown
that in this process mythical material of non-Israelite origin
must be understood as an interpretative vehicle for specifically
Israelite historical expectations: the hope of the conditions of
paradise were seen in Isa. 11.6ff. and Amos 9.13ff. to be devices
used to interpret the blessings brought by the kingdom of the
future descendant of David, the Messiah (cf. also the Syrian

[128] B. S. Childs, referring to Boman, Ratchow, Robinson, Marsh, etc.
has rejected the arguments of Weiser and Eichrodt in favour of a linear
understanding of time in the Old Testament, as a modern conception
inappropriate to the Old Testament (pp. 75ff.). He has also denied that
the relationship between the primal age and the final age in Israel is "one
of simple identity" (p. 77). In support of his arguments Childs refers in
particular to the concept of renewal in Deutero- and Trito-Isaiah, and
also in Jeremiah (pp. 78ff.).

[129] See in particular von Rad, *Theologie des AT* II, pp. 374ff., esp. pp.
381ff.; ET Vol. II, 1965, pp. 357ff., esp. pp. 363ff. In my article
"Heilsgeschehen und Geschichte" (1959), now reprinted in *Grundfragen
systematischer Theologie*, 1967, pp. 33ff. (ET "Redemptive Event and History", *Basic Questions in Theology*, 1970, pp. 15ff.), I raised the objection
to an earlier version of the idea of typology in von Rad on the grounds that
typological structural analogies were insufficient to represent the specifically
historical continuity of the course which the tradition took from Israel to
primitive Christianity. In spite of this, within the framework of an experience
of historical continuity with a different basis, the undergoing of analogous
experiences, and even more, the expectation of future happenings on the
analogy of the past, no doubt had an important function.

Baruch 29.5). The new *settlement* in the Promised Land – in
Joel 3.18, Ezek. 47.1ff. (and probably also Zech. 14.8ff.) – as is
shown by the conception of a fountain coming forth from the
temple and bringing fertility and salvation, is an interpretative
device for the saving power of a new cult, pure in the sense that
it is the worship of Yahweh. Again, in Isa. 65.17ff. the conception of a new creation is found in association with the hope
of the liberation of Jerusalem, in its transformation into "a
rejoicing" and "a joy". It is no accident that the elements of
the struggle with the chaos dragon occur first of all in a description of the historical saving act of the passage through the Red
Sea. Its transference to contemporary struggles, and then, in
Ezekiel and in the Apocalypse of Isaiah, to an indeterminate
future event, can be traced at every step as an expression of the
historical experience of the prophets. The related conception of
the rising up of the nations against Zion, of course, became a
stereotyped one at a very early stage (Ps. 2), because it had
formed part of the ideology of Zion, and was perhaps already
associated in pre-Israelite times with the king in the traditions
of the city state of Jerusalem. This kind of stereotyping of
themes, the function of which as interpretative devices is still
clearly visible in older texts, can be observed in various forms
in the apocalyptic literature. This is particularly true of the
paradisiacal fertility of the final age (Enoch 11.19) and the
appearance of Behemoth and Leviathan (Enoch 60.7; IV
Ezra 6.49ff.; Syrian Baruch 29.4).

The typological application of historical experiences of salvation, and of mythical themes in association with them, is always
directed towards a future which surpasses the event used as a
type and is no mere repetition of its model. Here typological
thought is distinct from genuinely mythical thought, which
knows of no future which surpasses and so supersedes the
mythical primal age. But the typological analogy makes possible
a consciousness of the future which has a definite content,
notwithstanding its complete novelty. For one can in fact speak
of the future only in the light of present experience or of
tradition. This does not mean that the novelty of what is to

come has to be played down; and the reason for this is that the significance of events surpasses the mere fact that they have happened. The more important an event is, the more strongly it points beyond its nature as an historical event which happened once for all. What tradition takes into itself because of its importance conceals a truth which as yet is unfulfilled, and points towards the future. If the Davidic king is understood as the Son of God, that is, as called to rule the world, and at the same time as the mediator of peace and righteousness, then precisely because something of the splendour of this idea became tangible in historical form at the time of David and Solomon, its splendour now surpasses the whole range of the concrete forms it has taken since then, and points toward a future in which it is realized to the full. Similarly, the covenant made by Yahweh with Israel, under the impression produced by the experience of the historical failure of the people to respond to Yahweh's will in the covenant, gave rise to the idea of a new Israel which will be faithful to the covenant. The temple of Solomon was desecrated by idolatry, and was never so pure a source of salvation as Ezekiel and others hoped would be the case when the worship of Yahweh was re-established in the new temple. Where there is still an awareness of the historicity and therefore of the imperfect and chance nature of the event that gave rise to the tradition, then – as opposed to the primeval event of the myth – its significance is experienced as pointing beyond its historical origins. Historical experience of this kind is a necessary assumption for an interpretation of the future in the light of tradition, an interpretation which can nevertheless look forward to the future as surpassing everything hitherto. Thus the eschatological conceptions of Jewish tradition do not anticipate, in the final events to which they look forward, a return to the first things, but are typological in meaning – in the image of the important things that have already happened they look for something hitherto unexampled which is still to come. This is also true of the mythical themes which occur in the visions of the events at the end of time: they too have lost their specifically mythical sense and are used as allusions to a future which is still hidden and only seen in ecstasy. Their function in the context of the eschatological consciousness is clearer when we compare them with a third group of eschatological conceptions, which in origin are neither mythical (that is, relating to the primal age) nor based on the tradition of earlier experiences of salvation or misfortune. These are conceptions which assume the typological framework, the final vindication of divine righteousness and the prophecies of salvation, but within this framework have come into being by a negative process as a contrary picture to the present experience of existence. This group includes the central eschatological conceptions of the resurrection of the dead and of judgment. Both came into being as contrary pictures to the present experience of unrighteousness in the course of the world process, in the face of the disparity between man's action and his fortunes, whether good or evil. Neither idea is specifically Israelite, but they should not be described as mythical simply because of the role they played in Persian eschatology and in Egyptian myth. The idea of the resurrection of the dead becomes mythical only when it is thought of as the re-experiencing of the primeval experiences of a hero or a divinity, as for example in the mystery cults of Hellenism, where the initiate partakes in the resurrection of Osiris or of Attis, originally thought of in terms of the vegetation myth. The idea of a judgment of the dead becomes mythical only when the god who is conceived of as the judge of the dead has this function because he is thought of as the primal image of the judicial power of the king, and in the case of belief in Osiris perhaps also because Osiris himself is thought of as the primeval example of the man justified in the judgment of the gods, because he won his case against Seth in the court of the gods sitting under the presidency of Geb.[130] Thus the conceptions of the judgment of the dead and the resurrection of the dead are not mythical in themselves, because they are not necessarily the repetition of mythical primeval

[130] This view is confirmed by S. Morenz, *Ägyptische Religion*, 1960, p. 137, by means of a series of Pyramid texts (cf. also p. 171) and may well explain the origin of the idea of a general judgment of the dead by Osiris.

events. Yet they can be conceived of as ideas deriving from a world which is understood in a mythical way, as seems to be the case in the Egyptian conception of the judgment of the dead, the basis of which is to be sought in the mythical idea of truth as the primal world ordinance (*maat*). But this mythical origin does not seem to be essential to the conception of the judgment of the dead. For although this conception always assumes the idea of a legal standard by which the earthly life of the departed as a whole is measured – with which the idea of a recompense for the disparity on earth between human actions and fortunes may be associated – the legal idea which underlines it need not always be a mythical one. The idea of law in the Old Testament can hardly be called mythical, even though the origin of the law is still thought of in mythical terms, since all legal traditions are transferred back into the primal situation of the events at Sinai. Thus the conceptions of the judgment of the dead and the resurrection in the context of Old Testament tradition have neither a mythical structure in themselves nor a mythical origin. But like the mythical themes with an eschatological application found among the conceptions of paradise, they possess the function of images which contrast with the present experience of reality. On the other hand the themes of the struggle with the chaos dragon and the rebellion of the nations can only be understood in part as such contrasting images, in so far as in them, by contrast with the present experience of misfortune, the future victory of God against the forces hostile to him is given visible expression. On the other hand, these themes also contain the expectation of an extreme intensification of the present experience of misfortune. But both the element of intensification and also the qualitative contrast between the future and the present belong to the structure of the typological correspondence between what follows and what has gone before. The element of historical novelty, which is the essential difference between the typological mode of thought – especially because of its openness towards the future – and mythological thought, is expressed above all in these themes of qualitative distinction between the future and the present. And oddly enough, even mythical themes can serve to emphasize the qualitative transcendence of the future over everything that has already existed, which distinguishes typological from mythical thought.

The typological interpretation of eschatology, by contrast to the mythical, makes it possible to understand how primitive Christian scriptural proofs, to which the idea of typological correspondence is essential, are related to the eschatological consciousness of primitive Christianity. For the earliest Christians lived in the certainty that in Jesus, and in a decisive sense in his resurrection from the dead, the events of the end to which Jewish faith looked forward were already inaugurated. In him, the "first fruits of those who have fallen asleep" (I Cor. 15.20), the eschatological resurrection of the dead had already happened. Consequently Jesus, who had spoken of the Son of Man who was expected to come in judgment as someone else who would come and confirm his judgments (Luke 12.8 parall.), was now himself identified with the Son of Man and subsequently also with the Messiah. Here the typological framework of Jewish eschatology makes it clear why primitive Christianity applied to Jesus not only the typologies already worked out in the Old Testament – such as the ideas of the new David, the new Moses and the new covenant – but also, in the face of the inauguration of the *eschaton* in Jesus, sought further foreshadowings of the appearance of Jesus and of the course of his life, in the history of the old covenant.[131] Thus Paul interpreted the rock from which Moses struck water to refresh the people of Israel in their journey through the desert (Ex. 17.6) as referring to Christ (I Cor. 10.4), and John saw in the apotropaic fixing of the image of the snake upon a pole (Num.

---

[131] The examples that follow are limited to the typological relationships between the figure of Christ and the history of the old covenant. There are in addition those between Christians as the eschatological people of God, and Israel. Here again the arch of typological correspondence stretches back into the primeval history, when the event of Pentecost is seen as the overcoming of the confusion of tongues brought about by the building of the Tower of Babel (cf. Acts 2.7ff. with Gen. 11.7ff.), or when the church is seen later as the new Noah's Ark.

21.8) a pre-figuring of the *lifting up* of Christ upon the cross (John 3.14). The epistle to the Hebrews related the whole cultic practice of Israel typologically to the one sacrifice of Christ, regarding it as both pointing forward to him and at the same time superseded by him. The most wide-ranging effect of all these Christian typologies has been that of Paul's interpretation of Christ as the new man (I Cor. 15.45ff.; Rom. 5). It was the basis of the historical picture of Christ which saw him as having overcome by his obedience and sacrificial death the sin of Adam and its consequences for mankind, and it consequently became one of the most important roots of the formation of christological doctrine.

This search for correspondences between the life of Jesus and events described in the Old Testament must be distinguished from scriptural proof in the strict sense, which treats as prophetic the words of scripture and not the events they describe. The appeal to prophecies and the assertion that they have been fulfilled has originally nothing to do with typology. A parallel between the primitive Christian proof from prophecy and the procedure of typology was first created when the former was extended to prophetic sayings which were intended in an explicitly eschatological sense. For here the deeper meaning lying behind the direct significance of the words of the scripture was read into them, just as a similar deeper meaning, pointing forward to Jesus and the new people of God, was typologically read into the events described in scripture. This use of scripture, which of course cannot everywhere be distinguished from the proof from prophecy in the strict sense, has profoundly influenced the narrative of the life and ministry of Jesus in the gospel. Sometimes it is difficult to decide where a meaning is being read into Old Testament sayings which was originally absent from them, in order to relate them to particular elements in what happened to Jesus, and where the story of Jesus has been elaborated and extended in order to bring it into correspondence with what are taken to be Old Testament prophecies of it. This procedure goes back to Jewish origins. Apocalyptic literature already identified a secret meaning behind some prophetic sayings: e.g. the use in Daniel 9 of the prophecy of Jeremiah that the exile in Babylon would last seventy years (Jer. 29.10; cf. 25.11ff.). Prophetic typology made use of the historical saving ordinances of God, that is, events of the past, as models for the future hope. But this practice in apocalyptic literature used traditional texts, in which a hidden meaning was sought. Here again we can perceive a transition, when we recall that Ezekiel took the still unfulfilled prophecy of Jeremiah, that an enemy would come from the north (Jer. 6.22ff.; 5.15ff.), as the basis for his own prophecy of a final struggle between Gog of Magog (Ezek. 38f.). This already anticipates the way in which later Judaism sought in the words of the scripture hidden references to the events of the end of time. The early Christian proof from scripture originated in this. In its turn, however, primitive Christianity went further than all the Jewish examples; for it believed that the end had already been inaugurated in Jesus Christ, and therefore read into the Old Testament scriptures, as the word of God, a very clearly defined hidden meaning, that of the prophetic foreshadowing of every possible individual feature of the story of Jesus.

IX

Under the influence of the "history of religions" school, and especially of the theology of Rudolf Bultmann, it has become fashionable to accept that mythical thought exercised considerable influence on primitive Christianity, and yet to state at the same time that these mythical features are alien to the true spirit of the gospel, so that a "demythologization" of the New Treatment can be regarded as the logical conclusion of the central purposes of early Christianity. According to Wilhelm Bousset, the mythical conceptions of the New Testament, and especially the mythologization of the person of Jesus, were wholly a matter of alien influences; first of the Jewish environment of primitive Christianity, and then of the Hellenistic Greek world, influences which were unconsciously adopted into the life of the church.[132] Thus the belief in the Messiah

[132] W. Bousset, *Kyrios Christos. Geschichte des Christusglaubens von den*

was there as a "ready-made royal cloak" which had only to be placed on Jesus' shoulders (p.18, cf. p.75). According to Bousset, the different christological conceptions are in general no more than alternative "outer garments" (p.77) for the figure of Jesus, and the motive for their adoption was not to be found in the inner development of faith in Christ, since they were simply derived from the surrounding world. Thus the myth of the redeemer-hero who came down from heaven was "not produced by Christianity" (p. 31), but only adopted by it. Bultmann has a similar view of the function of myth in primitive Christianity, except that he is mainly concerned with the allegedly mythical world view, including eschatology, which is found as the outward form, conditioned by the ideas of the time, of the self-understanding of Christians, but was already superseded by some tendencies in primitive Christianity itself, especially in John.[133] Now neither belief in demons nor the "three storey" world view of primitive Christianity is specifically mythical. While it is a world view which for modern mankind is obsolete, this fact is not enough to make it mythical, nor on the other hand can mythical thought be regarded as obsolete because this world view is obsolete. Bultmann's historical account of the mythical elements in the New Testament is likewise deficient. According to him, "the mythology of the New Testament is in essence that of Jewish apocalyptic and gnostic redemption myths".[134] But the eschatological conceptions of apocalyptic which are important in the New Testament cannot be understood as mythical without qualification, and the construction by the history of religions school of a gnostic redeemer myth which was ready and to hand for primitive Christianity to adopt, and which according to Bousset's theory was simply

---

Anfängen bis Irenäus, 1913, 5th ed. 1965, p. 103. The references that follow in the text are to this work. See also T. Koch, *Theologie unter den Bedingungen der Moderne* (inaugural dissertation, Munich, 1970) pp. 120ff., esp. pp. 130–40. Koch's account shows remarkable parallels to Gunkel's tendency to dismiss mythical elements in the Old Testament as external influences.

[133] Bultmann, "Neues Testament und Mythologie", in *Kerygma und Mythos* I, pp. 31f.; cf. p. 24; ET *Kerygma and Myth*, pp. 20 ff., p. 11.

[134] *Ibid.*, p. 27; ET p. 15.

an "outer garment" has been seriously criticized.[135] The question has in fact been raised whether the idea of a redeemer descending from heaven, if this is to be regarded as a myth, ought not to be understood as a specifically Christian creation. This is not necessarily to assert that it is something uniquely Christian, excluding other parallel or convergent ways towards the idea of a redeemer. But one must reject the assumption that in Christianity, as previously in Judaism, there could in principle have been no original creation of myth.

In primitive Christianity eschatology does not display mythical features, but the function which the figure of Jesus came to have for the Christian church is reminiscent of the archetypal elements of myth. For Christians, the destiny of man and the world has been definitively and irrevocably revealed in the figure of Jesus. Christian love is understood as an imitation of the attitude of Jesus. The central events of Christian worship are an imitation of the baptism which Jesus accepted and the last meal which he celebrated. From the time of Paul onwards, to die and rise with Christ is the essential theme of the Christian's understanding of himself. That the figure of Jesus should be understood in this way as an archetype is reflected in the normative character which the period of apostolic origins has maintained for the Christian consciousness. All these features show a striking similarity to the primal age of myth which is the basis of the present age. Of course they are distinct from genuine myth in that their origin lies in a non-mythical event, in what took place in a human life, a life in which the main consciousness was not mythical but eschatological in form. Consequently, the history of the origin of Christianity inevitably raises the question – as the history of religions school rightly saw – how the non-mythical story of the man Jesus of Nazareth could have turned into the characteristic "mythologization" of his person which is found as early as Paul. It is understandable that the attempt should have been made to explain this situation

---

[135] Cf. C. Colpe, *Die Religionsgeschichtliche Schule, Darstellung und Kritik ihres Bildes vom gnostischen Erlösermythus*, 1961, esp. pp. 15ff., 33, 57ff., 207ff.

by outside influence. But this view does not explain what took place, because the forms and conceptions which were used for the christological interpretation of Jesus' life and person were by no means so readily available in a complete form in the surrounding world as has been supposed. Moreover, if this were the case, it would still not be clear how Christians were able to adopt such alien conceptions as the expression of their faith, which they maintained in other respects in an obstinate conflict with their environment. Thus in understanding primitive Christian christology one must assume a considerably greater degree of intellectual productivity on the part of Christians themselves than has usually been assumed by the history of religions school. And this includes the production of something like a "new" Christian myth. Of course unlike the "new myth" in modern literature, it was not a purely literary invention, in which the poetic imagination sought to free itself by its own efforts from its unrelieved subjectivity. The Christian "new myth" came into being as an exposition of the meaning of an historical event, and it never lost contact with this origin, which remained its theme; it never took on independent form as a pure myth. Yet the process is remarkable enough.

The heart of the Christian "new myth" is the conception of the redeemer who came down from heaven. Elements of this conception are quite common in the religious "environment" of primitive Christianity. It may be that parallels to it can be found which are to a greater or lesser degree independent of it, although, as we have said, recent scholarship is much more uncertain on this point.

Here a peculiar feature of the eschatology of Jesus is of significance. As we know, Jesus was conscious that the coming kingdom of God which he proclaimed was at the same time already being inaugurated in his life and work. The reason for this strange situation may be that in the life of one who was already completely committed to the coming kingdom of God, God's will had already come to rule here and now. As a result, Jesus himself, with his message of the coming kingdom of God, became the event in which it was present, the presence of God

himself. There is an important similarity between this and the
way in which the news of the resurrection of Jesus, which led
to the formation of a Christian community, signified the onset
of the final glory of a new life in God, which devout Judaism
looked for in the future God was to bring about. In this way
the figure of Jesus became for believers not only a historical
figure, but at the same time the appearance of the absolute in
history, the incarnation of God. Because in him the future
salvation of the world was already present, everything now
depended for men upon becoming and remaining associated
with him: to be associated with the events of his earthly life,
with his sayings, with his suffering, and sharing in table
fellowship with him, was a guarantee of future participation
in the glory which overcame death and which had been
manifested in him; it guaranteed participation in the coming
kingdom of God. For this reason, the events of Jesus' life were
bound to take on an archetypal significance for his church.
Thus the interpretation of the events of Jesus' life in mythical
categories must not be condemned as a distortion of its original
meaning brought in from outside, but was demanded by the
very meaning of these events themselves – in principle at least,
though this affirmation does not necessarily specify the form of
the appropriate mythical interpretation. But the element in the
life and ministry of Jesus which demanded a mythical interpretation of his person in the sense of a presence of God in him,
an incarnation, a descent of God into the flesh, is oddly enough
the very one to which Bultmann appealed for his assertion that
"the age of salvation has already dawned . . . and the life of the
future has become a present reality".[136] Bultmann's interpretation of this situation as "demythologization" is explained by
the fact that he saw the mythical element in the New Testament
as in the first instance a future eschatology derived from Jewish
apocalyptic. Both in the case of Jesus himself, and also in Paul
and John, this is in fact reapplied to the present. But if, as was
usual amongst other scholars of the history of religions school,[137]

[136] Bultmann, *Kerygma und Mythos* I, p. 31; ET p. 20.
[137] E.g., in W. Bousset, *Kyrios Christos*, pp. 203ff., 333, cf. pp. 215, 31,

myth in the New Testament texts is seen above all in the conception of a divine being descending from heaven and manifested in Jesus, then a link between this primitive Christian conception and the remarkable idea of the presence of the kingdom of God – which means God himself – can scarcely be rejected as a historical fact. This characteristic feature of the eschatology of Jesus and of the earliest church must therefore be regarded not as the starting point for demythologization, but rather as the origin of the specifically Christian myth of the incarnation of the Son of God, regardless of the question whether or not a gnostic redeemer myth existed as a stimulus for the formation of the Christian doctrine.

However, the idea of the incarnation of the Son of God, regarded as a myth, contains an extremely odd and disturbing element. For it does not merely state that God *appeared* in human form, but that he became *identical* with a human being who actually lived, a historical person, and even suffered and died as that person. It is no chance that the profession of faith in the *vere homo* was disputed for centuries, and was rightly understood by Christians as the really distinctive and unique aspect of their faith. Hellenism had legends which told of epiphanies of heavenly beings in human or other forms, but never to the point of indissoluble identity with the form they took on. It also had myths of the dying and rising again of gods, but these always referred to an event which took place within the divine sphere itself. But the idea of the incarnation linked the substance of the myth, the nature of deity itself, to a historical event, a historical person. It has rightly been stressed, time and again, that this amounts not just to an arbitrary variation of basically mythical conceptions, but to something which is contrary to the nature of myth itself. For what is historically unique is as far as anything possibly can be from myth, which expresses what is archetypal and valid for

---

etc. We need not discuss here the fact that Bousset was not prepared to admit that this myth was a Christian construction, but derived it from a hypothetically constructed pre-Christian gnosticism.

every age. True though this may be, it is a judgment after the event, and does not explain the association of the language of myth with the unique historical event which is found in the Christian idea of the incarnation. This association can be understood only if the mythical expression, as an interpretation of the meaning of the historical figure of Jesus of Nazareth, is understood on the basis of his actual person, his specific significance. This is of course to admit that in the idea of the incarnation we do not have a normal myth, but an interpretation of the meaning of a historical figure. But this takes place not by the imposition upon the original gospel of the alien form of a mythology which flourished everywhere in the environment of primitive Christianity, but as a development of the specific significance of this historical figure. That the conception, in itself a mythological one, of a God who came down from heaven to redeem men could be understood as the only appropriate category results, as we have shown, from the distinctive nature of Jesus' eschatology, the presence of the kingdom of God, and so of God himself, in his coming and the events of his life.[138] The association of historical fact and myth in the idea of the incarnation might be thought quite incompatible with each other, but they can be explained without difficulty on this basis.

However, the meaning of the idea of the incarnation as an interpretation of the historical person of Jesus is not something of which Christianity was clearly conscious at the very beginning. The conception of a Son of God coming from heaven and returning to his Father after his redeeming work on earth is found in fully developed form as early as Paul (Phil. 2.6ff.; Rom. 8.3; Gal. 4.4). The priority in the relationship between

---

[138] The idea of pre-existence, which makes it possible to think of the presence of God in Jesus as the result of his coming down from heaven, is implicit in the eternity of God, whose presence in the life and ministry of Jesus is at issue. The fact that the idea of the incarnation has in mind not God in the absolute sense, but the "Son" of God, in distinction to the Father, as having become man in Jesus, results from the distinction which Jesus made between himself and the Father, and which was maintained by the Christian Church.

the events of Jesus' life and the idea of the incarnation was reversed in the Christian mind when the life and ministry of Jesus was thought of as having been derived from the ultimate ground of everything that happens, from God himself, as the sending of his Son in the flesh. As a result, the historical fact of Jesus, as the starting point of belief in the incarnation, was lost sight of, and this enabled what Christians said about the manifestation of the Son of God on earth to be expressed entirely in the language of myth, to the very point of the total and in- dissoluble incarnation of God. The theme of the incarnation prevented Christian theology from becoming identified entirely with myth. For in the idea of God's becoming man the theme of the epiphany coming down from above, and concentrated in the idea of the incarnation, intersects the "horizontal" orienta- tion of the life and ministry of Jesus in the history of mankind. The latter was expressed from the time of Paul onwards by the interpretation of Jesus as the second or last Adam, who by his righteousness and sacrificial death overcame the sin of the first man and the whole disastrous course of human history which resulted from it, and thereby paved the way for a new humanity which would be consummated on his return.[139] This specifi- cally Christian doctrinal development cannot be derived from a hypothetically reconstructed mythology of a primal man accord- ing to which, it has been supposed, the primal man redeems himself in his members (men). In fact the contrast between the second and the first Adam is characteristic of the Christian conception, and this contrast is clearly typological but not mythical in nature. A mythical component is introduced only with the archetypal significance of the second Adam, as of the first, for the individuals included in him. And it is here that the idea of the second Adam intersects that of the appearance of

---

[139] This idea in Paul was taken up by Ignatius of Antioch in the form of the idea of a divine plan of salvation directed towards the new man (Ign. *Eph.* 20.1), and found its classical theological expression in Irenaeus' theory of recapitulation (*Adv. Haer.* III, 17.4; 23.1). The passage from the *Protreptikos* of Clement of Alexandria (111.1ff.) also belongs in this context; R. Herzog, ignoring the christological tradition in which Clement stands, regards it as a Christian myth constructed by Clement himself.

the Son of God upon earth. It proved impossible, however, to reconcile the two interpretations of Jesus, as the new man on the one hand, and on the other hand as the heavenly Son of God. The inner logic of the mythical conception of a divine being who came down from heaven and returned thither inevitably remained alien to the idea of God's genuinely and irreversibly becoming man, even though this actually brought about a transformation of man himself into a "new man". It is this that gave rise to the numerous insoluble problems of christological doctrine. Thus the idea of the incarnation forms a corrective to several self-contained mythical interpretations of the figure of Jesus, both with regard to the idea of the epiphany of the Son of God upon earth and also with regard to a merely archetypal interpretation of the idea of a second Adam. And yet the step taken in the direction of a mythical interpretation of the figure of Jesus was not simply undone by virtue of the idea of the incarnation. Rather, it assumes this idea, and must be recognized as an intrinsically necessary and logical step. For how else was it possible to understand a literal presence of God, to be taken in the strictest sense, based upon the distinctive eschatology of Jesus and renewed by the experience of Easter? Even today it cannot be expressed otherwise than by the repetition of the primitive Christian interpretation of Jesus in the language of myth. Yet the function of the mythical language remains only that of an interpretative vehicle for the significance of a historical event. The irreplaceable sign of this in the history of Christian thought is the idea of the incarnation.

The conception of an epiphany of the Son of God at once became associated with the idea that in him the divine *logos* was manifested to men. It is not possible here to go over the complex previous history of the Christian doctrine of the *logos*. Let us only recall that the philosophical concept of the *logos* was used in pre-Christian times as an *interpretatio graeca* of non-Greek mythologies, notably in the process of applying the allegorical interpretation of the Greeks' own mythological tradition to the mythologies of other peoples. Thus Plutarch identified Osiris with the *logos*,[140] as he did also the Egyptian god of wisdom, Thoth (= Hermes).[141] The interpretation of the Son of God manifested in Jesus by the concept of the *logos* must be taken in the sense of this kind of philosophical interpretation of primarily mythical figures, though in this process the philosophical concepts in fact came to have a mythical potential, and led to the formation of a kind of secondary mythology. The best example of the form they took is found in the artificial myths of gnosticism. Just like Hermes, the guide of souls, Jesus was also thought of as the epiphany of the divine *logos* to save and redeem men, who had come under the domination of the visible.[142] The fundamental distinction remained, that Jesus as a historical figure was identified with the *logos*.

The "new myth" of the epiphany of the eternal Son of God in the figure of Jesus of Nazareth formed the starting point in Christian tradition for the adoption of the mythical thought forms of Hellenism, which in this way were incorporated into the Christian world. The importance of this process, which goes far beyond the theoretical sphere of theological reflection, can best be seen in the history of the Christian Sunday and the development of the church calendar, which has had a permanent effect upon the way Christianity perceives the connection between liturgy and life.[143]

Whereas the Jewish church kept the last day of the week, the sabbath, as a memorial of God's rest from his work of creation, the day after the sabbath, the first day of the week, on which according to tradition Jesus rose from the dead, became the day of the Christians, the "day of the Lord" on which the Lord's Supper was celebrated. Justin already em-

[140] Plutarch, *De Iside et Osiride* 49 and 54ff., cf. the commentary by T. Hopfner, *Uber Isis und Osiris*, Vol. 2, 1941, pp. 229.

[141] *Ibid.*, 54, and Hopfner, *op. cit.*, Vol. 2, pp. 243f. and 229.

[142] The Christian Fathers were also aware of the Platonic connection between the *logos* and Hermes. References in H. Rahner, *Griechische Mythen in christlicher Deutung*, 3rd ed., 1957, p. 174, cf. also pp. 183f.; ET *Greek Myths and Christian Mystery*, 1963, pp. 190f., 198f.

[143] Rahner, "Das christliche Mysterium von Sonne und Mond", in *op. cit.*, pp. 89–158; ET "The Christian Mystery of Sun and Moon", pp. 89–176.

phasizes that this day was also the day of the beginning of creation and the day of the sun.[144] We read later in Jerome:

The Lords day, the day of the resurrection, the day of the Christians, is our own. And if the heathen call it the *dies Solis*, we are quite ready to accept this description too, for on this day the light appeared; on this day the Sun of Righteousness shone forth.[145]

H. Rahner has put this very well: The early church "gave new content to this day of Helios by filling it with her own mystery of the resurrection".[146] The myth of the sun was not merely reinterpreted, but was superseded for Christians; this was because the resurrection of Jesus was understood as the epiphany of a divine reality greater than that of the sun. As a result, the rising of the sun could be used as a symbol of this even mightier reality, bringing a much more profound redemption, which had been manifested in the power of the external Son of God which overcame death and brought forth righteousness. For the church fathers, the good itself was manifested in him, an effective reality for which the sun could serve only as an image and likeness drawn from the visible world, as Plato's parable of the sun already stated.[147]

The same replacement of sun worship by faith in the risen Christ can be seen in the Christian festival of Easter, here related to the annual motion of the sun. When in the second century the Roman church transferred the Easter festival from 14 Nisan, the day of the historical memorial of Jesus' Passover, to the Sunday which followed, so that the weekly day of the Lord and the annual festival of the resurrection of Jesus

[144] Justin, *Apology* I, 67. The fact that the day of the resurrection of Jesus was the same as the day of the sun not only gave rise to the early misunderstanding that Christians were sun worshippers, but explains at least in part the special promotion of the day of the Lord by the Emperor Constantine, the heir of the late imperial veneration of the *sol invictus*, which from now on he regarded as identical with the crucified Son of God.

[145] Quoted by Rahner, *op. cit.*, p. 104 (ET, p. 108), together with other references, from *Anecdota Maredsolana* III.2, ed. G. Morin, 1897, p. 418. Also in PL 30, col. 212.

[146] Rahner, *ibid.*

[147] Plato, *Republic*, 508 c. The passage is quoted in Gregory of Nazianzen, *or.* 28.30 and 40.5 (PG 36, col. 68f., 364 B).

coincided, the connection of the former with sun worship was transferred to the Easter festival, with particular reference in this case to the way the sun rises in the course of its annual motion following the spring equinox. Thus a sermon of the fifth century was able to anticipate the theme of the walk which Faust and his servant take on Easter morning in Goethe's play. But the Christian Easter joy is not, as in Goethe, an expression of the new life of nature. Instead, the return of nature to life is seen as an echo of the resurrection of Jesus: "The whole of nature, which hitherto was as though dead, celebrates resurrection together with its Lord."[148] And just as Easter day could be associated with the return of the sun, so the death of Christ was illustrated by the image of the setting of the sun. "As the sun returns from the west to the east," said Athanasius, "so the Lord ascended to the heavens from the depths of Hades."[149] As early as the end of the second century, Melito of Sardis called Christ "the sun of the eastern sky who appeared both to the dead in Hades and to mortals upon earth. As the one true sun he went up to the highest heaven".[150] Of course one cannot look in such statements for a dependence of the Christian Easter faith on an ancient sun myth. Christians used them as images and symbols in order to express the fact that everything towards which the religion of antiquity was only groping had now become a higher reality in Christ.[151] They were not mere rhetorical flourishes, but expressions of the conviction that there was a real correspondence between what takes place in the heavens and the history of him through whom all things were created. The expression of this is the liturgical consequence of the idea of the correspondence between Christ and the sun which has a formative influence on the Christian festival calendar. This can perhaps most clearly be seen in the history of the feast of Christmas. This feast, and probably also its older predecessor and doublet as the celebra-

[148] Ps.-Augustine, *Sermo* 164.2 (PL 39, col. 2067), quoted by Rahner, *op. cit.*, p. 107; ET, p. 112.

[149] Athanasius, *Expos in Ps.* 67.34 (EVV 68.32f.) (PG 27, col. 303D).

[150] Melito of Sardis, in Rahner, *op. cit.*, p. 111; ET, p. 115.

[151] Rahner, *op. cit.*, p. 112; ET, p. 118.

tion of the birth of Jesus, the feast of the Epiphany on 6 January, is the result solely of the correspondence between Christ and the sun; for there is no question of any historical tradition about the day on which Jesus was born. After his victory over Palmyra in 272, the Emperor Aurelian instituted in Rome, on the winter solstice, which fell according to the Julian calendar, on 25 December, a feast of the *sol invictus*, identified with Mithras. It actually took the form of a festival of the birth of this god, in which the solar monotheism which Aurelian had in mind was given concrete expression. The Roman church then adopted this feast as the feast of the birth of Christ. Thus from one point of view the feast of Christmas, which is found from the middle of the fourth century on, represents Christian competition with the sun worship of the later Empire. On the other hand, the adoption of the feast was only possible because Christ himself was regarded as the true sun, so that the winter solstice seemed appropriate for the celebration of his birth. Thus we read in a Christian treatise attributed to the beginning of the fourth century, in an allusion to the institution by Aurelian of 25 December as the birthday of the unconquered sun:

Yet who is as unconquered as our Lord who threw down death and conquered him? They may call this day the birthday of Sol, but he alone is the Sun of Righteousness of whom the prophet Malachi said: There shall arise to you who fear his name the Sun of Righteousness, and there shall be healing under his wings.

Both in this assimilation of ancient sun-worship, and also in the interpretation of the cross as the tree of life and the world tree, the conception of the crucified Jesus as the "true Orpheus" who liberated mankind from the depths of Hades,[153] and the pictures which represented Christians as Odysseus[154] chained to the mast (of the cross), it is possible to see an expression of extreme Hellenization and the swamping of Christianity by myth. But this judgment overlooks the hermeneutic function which mythical conceptions did not merely have for Christian

[152] Quoted by Rahner, *op. cit.*, p. 135; ET, p. 148.
[153] *Ibid.*, pp. 65f.; ET, p. 58.
[154] *Ibid.*, pp. 281–328, esp. pp. 315ff.; ET, pp. 328–86, esp. pp. 371ff.

faith as matter of fact, but were bound to have as a result of the eschatological significance of the life and ministry of Jesus. Myth, however, was reduced to a device for interpreting history, and this explains the dazzling combination, foreshadowed by Hellenistic syncretism, of fragmentary mythical elements in patristic literature. But the mythical themes used in this way are by no means merely redundant ornamentation, reflecting the Hellenistic education of the church fathers. In the basic content of the theology of the incarnation at least, they are also a necessary element in a reflective consideration of Christian faith. Even in what seem to be only playful allusions to themes and figures of mythical tradition, they therefore represent a meaningful exposition of the significance of the life and ministry of Jesus. And the easy facility in using mythical themes which had long become the material of literature corresponds, in the consciousness of someone like Clement of Alexandria and later representatives of Christian Platonism, to the awareness of the provisional nature of the present life of Christians and therefore of their knowledge of God. This remains symbolic theology in the sense in which the expression is used in the Areopagite; for it possesses the revelation of God only in a concealed form, and to see him face to face is something still to come.

2

ANTHROPOLOGY AND THE QUESTION
OF GOD

Guest lecture to the Theological Faculty at Groningen, 3 November
1970; first published in *Kerk en theologie* 22, 1971, pp. 1–14.

I

AT THE END of the *Laws*, written in his old age, Plato sums
up the last contribution to the dialogue by the guest from
Athens by saying that two things lead to belief in the gods, the
soul and the movement of the stars (*Laws* 966d 6ff.). For, he
says, the necessary order of the movement of the stars does not
lead the observer to fall into atheism, as many suppose, but
rather brings him to accept the existence of a reason which
brings about this order. But the soul is the oldest and most
divine of all those things, the movement of which has had a
beginning, and yet has produced a being which will last for
ever. This comparison may remind the modern reader of the
conclusion of Kant's *Critique of Practical Reason*, and his famous
statement that there are two things which fill "the mind with
ever new and increasing wonder and reverence: the starry
heavens above me and the moral law within me." But the very
analogy with Plato's words shows unmistakably the great distance
which separates Kant's thought from the Platonic view of the
world. Kant, of course, like Plato, regarded it as impossible to
derive the soul or the subject from the course of events of
material nature. But according to Kant this is so because the
subject must already be presupposed in any explanation of
nature, whereas Plato declared that the soul could not be
derived from material processes because it is self-moving. And

Plato also followed the reverse course of considering the self-moving of the soul as the condition of every other movement which requires an impulse from outside. In this way he was able, and indeed obliged, to assume the presence behind all corporeal movement of a soul, a spiritual principle as its origin – behind the visible course of the sun in the sky, the invisible sun-god (898d 9ff.), and behind the ordered movement of the cosmos, a supreme reason ordering everything. For Kant, however, it was no longer possible to couple together in this way the two spheres, the soul and the processes of nature. It is true that even according to Kant, the argument from the order of nature and the "majesty of the universe" (*Critique of Pure Reason*, B652) to a supreme reason which orders everything, "always deserves to be mentioned with respect", particularly as it "extends our knowledge of nature by means of the guiding concept of a special unity, the principle of which is outside nature". (651) But for Kant the argument still has no apodeictic certainty, and is the mere expression of a faith (652f.); for it already presupposes the acceptance of a necessary being as the first cause of nature. But for Kant the acceptance of a first link in the chain of causation is no longer compelling; the chain of causation might well reach back into infinity. And in addition Kant advances his specific argument that the category of causation can only be applied to relationships between phenomena in space and time (B637f.). Thus for Kant, unlike Plato, the chain of movement in the material world no longer points back to something self-moving, like the soul, or to an unmoved mover like the Aristotelian reason. Thus in Kant not only is the link between material nature and the soul broken down, but he has also no further reason for supposing that all phenomena have as it were a soul within them. Something like a soul is only to be found in man, in so far as man is a subject. Even in Kant, the consideration of the soul still leads to belief in God – but not because, being self-moving, it is the "oldest" of all existing beings, independent of everything which is only moved from outside. Rather, for Kant, belief in a God is required by the task of the self-understanding of the subject, particularly in its moral experience. Because its basis is restricted to man's self-understanding, the idea of God takes on the character of a postulate, the truth of which is no longer separable from the actual course taken by man's understanding of himself, and in this sense it can claim to possess mere practical validity.

Plato stands at the beginning, and Kant at the significant turning point for modern man, of a process which can be described as one of the continuous anthropologizing of the idea of God. Of course for Plato, the human soul was already distinguished by being particularly close to divinity, and this theme can be traced through Augustine and the Christian Middle Ages to Descartes, and on to Kant. But for Plato the soul was still embedded in the world of nature, and rooted, together with this world, in a divine origin. The philosophical theology of the modern age, on the other hand, has been guided by the apprehension that there is no assured way leading from nature to God, and that therefore the whole burden of proof of the truth of faith in God falls upon the understanding of man, upon anthropology.

We cannot discuss in greater detail here how this has come about. An important step was certainly the realization, achieved particularly by William of Ockham, that no first link is necessary in the chain of moving and creating causes, because, as in the succession of generations, the earlier causes may already have lapsed completely into nothingness, while the effects they have produced still persist. Thus for Ockham the problem of a first impulse to the movement of the universe, which still preoccupied Newton, no longer existed. Only in the series of maintaining causes did Ockham's acute perception still regard a first link as necessary, because a body which is moved can go on moving only as long as it is maintained in movement, so that the moving power which maintains its movement must be simultaneous with it as long as that movement persists, by contrast to an impulse of movement which is transferred from the cause to the effect. Consequently, according to Ockham, one cannot go back infinitely in the series of maintaining causes without coming upon a first cause. Thus in this case one cannot ignore the question whether there is a first cause at all. For, in Ockham's view, if there is not, all movement would die out in this very moment, and everything would fall back into nothingness. But for the modern age even this argument falls. The acceptance of a first maintaining cause became superfluous as a result of the formulation of the principle of inertia. For if every body has in itself a tendency to persist in the state in which it is – be it a state of rest or a state of movement – and if this state is altered only under the influence of other forces, then the persistence or continuance of a state that has once come into being no longer needs any particular cause, and neither does a persistence in movement at the same speed and the same direction. It was the principle of inertia which made the idea of God superfluous to physics, not the fact that a first moving impulse was no longer indispensable. When Newton and the deists still sought to assure a place in their image of nature for God as the author of the necessary first impulse of the movement of the planets, Ockham had long before recognized the fallibility of this kind of argument in theology. If continuance in being and in movement had become something that could be taken for granted, then there was no longer any place for God in an account of nature. Descartes did not feel that inertia could be taken for granted so easily. He still found it necessary to base the acceptance of the continuance of all beings in their present state on the immutability of God in his creative action. But in the period that followed inertia became a principle, that is, something which no longer required any further explanation. It may be asked whether the rediscovery of the fundamental importance of the contingency of everything that happens in modern physics may not lead to revision of the way the principle of inertia is taken for granted. But until this happens, no valid renewal of the cosmological proof of God in the context of the understanding of nature is possible. The purely logical argument from the contingency of everything finite to the existence of a necessary being may be the expression of an ineluctable need of our mind and thought, without permitting of itself the conclusion that the reality of nature on which human thought is exercised needs such an original cause. But this brings us face to face with nothing less than the anthropological interpretation of the cosmological proof of God, an interpretation which in essence is present in Kant, although the argument in the *Critique of Pure Reason* so emphasizes the critical element that the positive conclusion of the *Critique* is often overlooked. The necessary being which is the conclusion of the cosmological proof is in Kant no longer a demand of nature itself, but only a requirement of the human understanding of nature carried out by means of the ideas of reason, that is, in Kant's term, a transcendental ideal. Kant did not believe that such an ideal was arbitrary, so that everyone had the choice of using the concept of God or not. Rather, for Kant, the idea of a necessary being was an idea that was necessarily involved in reason, but on this account was only an idea of reason. And apart from the reality of reason man cannot determine anything certain, even though according to Kant man cannot understand himself – particularly with regard to his moral constitution – without assuming the reality of this idea in his actual existence.

Hegel's renewal of the proofs of God must be understood as a completion of the anthropological interpretation which Kant began. In Hegel's interpretation, the cosmological and physico-theological arguments no longer relate directly to the processes of nature, but express the relationship of man to nature, man's elevation above the finitude of natural phenomena to the idea of the infinite, which as the truly infinite is the absolute. Here the proofs of God are for Hegel merely the formal expression of the elevation of man in religion above everything finite to the infinite. This is an extraordinarily profound thought, even if one finds the association of different forms of proof with different types of religion, in the form in which Hegel presents it, to be artificial. The conception of the proofs of God as the expression of man's elevation to the thought of God made it possible for Hegel to admit that forms of proof in which finite reality appeared as the starting point and the existence of God as the conclusion were inappropriate, and yet to recognize a meaningful process of thought in these proofs. F. H. Jacobi criticized the form of these proofs on the ground that in them God seemed to be dependent upon the finite data from which the proofs proceed. For Jacobi this was the decisive argument for the absurdity of all proofs with regard to God. But Hegel's interpretation of the proofs of God made it possible for him to show that behind the apparent absurdity produced by the logical form of the proof there lies a more profound meaning, for in fact the religious elevation of the mind must proceed from the experience of nature and the finite, in order to lift itself up to the idea of God. According to Hegel, the form of argument appropriate to this movement of thought must be to assert the existence of the infinite on account of the transitoriness of the finite, whereas in the traditional proofs of God, which proceed from the being of the finite to the being of the infinite, this element of negation is absent. The deductive forms of proof cease to be inappropriate only when God himself appears as the starting point of the proof, so that the form of the proof becomes a description of God's proof of himself. In Hegel's view this is so in the case of the ontological proof, which proceeds from the concept of God to his existence, and which was considered by Hegel to be the highest of the proofs of God, precisely because it resolved the contradiction between the content and the form of the proof. But in Hegel even this proof is related to the religious process of the elevation of man to God. Hegel did defend the ontological proof against Kant's criticism that one could not draw a conclusion about the existence of God from the concept of God. Kant had illustrated his criticism by the well-known example that if you think of a hundred thalers, it does not mean that you already have a hundred real thalers. Hegel replied that what distinguished the concept of God from all finite things is that in God essence and existence are identical. Thus only in the case of God can his existence be concluded from a concept, i.e. from this one particular concept of God. But to Hegel the difficulty of the ontological proof lies in the way we reach the concept of God which has to be assumed. So long as it appears as an arbitrary assumption which is made, but which can be omitted, there is no necessity for the idea of God and therefore for concluding from it his existence. Thus the concept of God, as the assumption of the ontological proof, must itself be shown to be a necessary and not a merely arbitrary idea, in order for the ontological argument to be conclusive. This means that the elevation of the human mind above all finite reality to the idea of God is itself an assumption made by the ontological argument, and provides the basis of it. And this elevation to the idea of God must be shown to be something which is inevitable and necessary for the human mind. Otherwise, the starting point of the ontological proof is an arbitrary and purely subjective idea without any real power of conviction.

Thus in Hegel himself the whole complex of problems associated with the proofs of God goes back to anthropology, that is, to the religious elevation which takes place in the life of the human mind. This makes it of decisive importance whether the elevation above the finite to the idea of the infinite and absolute is in fact, as Hegel asserted, a necessity for the human mind, and whether in fact it leads to a divine being different from men. Within the sphere of anthropological argument, the first and fundamental decision that has to be taken is whether what is said about God can claim a theoretical content of truth or can be taken to be the irrational expression of human attitudes which need to be explained differently – for example, in terms of psychology or social psychology.

II

The concentration upon the understanding of man of efforts to demonstrate the truth of the idea of God is paralleled by a similar development in the atheist criticism of belief in God. It is no accident that the arguments of modern atheism since the time of Feuerbach have been entirely anthropological. This is true not only of the Marxist criticism of religion, but also of Nietzsche, Freud, Nicolai Hartmann and Jean-Paul Sartre. The question that is really at issue here is not whether the idea of God is a product of the human mind, but whether it is an unessential product of the human mind, that is, an idea which is not part of man's understanding of himself which belongs to his essential being. The arguments of every form of modern atheism set out to demonstrate that no form of the idea of God is a necessary idea for the enlightened exercise of human existence, but is much more the expression of a misunderstanding on the part of man about his own nature which is transitory, even though it has dominated a long period of human history; an illusion which can be shown to be an illusion by the fact that it does not belong to the essence of man as such, but only to one phase of his history, however long that might have been. It is necessary in this case to demonstrate that the essential being of man can be completely described without calling upon the aid of religious categories, and that the idea of God is not an indispensable condition of a self-understanding adequate to man's nature, but has alienated men from themselves, and in particular has barred the way to a recognition of their freedom.

Amongst the examples of an excessive adaptation of theology to the intellectual fashions of the age was the belief of dialectic theology that it is possible to accept atheist arguments and trump them by a radical belief in revelation. It was held that the efforts of nineteenth-century theology to find a basis for theology in an anthropological theory of religious experience could be abandoned, together with the arguments of Feuerbach and his followers, as an expression of human self-deification, in which man simply projected himself into an imaginary heaven. It was supposed that instead it was possible to speak of God as the Wholly Other, inaccessible to an approach from the human side and revealed solely by his own initiative in Jesus Christ. Where this falls down is in the fact that to speak of God in this way can never be more than an empty subjective assertion, and is therefore, contrary to its intention, an extreme example of the way in which the question of God in the modern age has become dependent solely upon man's understanding of himself, even when this is manifested solely as the subjectivity of his assertions. When one speaks in this way of God, one is unprotected against the argument that one's language and use of the word "God" can be refuted by the same atheist argument that it is a projection. Dialectic theology in fact recognized the truth of this argument when it claimed that the way it spoke about God represented an exception. All atheist criticism has to do in this case is to show that the claim of theology, to speak about God in the way which forms an exception to the theory of religion which both accept, is baseless. This can be shown with little trouble by numerous analogies between Christian and non-Christian ways of speaking about God. If theology can do no more than protest, as H. Gollwitzer believes, against being taken over in this way by the atheist theory of religion, but is no longer able to assert the force of the argument against that theory, then its position is hopeless. And this is the position in which it finds itself in the public mind, following the great disillusionment with the uncompromising theses of dialectic theology. Theology is a good deal to blame itself for this situation. A theologian cannot appeal with impunity to the atheist criticism of religion. The intellectual situation of the present day, which is so strongly characterized by the tradition of modern atheism, does not require a theologian to take his stand on the ground of atheist theory. In terms of the intellectual effort a theologian has to expend, this represents the cheapest form of modernity. Yet theology pays a high price for it. If theology is not to abandon its task altogether, it must accept the challenge of atheism in such a way that it comes to grips with the atheist theory of religion. But in the historical situation of the modern mind it cannot come to grips with it in an area of its own choice, but only in the field which thoughtful concern with the question of God has, for quite good reasons, come to occupy in the course of the centuries. The arguments of atheism have consequently also established themselves in the same field. But it is that of anthropology, or more precisely that of the status of religious concerns and topics with regard to the nature of man. If it cannot be shown that the issues with which religion is concerned, the elevation of man above the finite content of human experience to the idea of an infinite reality which sustains everything finite, including man himself, are an essential of man's being, so that one is not really considering man if one ignores this dimension – if this cannot be shown with sufficient certainty, then every other viewpoint with which one may concern oneself in this field is an empty intellectual game, and what is said about God loses every claim to intellectual veracity.

Unfortunately the centrally important and urgent necessity for theology to come to grips with this topic, and the scale of the work to be done there, is too often underestimated in present day theology. This is partly because many theologians clearly still believe that statements with regard to God can be justified by appealing to a direct assertion of faith, however many other different grounds there may be for them. There are nevertheless issues on which it is possible to open a debate with atheism concerning the understanding of man. Such a starting point can be found in the widespread thesis of the problematic character of human existence. Oddly enough, this thesis is widely to be found even in dialectic theology – with the exception of Barth's middle period – but is also advanced elsewhere, e.g. in Tillich. But it is far too metaphorical a formulation, and except in the works of Brunner and Tillich it is often questionable whether we have an argument based on the observed phenomena of the structure of human existence, or just another theological assertion. Brunner sought support in the arguments of the personalistic anthropology of Buber and Ebner, but their thesis, which was also adopted by Gogarten, that the human "I" is unthinkable without a "thou", and is ultimately constituted not by the "thou" of our fellow men, but by the absolute "thou" of God, depends upon separating personal I–thou relationships from the practical concerns of the human experience of the world, in a way which is nowadays no longer possible. Tillich's thesis of the absolute concern which preoccupies every human being seems plausible by contrast, but forms too narrow a basis. And the development of this idea is burdened down in Tillich by a philosophical language adopted with too little reflection, the terminology of essence and existence. The analyses of intellectual life which Tillich has given in the third volume of his *Systematic Theology* go further. They would need to be discussed at a more profound level which explicitly took into account the relevant anthropological disciplines. Tillich's distinction between spirit and Holy Spirit in particular makes it unusually difficult to co-ordinate religious concerns and topics with other aspects of human life. The anthropological justification of religious concerns and topics is developed in a much more concrete way in the Catholic theology of Karl Rahner, though here it is burdened by the guiding thought of a "transcendental" structure of human nature prior to all concrete historical human experience. Similar difficulties are associated with the hypothesis of a religious *a priori*, an argument still advanced at the present day by Anders Nygren. In both cases we have extrapolations of the Kantian transcendental philosophy, which are intended to avoid the narrow restriction of the philosophy of religion to an ethical basis in Kant, but which overextend the concept of the transcendental or the *a priori* in a way for which there is no theoretical justification. The most impressive degree of success in developing a supranaturalist theology starting from the narrow Kantian concentration upon ethics is nowadays being achieved by G. Ebeling, in working out the theological implications of man's moral self-experience.

These various attempts to achieve a theological interpretation of the human situation all present points of view which must be accepted as positive contributions by a theological anthropology which is prepared to face up to the challenge of atheism. In the situation brought about by the atheist challenge, such a theological anthropology is in no sense merely a theological side issue. The anthropologizing of the idea of God, and the corresponding concentration of the atheist arguments against it upon anthropology, mean that theological anthropology nowadays has the status of a form of fundamental theology.

In order to do justice to the task this poses, it is absolutely necessary to pay full and detailed attention to the various empirically based disciplines of anthropology, human biology, sociology and psychology, with their methods and the problems associated with them. A thesis appealing to man's self-experience as it is accessible without scientific study, such as Tillich's thesis of the importance of an absolute concern in human life, is now too general to be satisfactory, however correct it may be. The same is true of metaphorical forms of expression such as the statement that human existence is problematic. What such turns of phrase imply must be demonstrated on the level of the problems of human biology, sociology and psychology as a constituent element of human nature. I have made an attempt in this direction, by taking further, in debate with Arnold Gehlen, the anthropological outline given by Max Scheler, and studying the theological relevance of the phenomenon of man's openness to the world. Reasons were found for understanding this phenomenon, which includes numerous characteristics of human organization and human behaviour, as an expression of the dependence of man upon an infinite reality which transcends everything with which he is in direct contact, and everything finite in general. Only on the basis of this reality, it appears, can human self-transcendence look forward to the fulfilment and totality for which it calls in its openness to the world. Similar studies are required of the importance of what may be called "basic trust" for the formation of personality, and of the need of social institutions for legitimation, to name only two examples. A number of tasks of a similar kind arise in the fields of cultural anthropology and the history of civilization, with regard to the role of religions in the development of man in the course of his history. A kind of first impression of the complex of problems that exist here is found in J. B. Cobb's book, *The Structure of Christian Existence*, 1967.

In working out the religious aspects of anthropological topics, which in non-theological study are usually raised only implicitly, the participation of theology must be associated with philosophical reflection upon one's own subjectivity. This requirement assumes that the modern problems of subjectivity have not merely been introduced by philosophy as a matter of historical fact, but that in their central concern they are a matter for philosophical self-reflection and cannot simply be left to psychology. Theology does not deal adequately with the task this poses by taking as its own basis a single one of the modern attempts at a philosophy of subjectivity, or outwardly modifying its perspectives to suit the needs of theology, as has happened in various ways in particular with the transcendental philosophy of Kant. Rather, philosophy must become involved in the philosophical debate about the ultimate basis of subjectivity, and it must do so in such a way that a theologian, in the case of the whole history of thought down to the present day, can form an independent judgment upon the whole course of the history of these problems, leading from one philosophical assertion to another, and on to the next. Only by independently mastering the history of the problems of philosophical thought, but not by adopting one or another single form of philosophy, can theology make a serious contribution to the problems of the basis of subjectivity. Here the central issue must be the question of the possibility of the freedom which first constitutes subjectivity as such. The central importance of this theme for theology is confirmed by the attention which modern atheism, in its various forms, has devoted to it. Is freedom possible as something constituted by the subject as such, or can it only be thought of as a freedom given to him, or even only as the experience of a liberation at some particular time? This problem has been posed since the time of Fichte, and still remains unresolved. It is this question which decides whether any faith in God must imply the denial of freedom, or whether the origin of freedom itself is to be sought in the religious concerns of life. Even in the latter case, the traditional doctrine of God must undergo a profound revision in the light of the problems of freedom; for there are unquestionably forms of the conception of God which exclude human freedom, even though this is not true of every possible understanding of God. For example, in the case of the classical conception of God in Christian scholasticism it is not possible to assert that it must be understood as the condition of human freedom. It is even very questionable whether it can be reconciled with freedom, as is indeed shown by the medieval discussion about the relationship of divine foreknowledge and predestination to human freedom. If God is understood as an omniscient and omnipotent being complete and perfect at the beginning of the created world, then in fact no human freedom would be possible; and on the other hand the experience of freedom excludes belief in the existence of such a God, as Nietzsche, Nicolai Hartmann and Sartre have rightly emphasized. The question is only whether we have here an insoluble difficulty involved in every idea of God, or whether the understanding of the reality of God can be developed in such a way that God is conceivable as the basis of human freedom, and no longer as its negation. In answering this question, however, it is scarcely possible for theology to avoid re-examining the way it speaks about the being of God. Thought of as an existent being on the analogy of tangible things, God, even if such a God existed, could only belong to the totality of everything with which freedom is concerned. But the basis of freedom cannot be a being that already exists, but only a reality which reveals to freedom its future, the coming God.

Thus a theological anthropology which is to serve as a fundamental theology must, if it is seriously to face the challenge of athesim, deal at appropriate length with the different fields of anthropological study, with their methods, results and problems, and with the history of the problems resulting from philosophical reflection upon human subjectivity; and it must also discuss them with regard to their implications for the religious dimension of human existence. And the more empirical aspects and the philosophical problems of subjectivity must not be kept apart, but must be dealt with in accordance with the ways in which in practice they are associated. Moreover, this association in practice is already implicit in the fact that the distinctive features of human organization and behaviour, cursorily described as "openness to the world", amount simply to the outer aspect of the freedom, the inner aspect of which is the theme of the problems of subjectivity.

III

A reasonable view of the necessity and possibility of a theological anthropology appropriate to the modern concentration of the question of God on man's understanding of himself, and to the challenge of atheism, must include the question of its limitations. A general theological anthropology cannot be expected to do more than demonstrate the religious dimension of man's being. It can show that what takes place in religious experience is as much a constituent part of man's being as walking erect, or the ability to use fire and tools. But it cannot be expected to supply a proof of the reality of God. Kant's thesis that a theoretical proof of the existence of God is impossible is not invalidated by the abstract dualism of Kantian philosophy, with its separation of subject and object, criticized by Hegel. Hegel rightly objected to this separation on the grounds that in every act of knowing, in so far as it is an act of knowing, subject and object are united. It is virtually this which constitutes the concept of truth. The question is only whether an act of knowledge ever definitively achieves possession of the truth. The process of knowing seems rather to be such that what is directly apprehended as true is always seen by the reflective thought, which occurs as the experience is continued, to be merely a partial truth. This is also true of the sphere of religious experience. Hegel believed that the religious "elevation of the subjective spirit to God directly implies that in this very act of elevation the one-sidedness of knowledge, that is, its subjectivity, is abolished, and that it is itself essentially this process of abolition and absorption".[1] In fact the meaning of the elevation of man in religion lies in his union with the divine reality to which he elevates himself. So faith too unites the believer with God, even though *extra se*. If the reality of

[1] *Vorlesungen über die Beweise vom Dasein Gottes,* ed. G. Lasson, *Werke* 14 (PhB 64), 1930, p. 44; ET *Lectures on the Philosophy of Religion* III, 1895, p. 190.

God remains simply inaccessible to man, then religion becomes a self-contradictory concept. In the self-elevation of religion, in so far as it possesses truth, man is united with the reality of God, just as someone who knows is united in the act of knowing – in so far as it is true, and is therefore really knowing – in his consciousness with the object which he knows. But this implies that the truth of religious knowledge is the measure of its power to unite. This is also true of faith, in so far as faith without any knowledge of him who is its object is not possible. But this does not mean we can conclude, from the fact that the religious dimension is one of the constituent elements of man's being, that God exists. It is possible that man's very nature is dependent upon an illusion, which, contrary to what is held by atheist theories of illusion, he is not able to detect as such, because it is in the nature of his being always to be subject to it. General anthropological considerations can never take us further than the assertion that when man's being is fully aware, man is conscious that he is dependent upon a reality which surpasses and sustains everything finite, and in this sense is a divine reality. This is what Kant had in mind when he restricted his moral argument to practical rather than theoretical validity. This limitation is intimately associated with the fact that the modern consideration of the question of God has been entirely dependent upon man's self-understanding: only in so far as man's statements about God have some points of contact with extra-subjective reality as well, can he assume that he is not trapped in an illusion brought about by the structure of his subjectivity, and instead experiences God as a reality. The divine reality, on which a person whose religion is lively and self-conscious finds himself dependent in the structure of his subjectivity, is encountered as a reality only in the context of the experience of the world. The way it is encountered is that in the context of the historical world of any person, freedom is something which actually comes about in a particular way on some occasion. Thus the divine reality, on which man finds himself to be dependent in the structure of his subjectivity, reveals itself in the actual coming about of freedom as a power over the world in which he finds himself, and therefore as a reality. Moreover, only in this experience is there any place for the knowledge of the divine reality as personal, as God, in so far as it is experienced as a liberating action which bestows freedom. But the concrete way in which man finds his freedom has undergone many changes in the course of the history of individuals and nations. It is the subjective aspect of the history of religion, and forms a complement to the understanding of the reality of the world, as religious experience has apprehended it in its totality at any particular time.

These latter considerations are not in their turn invalidated by the modern concentration of the question of God upon man's self-understanding. There can no longer be any corroboration of the reality of God which ignores the problems of man's self-understanding. There is no longer any direct route from the knowledge of nature to the knowledge of God, and even an interpretation of inertia in the light of the contingency of natural events will not lead in the end to proofs of God from physics. But besides the direct relationship to the phenomena of the world, there must be another kind of relationship of man to the world which is not isolated and opposed to his relationship to himself, but in which man experiences himself by experiencing his world. And this experience of man's world, mediated by his relationship to himself, is that in which he perceives, or fails to perceive, the reality of the dimension upon which he is dependent in the structure of his subjectivity. This is just as true of the historical fact of individual experiences as of the general considerations of theological reflection: an abstract concern with the structure of subjectivity cannot go as far as the reality of God, but only as far as to see the evidently problematic nature of man's being as a question about God. The reality of God, on which man is dependent in the structure of his subjectivity, is encountered only where, in the context of his world, he receives himself as a gift in the experience of freedom.

This does not mean that what we have just called the

abstract consideration of the structure of subjectivity – either of subjectivity in general or the existential concern with one's own self – is without significance for the experience of the reality of God. For at the present day only someone who by self-reflection has come to be conscious of the dependence of his subjectivity upon a divine reality which sustains it can realize that both the gift of freedom and its continued absence in the context of his historical world have to do with the reality of God.

But in so saying, we have already affirmed that to take the question of the reality of God beyond anthropology to the experience of the gift of freedom in the context of the experience of the world does not make belief in God in any sense a question of an act of piety or a supernatural interpretation of life. It is a question of a sober concern with the historical facts, at any time, of man's experience of the world and of himself. The material of a theology which reflects upon this complex of experience is not a religious subjectivity which is dependent upon an act of faith, nor a religious interpretation of the world laid down in advance by an authoritative revelation. It is the history of religion as the record of men's historical experience of themselves in the context of the totality of their world, and thus of the reality of God and the gods. The truth of such an experience depends upon its power to illuminate the situation of men in their actual historical world. Religions have come into being within the limits of the illuminating power of the experiences on which they were based, and they have died when their light failed. But we can no more close the files on the truth or untruth of such experiences than upon the truth and untruth of any and every piece of knowledge we possess. Nor does the continuing process of experience always bring with it a growth of knowledge. All too often, one prejudice is merely replaced by another. Thus, like all intellectual life, the life of religion possesses no final truth, nor does it make unambiguous progress in the knowledge of truth. The final validity of truth and untruth, and the closeness or distance of various historical periods to the truth, will only become visible in the light of the end of all things. But all human experience is still in progress. It is not cut off from the truth. But as we progress through the changing horizons of new experiences, the truth which our experience has perceived must always be tested to see if it can still be sustained.

3

SPEAKING ABOUT GOD IN THE FACE
OF ATHEIST CRITICISM

First published in *Evangelische Kommentare* 2, 1969, pp. 442–6.

NOT LONG AGO, the question of the "natural" knowledge of God seemed to be one of the doctrines which determined the denominational differences between Protestants and Catholics. Karl Barth saw in all "natural" knowledge of God and "natural" theology the enemy of a theology based upon the revelation of Christ, because it was an inalienable feature of revelation that it provided man with his knowledge, his first knowledge, of God. Barth's attack upon "natural" theology formed the climax and conclusion of a growing criticism in Protestant theology, since Schleiermacher and Ritschl, of the traditional philosophical doctrine of God and its use in theology. Schleiermacher actually described the "natural" knowledge of God as a mere abstraction derived from concrete historical religions, or more precisely as an abstraction from the features common to the religions of the highest, monotheist stage. This deprived "natural" theology of its independence of positive religions, and turned it into something secondary and merely derivative from them. Ritschl, and Wilhelm Herrmann even more, intensified Schleiermacher's criticism by rejecting along with "natural" theology all metaphysical elements in the doctrine of God, and attempting instead to base it upon ethics. Finally, although Barth began in the school of Ritschl, he came to include even an ethically based knowledge of God on Kantian lines in "natural" theology, and argued instead that it should be replaced by the revelation of Christ as the sole source of a true knowledge of God. Thus the road leading from Schleiermacher to Barth showed an increasing extension of the concept of "natural" theology as a polemic conception opposed to the Christian theology of revelation, together with a progressive narrowing down of the way the Christian theology of revelation was itself understood by those who maintained it.

In Barth the rejection of "natural" theology took on a new function, not found in Schleiermacher, but already hinted at in Ritschl. It became an instrument of theological apologetics against the atheist criticism of the metaphysical idea of God, and of that which religions teach. If a theologian cannot count on any knowledge of God outside the sphere of influence of the revelation in Christ, then it is perfectly comprehensible that a non-Christian should not want to know anything about God. Thus atheism can virtually be considered a confirmation of the exclusiveness of revelation, a corroboration of its claim and promise to be the sole source of the knowledge of God. In this sense it has rightly been said that Barth's theology assumes the atheism of Feuerbach in the same way as scholastic and orthodox Protestant theology was based upon a natural knowledge of God and a natural theology. When Dietrich Bonhoeffer demanded a religionless preaching of Christ, in theological terms he was only drawing the consequence of the standpoint of his teacher Barth.

The way in which Feuerbach's criticism of religion was accepted by Barth and his followers was from the first open to serious objections. Ultimately, the main intention of Feuerbach, as of his atheist successors Marx and Freud, was to unmask *Christianity* and the *Christian* idea of God as the product of human self-alienation. This was bound to raise the question whether one has any right to apply the description, by Feuerbach or his successors, of religion as the projection of human anxieties and longings into an imaginary heaven, to *non-Christian* religions and *non-Christian* philosophy, but to postulate Christianity as an exception. In view of the extensive analogies between Christianity and the holy scriptures which it asserts as a testimony of revelation, and other religions and their documents, the postulate that in the case of Christianity we have something quite different, not a human religion but a divine revelation, could only appear to be a bare assertion – and what is more a completely human assertion. It seemed to make it far too easy for theology to dismiss at a single stroke both atheist criticism and the encounter with non-Christian religions and with philosophy.

Of course such considerations did not shake those followers of Barth who adopted the extreme position of the theology of revelation. The blows bounced off them. It was relatively simple for the theology of revelation to defend itself against such doubts by insisting upon the uniqueness and exceptional nature of the revelation in Christ. The situation became more serious when the untenability of a point of view based exclusively on the theology of revelation was demonstrated from within, on the basis of the theme and concerns of theology itself. This came about through the recognition that the use of the idea of God can itself no longer be justified on the basis of an exclusive theology of revelation. The present-day tendency to argue away and exclude the idea of God in Protestant theology must be understood as a consequence of the movement which began with the rejection of "natural" knowledge of God, and with it of all philosophical theology. But the dismay at the conclusions to which this movement has led must not be allowed to provoke the reaction that it was in every respect a movement in the wrong direction. It is very doubtful whether one can simply take up again the threads at the point at which the "natural" theology of scholasticism and the Enlightenment began to be criticized. The decisive issues and arguments which led to their breakdown under criticism must not be forgotten: Schleiermacher's realization that all concrete religion is historical, and that philosophical or "natural" theology is the result of a process of abstraction; Ritschl's understanding that the idea of God cannot be based solely upon the world which exists here and now, and with which our theoretical knowledge is concerned; and finally, Barth's argument that the concept of revelation is emptied of significance if it is possible to find elsewhere what can seriously be called definitive knowledge of the God to whose revelation the scriptures bear witness.

These insights make it impossible simply to return to the course followed by the old "natural" theology – even if this were possible in the present day philosophical situation. But however highly we value the motives which led Protestant theology to an increasingly intense criticism of all non-Christian knowledge of God, it must be realized that the consequence of this course was in fact the breakdown of the idea of God: Herbert Braun's demythologization of the idea of God, Robinson's *Honest to God* and the American "Death of God" theologians are the heirs of Barth and Bultmann. For if all philosophical theology is to be dismissed, what justification is there for continuing to maintain and believe what Jesus says about God? The human authority of Jesus alone? Would this not mean that the idea of God was one of the features of his ministry and preaching which were conditioned by his own time, particularly as it is clear that Jesus usually presupposed the idea of God and of his coming Kingdom which he found in his environment. But if Jesus' idea of God, which unquestionably forms the centre of his message, is abandoned, then there is virtually no point in continuing to assert any connection, any continuity of meaning worth calling "Christian", with what was central for Jesus himself. And what is the real position of the human authority of Jesus, when one looks at it in isolation from his preaching of God? The light cast by the humanity of Jesus on the nature of true humanity, the example of unconditional love untrammelled by the law, is only partially relevant. For it is clear, as for example Karl Jaspers has pointed out, that whole areas of the reality of man's existence, and especially his place in the whole framework of the universe, were never dealt with by Jesus. The humanity of Jesus can only be of universal validity if he is understood in the light of his message about God and his imminent kingdom. In this case the general relevance of the humanity of Jesus is related to the idea that man as a whole is destined for fellowship with God in everything whatsoever which belongs to his human nature. If we

reject a relationship between man and a reality which transcends him and everything finite, which to this extent is
mysterious, and which we call God, as irrelevant for the understanding of the being of man, then it is also impossible to
attribute general validity to the humanity of Jesus. It is no
more than the logical consequence of this that Thomas Altizer
should abandon, together with the idea of God, the historical
Jesus of Nazareth as well, and maintain only an idea of Christ
distinct from Jesus. Anyone to whom Jesus' message concerning
God no longer means anything would do better to look round
for other exemplary figures of humanity, towards which the
self-realization of man in the world can be more securely
orientated than Jesus.

If the possible general relevance of the humanity of Jesus,
that is, its human authority, must be seen by us as related
from the first to man's search for God, then it can neither be
isolated from Jesus's preaching about God, nor serve on its
own as the basis for what Christians say about God. If people
are to believe in the God whom Jesus preached for his sake
alone, and on the basis of his authority, the result would be a
kind of self-deception. As we have said, the human authority of
Jesus has a tenable basis only in his message about God and
the coming of his kingdom. But this means that the authority
of the person of Jesus – like the message of the historical Jesus
himself – already assumes a preliminary knowledge of God.
A well-founded authority can be accorded to the man Jesus
only by people who are already concerned with the question
of God, or at least brought into contact with it by Jesus. The
authority of Jesus is based on his message of the coming of the
kingdom of God, and not the other way round. Present-day
theologians who abandon the idea of God, but still wish to
venerate Jesus, or to find the way back to God through the
human authority of Jesus, show a devotion to the figure of
Jesus which must be respected as genuinely Christian. But they
deceive themselves in supposing that the influence of the
human features of the person of Jesus on Christian tradition
and devotion was not mediated by the divine light which they

are no longer willing to see in his face. We do not wish to share this self-deception, but to make it clear that the abandonment of God would bring the end of Christianity altogether in the foreseeable future. The relativization of a figure of Jesus deprived of its central concern, the message of the coming of God, would be child's play for the critics of Christianity by comparison with the struggle over the idea of God. The abandonment of the idea of God would not make the task of apologetics any easier for Christian theology, a curious view which many Christians seem to hold, but would make it incomparably harder, and indeed completely hopeless.

Look closely at the situation in which the struggle against an awareness of God which must already be assumed by Christian faith and is prior to faith is associated with the demythologization or rather the critical elimination of the idea of God from theology. Try then to measure the full burden of the consequences which result from this for the Christian message of salvation. Anyone who does so can remain a theologian only if he takes up again the question that has already been abandoned, of the relationship of man to God which is already assumed by Christian faith, and of which it always has a prior consciousness in some form or another. Only if man, even outside the Christian message, is related in his being as man to the reality of God on which the message of Jesus is based can fellowship with Jesus mean salvation to him. But if, even outside the Christian message, man already has a relationship with the God whom the message of Jesus presupposes, then man must always have had, in some form, a consciousness of this relationship which constitutes his being as man. For a creature endowed with self-consciousness may be mistaken about what makes him himself, but he cannot simply remain unaware of it.

In other words, theology must once again become aware of the world of non-Christian religion as a central concern, if it is to assert that a relationship to the reality which we call God is everywhere a constituent element in man as such. The world of religions, and the religious attitude of man in general to which it bears evidence, is the field in which theology must take its stand against atheism. The theologian who fails in this is acting like a revolutionary who makes a pact with the establishment in the hope that it will fall apart by itself. If the religious tendency of man is asserted to be decisive for the justification of any way of speaking about God, this implies that the tenability or untenability of our speaking about him must be decided on the basis of man's self-understanding.

It is no accident that, at least since Feuerbach, modern atheism has concentrated its arguments upon anthropology, as can clearly be seen in Marx, Nietzsche, Freud, and Sartre. Here the arguments of atheism run parallel to the concentration upon anthropology which has taken place in the recent history of philosophical theology, and in particular of the proof of God. Kant's criticism of rational theology was aimed at the theoretical arguments for the existence of God based upon the framework of the objective knowledge of the world. His own moral proof of God, on the other hand, centred upon the question of an appropriate self-understanding of man in his moral constitution. But the idealist renewal of the ancient proofs of God was brought about by interpreting them too in an anthropological way: Hegel interpreted the cosmological and the cosmo-teleological proofs as the abstract philosophical expression of the religious self-elevation of man above the finite to the idea of the infinite. And he considered that the main problem, even in the ontological proof, was how the human mind could elevate itself to the particular concept of God which itself included his existence.

It can be shown that even in forbears of modern thought who differ as much as Descartes and Locke there are likewise recognizable first steps towards an anthropological concentration or reformulation of the proofs of God. This trend is no doubt associated with the fact that the theoretical knowledge of the world in modern physics – by contrast to the physics of Averroes and in spite of Newton – no longer needed the idea of a first cause. The methodological atheism of modern natural science shifted the whole burden of the question of God upon man. Thus it was only logical for modern atheism to concentrate

its arguments upon anthropology, and to try to show that
the idea of God expressed in the religious and philosophical
documents of humanity was to be understood in its entirety as
a projection of human conceptions into an imaginary heaven.
However, the idea that all human conceptions and statements
about God were products of the human mind was not itself a
sufficient basis for atheism. Kant and the idealists also regarded
man as a productive subjectivity, in his religious thought as in
the whole of his intellectual life. But the decisive question is
whether the development of an idea of God is of the essence of
man's being, or whether it can be shown to be a misunderstanding of man on his own part, and consequently an error. Kant,
then later Fichte, Schleiermacher, and Hegel saw man as a
being looking beyond himself and everything finite to a reality
transcending the finite, so that only his elevation to God can
set man free from his entanglement in the finite. By contrast,
Feuerbach and his successors down to Sartre resisted the idea
of God as a hindrance to human freedom. The basic question
posed by modern atheism is this: Does man, in the exercise of
his existence, assume a reality beyond himself and everything
finite, sustaining him in the very act of his freedom, and
alone making him free, a reality to which everything that is
said about God refers? Or does the freedom of man exclude
the existence of God, so that with Nietzsche, Nicolai Hartmann
and Sartre we must postulate the non-existence of God, not his
existence, for the sake of human freedom? This must be the
central question by which modern atheism stands and falls.
And a decision on this question is an indispensable basic condition, though not a completely sufficient condition in itself,
for any justification of our speaking about God.

This statement means that the first and fundamental choice
between theology and atheism in fact lies in the understanding
of man, in anthropology.[1] The objection may be made that the
idea of God is never concerned solely with man, but always with
the world as well. This remains true even if knowledge of the

[1] In this sense one can agree with Herbert Braun's formulation: "The
atheist does not do justice to *man*", *ZThK*, Beiheft 2, 1961, p. 18.

world, taken by itself, no longer leads to the idea of God. But the starting point must lie in the question of a proper understanding of the being of man. Even arguments which are not in a form that makes this immediately obvious have in this sense an anthropological basis, in so far as they are meaningful at all. Hegel showed this for the cosmological and the cosmo-teleological proofs. But the argument from the contingency of all experienced data is conclusive for man only if he is asking about something which exists in itself as the ultimate basis of all that is real. The idea that everything contingent pre-supposes for its existence something that exists in itself is already a form of elevation of man above his situation in the finite to the idea of something non-finite.

Thus it is clear that in the conflict between theology and atheism, the decision about whether any way can be found to the idea of God depends upon the understanding of man, upon anthropology. This is true, even though the final tenability of any idea of God which is put forward depends in addition upon the understanding of the world, that is, upon how far the God who is asserted is comprehensible as the reality which determines everything.

The atheist assertion that the idea of God is the expression of a self-alienation of man, and is a threat to human freedom and therefore to humanity itself, cannot be taken lightly. If theology appreciates the force of the argument at all, it is forced at least to make a far-reaching reformulation of the idea of God. For the key problems of divine foreknowledge and predestination show that in fact there is an antinomy in the attitude adopted by traditional Christian theism to human freedom, however much the understanding of man as the image of God may have encouraged the idea of man's destiny to be free as the image of the creative freedom of God. The disputes in scholasticism concerning divine foreknowledge and predestination are evidence that as early as this there was an awareness of the tension at this point between the understanding of God and human freedom. And one can hardly say that the difficulties which arose in traditional theology over this issue were ever satisfactorily resolved. They display the ultimate effects of an ontology of the being of God which is associated with traditional Christian theism, although it is not perhaps absolutely essential to the Christian idea of God. This ontology thought of God on the analogy of everything else that exists. If the eternity of God is thought of as the unlimited continuance of a being which has existed from the first, then the omnipotence and omniscient providence of this God must have established the course of everything that takes place in the universe in all its details from the very first. In this case there is no room for genuine freedom on the part of any creature. The great efforts of Christian theology to avoid this consequence are well known. It was bound to conflict with a whole series of genuine Christian convictions, such as the fact of sin, which it was very difficult to fit into a divine plan for the world which had existed from the beginning, and was equally difficult to reconcile with the idea of the redemption as an act of grace, a free act of God not laid down in advance. The conflict between the contingency of historical experience, and particularly of human freedom on the one hand, and the idea of divine providence and predestination on the other hand, could not simply be dismissed. Neither the solution that God foresees free actions as such, nor the consideration that the eternity of God is simultaneous at any point in time and therefore does not predetermine temporal events, could be convincing as long as the being of God was thought of as already perfect and complete in itself at every point in past time and therefore at the beginning of all temporal processes.

This view, which might seem to be directly implicit in the idea of the eternity of God, seems to have been somewhat questioned in traditional Christian theism. But if it is adopted, then no subsequent precautions are of any value in averting the undesired consequences of this assumption. An almighty and omniscient being thought of as existing at the beginning of all temporal processes excludes freedom within the realm of his creation. On the other hand, if freedom is the ability to go beyond what already exists, to set it aside or change it, then such a freedom means the ability to go beyond a God who in some sense belongs to the totality of what exists. Thus Sartre was able to concentrate atheism into a remark that is as intolerable as can be to the ears of believers: "Even if God existed, it could make no difference"[2] – that is, to man's situation of being at the mercy of his own freedom and therefore always as such transcending himself, going outside himself, and going beyond all that already exists. But because man transcends a God thought of as an existent being, and can get away from him as he can from everything that merely exists, then ultimately such a God would not be God at all. He would be no longer conceivable as the reality which determines everything, for he could no longer by definition determine the freedom of man, but could be transcended by it. In this sense Bultmann's statement that God cannot be thought of as an object, that is, as existing as any other being exists, is correct.[3] To think of God in this way would be to no longer think of him as "God". But it is this very monstrous conception of a God who is an existent being equipped with omnipotence and omniscience, which atheist criticism attacks in the name of human freedom. One cannot say that this displays a total misunderstanding of traditional Christian theism. Rather, the Christian doctrine of God has in fact, and in all innocence, thought of God on the analogy of what exists. It has linked this idea with the biblical conception of the omnipotent actions of God in history, and has then endeavoured in vain to avert the disastrous consequences which have resulted from this combination. Here atheist criticism is justified. An *existent* being acting with omnipotence and omniscience would make freedom impossible. But such a being would also not be God, because it could not be the reality which determines everything, for the reality of freedom, of human subjectivity, would remain outside its grasp.

Thus the biblical idea of the omnipotence of God is in

[2] *Existentialism and Humanism*, ET by P. Mairet, 1948, p. 56.
[3] *Glauben und Verstehen* I, 6th ed., 1966, pp. 26ff.; ET *Faith and Understanding*, 1969, pp. 53ff.

irreconcilable conflict with the understanding of God as an existent being. Theology should think of God rather as the origin of freedom, as the reality which makes possible the subjectivity of man.[4] This would be in accordance with theological tradition in regarding man as the image of God because of his freedom. It would also follow both Paul and John in using the word freedom as a term to sum up the whole of the salvation which has even now been made possible by the event of the atonement, by the incarnation and death of the *logos*, and by the activity of the Spirit of God. But if Christian theology is nowadays to think of God as the origin of human freedom, then it can no longer think of him as an existent being. The age of metaphysical innocence concerning this question is over. And it is modern atheism which forces us to make a break with it. Here atheist criticism can be given credit for having assisted theology to be more clear about its own subject, about the reality of God, which is no longer to be confused with an existent being.

But how can one speak of God as a reality without speaking of him as an existent being? Is there an alternative? Is not the scope of the real identical with what exists at the present moment? Or is what is no longer or not yet existent at the present moment "real", that is, effective in the present moment? Whereas the past can always be thought of as formerly existent, as though the basis of its reality were that it was once existent, the future in particular seems to offer an alternative to an understanding of the real which is concentrated entirely upon what is existent. For what belongs to the future is not yet existent, and yet it already determines present experience, at least the present experience of beings who – like man – are orientated towards the future and always experience their present and past in the light of a future which they hope for or which they fear. Thus the future is real, although it does not yet exist. This can moreover be significant for the question of the reality of God with regard to the fact that Jesus proclaimed

[4] See T. Koch, "Gott – der Grund der Freiheit", *Pastoraltheologie*, 1968, pp. 45ff.

the kingdom of God, which cannot be separated from the deity of God, as a future kingdom.

The reality of the future in contrast to what exists here and now is expressed not least in the freedom of man. The realm of human freedom consists of possibilities not yet realized, in which man is concerned for his future and the future of his world, and through which he makes his own self the future of what now exists. Thus the reality of the future and that of freedom belong together, by contrast with what exists here and now. Neither exist themselves, but they have power over what exists here and now.

In such a correspondence between the reality of the future and the nature of freedom, is *God* already implicit as the origin of freedom, especially if God is thought of as the power of the future, as the God whose kingdom is *coming*? Or is there not a considerable leap which separates the association of freedom with the future from the idea that it is God who makes freedom accessible? The gap between the two ideas seems to arise particularly from the ineffaceably personal note of the word "God". But freedom and personality are intimately related. If personality can be distinguished from the modes of existence of what exists here and now, it is perhaps not so completely hopeless to look for God, as the origin of freedom, in the fact that freedom refers to the future.

This question affects our theme over a considerable range. For as we have said, the word "God" is inescapably personal. A non-personal basis for the universe cannot rightly be called "God". The fact that traditional philosophical theology has often so loosely used the word "God", when what was really meant was the non-personal basis of the world, may be a sign of its derivation or formal adaptation to receive religious language, but fortunately there is no need to attempt to justify it. Anyone who says "God" says "person". The personal character of what is said about God has often been felt burdensome – even by theology – because it seems to discredit the idea of God, as being of its nature anthropomorphic. Modern criticism of the idea of God has in fact to a large extent sought to lay bare the anthropomorphic aspects of the idea of God as a personality which might seem to be a mere reflection of the human personality, particularly as the personal self-consciousness of man, dependent upon another self-consciousness outside himself, seems to be in contradiction to the alleged infinity of God. But the personality of God becomes relevant in a new way to the question of a reality which is not an existent being: a person is the opposite of an existent being. Human beings are persons by the very fact that they are not wholly and completely existent for us in their reality, but are characterized by freedom, and as a result remain concealed and beyond control in the totality of their existence. A person whose whole being we could survey and whose every movement we could anticipate would thereby cease to be a person for us, and where human beings are falsely taken to be existent beings and treated as such, then their personality is treated with contempt. This is unfortunately possible, because human beings are in fact also existent beings. Their being as persons takes shape in their present, bodily reality, and yet it remains invisible to one whose vision – unlike the vision of love or even that of hate – looks only at what is existent in man.

It is of decisive importance not to see the personality of man in its turn as no more than an existent being of another kind. To do so leads to such ideas as that of a metaphysical soul-substance, which is supposed to exist in parallel to or within that of the body, but which cannot be demonstrated to exist. The subjectivity and personality of man are not something existent, although they endeavour to take form in what exists. When we consider this, it becomes clear that man is not a person of himself, not by the constitution of his ego, as though it were an existent being and not rather a name for the person who is present, but is not an existent being. But if the origin of freedom is sought in man himself, in what man already was before the act of his freedom, then his being as a person – the subject of his freedom – has already been thought of as an existent being, instead of as a subjectivity which is realized only through freedom.

The basic and widespread failing of atheist descriptions of human behaviour is that they take man's personal being, his subjectivity, as something existent, as an existent self, which, however, first constitutes itself in the act of its choice. Thus in one breath the self is asserted to be already existent and at the same time constituted only by the act of its choice. The question of the identity of the self in these two elements must be seen in this light. In the act of his freedom man goes beyond what he already was; that is, the origin of freedom lies in someone or something other than the self which already existed. In other words, human freedom is always received as a gift. Because man is always and in the first instance a being existent for others and for himself, his freedom cannot derive from himself. And the identity of his freedom with the self that is already existent cannot simply be assumed, but is based on the fact that in the act of his freedom man constantly transcends himself. Consequently, the someone other to whom man owes his being, cannot himself be an existent being, if he is to be the origin of man's freedom. Thus man achieves his being as a person, as a free subjectivity, only from the encounter with other persons, and in fact basically by turning in love to others. The basis of this is the fundamental trust found at the beginning of the life of the individual, which the personality of the child needs for its formation. Common humanity, language and society are conditions of personal life, and form the atmosphere in which alone freedom can breathe.

The sphere of common humanity, of society, is of course also the sphere of the suppression of freedom. The other person, to whom I can turn and so obtain freedom, needs to be set free in order to become himself. For he too does not derive his freedom from what he already is or was. He can impart only the freedom towards which he himself is open, and which is in the balance at any moment, and must be given and received anew. Where this does not take place, a lack of freedom deforms the relationships between one man and another. This occurs above all where the name of freedom is called upon to justify the self assertion of the existent ego, and the "freedom" of the one is obtained at the cost of the freedom of the others.

Since in the end my fellow man is ultimately as dependent as I am upon the gift of freedom, the "thou" of my fellow man cannot be the ultimate basis of freedom. Freedom can continue to flourish amongst men only where its origin lies, independently of the arbitrary desires of individuals, in a commonly recognized truth. But this requirement is not satisfied by the universality of an idea (in the Kantian sense), for the carefully defined and therefore limited way in which it is formulated restricts the freedom of individuals; and it is in addition always thought of as something existent, which thought itself can transcend. The basis of freedom as something held in common can be provided only by a personal reality of a supra-human kind, which by contrast to a human reality would be a pure act of freedom.

This does not mean that the existence of a divine person or of a personal God can be postulated as the basis of freedom. Moreover the form of the proof must be regarded as the most impermanent element in the so-called "proofs of the existence of God". What they prove is at best the finiteness of man and the world, and not the existence of God, even though the demonstration that everything that exists is finite, and that nothing finite can exist of itself, may raise and make explicit the question of the reality with which religions are concerned. It is not the purpose of these considerations to prove the existence of God. But perhaps the idea of a divine person as the origin of freedom may appear less incredible and unthinkable at the end of this argument than before. The history of humanity shows that freedom with regard to what exists, with the corresponding step in the realization of human personality, was in each case won only through a particular experience of divine reality. The history of human personality appears as a function of the history of religion, that is, of the changes in man's experience of God. This situation suggests that the relationship between divine reality and human freedom is not so much one of contraries as modern atheism argues. The positive connection between the two, the evidence for which is found in the conditions imposed in the history of religion on the development of human personality and freedom, can be understood when one considers that for divine reality to be personal does not imply that it is an existent being like others. The "existence" of gods – which is not necessarily to be interpreted as their being existent beings like others – is subordinate in religious experience to the apprehension of their activity. By contrast to man, who in one respect is also an existent being, the existence of the gods as a reality lies only in their activity, in the demonstration of their power. And therefore the existence of the gods has always been a matter of dispute in the religious experience of mankind, so that men have changed their gods and come to have different conceptions of them.

In the history of religion, the divine reality is an element which is always subject to dispute, and it is in this way that the history of religion can be understood as the course taken by God to reveal himself. Not until the true nature of the divine is revealed will the question of the existence of God be finally decided – and even since Christ has come, man is still moving towards this event, in so far as the kingdom of God and therefore the full demonstration of the deity of the God proclaimed by Jesus is still to come. But as the God who is to come, the God of Jesus is already at work as the God of reconciling love, who raise the dead and is therefore also the origin of the freedom which overcomes what exists, and yet redeems it.

4

CHRISTIAN THEOLOGY AND PHILOSOPHICAL CRITICISM

First published in *Revue de Théologie et de Philosophie* 18, 1968, pp. 249-71.

IN FOUR hundred years of the history of Protestantism, the relationship of theology to philosophy has repeatedly been questioned and disputed. Consequently, there is no attitude to philosophy and its intellectual heritage which is characteristic of Protestantism as a whole. Instead, there is a great diversity of attitudes which are in part in direct opposition to each other. The issue is not merely that of the relationship of Christian faith to attempts to describe the ultimate basis of experience and thought which are philosophical in the narrower sense. It is also that of the relationship of theology to the whole body of critical thought which has developed since the beginnings of Greek philosophy, and of which there is a greater awareness in the modern period than ever before. In historical terms the issue is on the one hand the attitude of the Christian mind to the heritage of Greek thought. It is a question which for theology is constantly raised by its own tradition, because in its classical period, in late antiquity, theology explicitly and with some success claimed this heritage for its own, and because the assimilation was bound to become the essential element in the self-understanding of a Christianity which had grown away from the sphere of Jewish tradition. The other and more urgent issue is the attitude of the Christian self-understanding to the problems which were brought to a head in the Enlightenment and have since been characteristic of the modern consciousness. Ought Christian theology to endorse the way the modern mind has turned against the authoritarian claims of a sacred tradition? Or ought it to identify itself with the points of view attacked by the criticism of the Enlightenment on the grounds that these are representative of Christianity as a whole?

In Protestantism, opposition to the Enlightenment tendency towards intellectual emancipation has usually taken the form of dualist definitions of the relationship of theology to philosophy. In this respect Catholic theology found itself in a different situation, since the assimilation of Aristotle by the Christian Middle Ages identified one of the representative figures of Greek philosophy with the claim of the Christian tradition to be authoritative. In this case the struggle of modern thought for emancipation came into conflict first of all with the authority of Aristotle, before it came up against Christian doctrines in the narrower sense. In classical Protestant theology such preliminary philosophical conflicts could not take place on any significant scale, since officially at least its theological traditions, and the philosophical conceptions which they incorporated, had no independent authority apart from scripture. In this case it was not the transitory link between orthodox dogmatics and Aristotelian metaphysics which was the main target of the earliest modern criticism, but the authority of revelation itself, and above all the classical Protestant conception of the doctrinal unity, free of contradiction, of the inspired canon of scripture. In so far as Protestant theology identified itself with the attitude of traditional authority attacked by the Enlightenment, its relationship to philosophy and to a religious doctrine based upon philosophy tended to be somewhat dualistic. An acute expression of this was the conflict between supranaturalism and rationalism towards the end of the eighteenth century. In the face of the supranaturalist view, however, it was possible for Protestantism – which once again differed in this from Roman Catholic theology – to develop theological conceptions which were firmly based upon the criticism of authority by the Enlightenment. These conceptions showed a general tendency to borrow from particular philosophical systems. This is equally true of the constructions of liberal theology in the nineteenth and twentieth centuries, which by contrast with earlier rationalism appealed to the peculiar nature of religious experience as the characteristic distinguishing theology from philosophical thought. For the contents of this religious experience had to be described in a set of concepts borrowed from philosophy, that is from particular philosophical systems, if they were not to be asserted, against the whole purpose and intention of liberal theology, as truths of revelation immune from philosophical criticism.

Besides these two types of approach to the relationship between theology and philosophy, which differed from each other and were conditioned by the attitude they adopted to the questions raised by the Enlightenment, there is a third view within Protestantism which more than the others could be called specifically Protestant, and which has had widespread effects. It does not directly oppose theology to philosophical thought, neither does it treat the inevitably philosophical form of the concepts used by theology as trivial and irrelevant to the content of theological statements. But it restricts the theological relevance of the questions posed by philosophy to the themes of a practical philosophy, to man as ethically constituted, and to the resistance of his disposition to his constitution as an ethical being. Thus, as E. Mühlenberg has shown in a recent article,[1] Melanchthon's *Loci Communes* already placed at the centre of theology, as *topoi* of Christian doctrine, those factors in Christian tradition which were suitable for influencing the affective dispositions of man and overcoming his resistance to the love of God. The fact that the practical philosophy of Kant was later to have an epoch-making effect upon Protestant theology, as the starting-point not only of rationalism, but also of supranaturalism, was something that went right back to the specifically Protestant concerns of theology, the topics of guilt and forgiveness, the law and the gospel. The concentration of religion upon questions of ethics

---

[1] "Humanistisches Bildungsprogram und reformatorische Lehre beim jungen Melanchthon", *ZThK* 65, 1968, pp. 431–44.

can be regarded as a distinctive characteristic of the Protestant theological tradition as a whole. It can be traced in the Reformers, in the classical Protestant understanding of theology as a practical science, and in the Enlightenment as well as in pietism; and it is characteristic of rationalism, especially in the successors of Kant, as well as of supranaturalism. The only difference is that the latter, instead of *reducing* theology to ethics, *complemented* philosophical ethics by the revelation of the holy and forgiving love of God in Jesus, arguing that philosophical ethics was not in a position to resolve the ethical dichotomy in man. This kind of supranatural thinking followed at least three lines of development in the theology of the nineteenth century. One line can be traced from G. Storr, through Tittmann, Tholuck and Julius Müller, to the new Lutheranism of Erlangen. Another leads to the biblical theology of E. Cremer and M. Kähler, while the third leads to A. Ritschl and W. Herrmann. Through the latter its influence can be felt to the present day, particularly in Bultmann and his disciples, amongst whom E. Fuchs and G. Ebeling have returned to the ideas of W. Herrmann. Thus at the present day it is the existential interpretation of the school of Bultmann which is the heir of an ethically based supranaturalism. By contrast to "neo-orthodoxy" in its Barthian form, which resists any philosophical justification or even point of contact for theological statements in philosophy, the existential interpretation recognizes in ethics, or in an analysis of existence based upon ethics or drawn up with an ethical emphasis, a common ground which it shares with philosophy. But this concentration upon ethics overshadows the way in which the themes of ethics are interwoven with other groups of theoretical topics of the philosophical tradition. The one-sided ethical emphasis in the adoption of Heidegger's analysis of existence, and subsequent questions of linguistic philosophy provoked by the existential interpretation, are very instructive in this respect.

An attempt to pass judgment on the different typical expressions of the way Protestant theology regards its relationship to philosophy must begin with the standpoint of pure revelation; for if this seems justified, then any further discussion of the relationship of theology to philosophy is superfluous.

For theology to be concerned with revelation means at the very least that it cannot be reduced to insights which can be obtained without the manifestation of divine reality in a historically concrete form, "revelations" in the broader sense in which the term is used in comparative religion. This is certainly a truth of which theologians, in their endeavours to make the Christian tradition comprehensible, ought constantly to be reminded. In this assertion, which accepts the historical justification for "neo-orthodoxy", we have used the term "revelations" in the plural, and in association with religions in general. Our first criticism is already implied by this usage. The revelation of God to which the biblical writings testify (however high a status is according to their content and unity) cannot be isolated by an act of irrational and arbitrary choice from the sphere of other religions and their claims to be revelations. The specific characteristics of Israelite and early Christian belief in revelation can be established only by comparison with them, and not by an *a priori* postulate. This is true both of the whole of the history of Israelite and Christian tradition, and of the literary records of it in the Old and New Testaments; it is equally true of the smaller number of characteristic complexes which by contrast with the unmanageable variety of conceptions which occur in the biblical scriptures, are regarded as theologically central, that is, as a canon within the canon – e.g. the message of Jesus and the theology of Paul. Only on this basis is it possible to deal with the question of the truth of this belief in revelation – that is, the question whether we have here a merely human religion or a self-revelation of the divine reality in the form of human religion, which is what it claims to be. A comparative study of this kind, and still more the judgment it involves concerning the truth of a belief in revelation which we first encounter as one amongst many religions in the world, is quite impossible without a philosophical theory of religion. Thus a basis in the philosophy of religion is necessary for a theology of revelation. This requirement does not mean that theology has to accept any philosophy as an authoritative basis for its own work. Rather, in each particular case it has to test whether or not the categories and judgment of the philosophy of religion which are available to it are appropriate to its own subject matter in any particular case, and in some circumstances it must develop its own alternatives. But this can take place in a meaningful way only on the basis of a discussion of the philosophy of religion, and not on that of the principle of revelation which is already assumed in advance.

Thus the theology of revelation always implicitly assumes an understanding of revelation and religion, that is, a philosophy of religion. At this point theological thinking which is self-critical has no alternative but to deal explicitly with philosophical problems. And any self-isolation for philosophical thought on the part of a theology of revelation is also untenable in a further respect. Theology appeals to revelation in order to make assertions about man and his situation, but also about the world and history – every one of which are themes which are also the subject of scientific and philosophical statements. In so far as there can only be one truth with regard to one and the same thing, a conviction of the truth of such theological assertions is possible only on the assumption that the theological assertions are reconcilable with the truth of non-theological statements about man, the world and history. And this assumption itself must become the object of theological reflection, for otherwise the truth of all theological statements remains undecided. This in its turn requires that theology should participate in the whole range of philosophical discussion, and in the concern of philosophy with the study of individual branches of knowledge.

There is a third way in which what purports to be a pure theology of revelation cannot honestly avoid philosophical inquiry and responsibility. It must be able to give an account of the meaning of the sentences and language it uses. Thus we have already said that theological sentences – in part at least – have the character of assertions, and thus do not have a merely performative function. The result is that they are also subject to the criteria which apply to assertions; in particular, it must be possible to lay down criteria for their truth or untruth.

The arguments which can be advanced against a dualist definition of the relationship of theology to philosophy in the sense of a pure, that is, authoritarian theology of revelation, also cast doubt from the first on whether it is defensible to restrict positive contacts between theology and philosophical thought to the field of ethical problems. For the assertions of theology all go far beyond the themes of ethics. They call for an understanding of reality as a whole. For even if human action goes beyond what already exists, yet it is related to what exists and raises questions about the conditions of its own reality and its power over the world on which it acts. Thus although every attempt at an intellectual consideration of the problems of ethics implicitly assumes a theoretical understanding of reality as a whole, it is necessary to consider the element of truth in the limitation to ethics of the use made by theology of philosophy. This is unavoidable, if only because of the dominant significance of this way of thought in theological tradition.

The strength of this approach lies in its concentration upon man and his existential problems. Thus in the Reformation it unquestionably led to the renewal of primitive Christian elements. Moreover, there are clear and significant parallels between Protestant theology and modern philosophy in the way they turn to subjectivity as the locus of truth. But by contrast to the modern philosophy of subjectivity, theology, with its concentration upon the sin, justification and sanctification of man, has increasingly withdrawn from the battle about the understanding of the world, in proportion as the long standing belief in miracles and a teleological view of nature have progressively disappeared. The themes of ethics were not understood as a starting point for a completely new understanding of reality including the processes of nature, but became a fortress into which theology retreated as the world of nature was withdrawn from its competence. The result was the development of a division between the world and man's understanding of himself which was bound to be untenable in the end. A classic example of such a division has recently been given by Bultmann, in his thesis that as far as we are concerned the world view of primitive Christianity is obsolete, while the primitive Christian self-understanding represents as it stands a possible self-understanding of man even at the present day, once it is liberated by demythologization from its association with the obsolete mythological world view. This thesis, and every similar isolated concentration upon man's self-understanding, are untenable, because man's understanding of himself and of the world are always related. It is unhistorical to state that one is obsolete, while the other can be adopted as it stands. Man's struggle for an appropriate understanding of himself comes about largely when he comes to terms with his relationship to the world, and when he achieves this his relationship to himself also changes. Man's changing of the world brings about a change in man himself.

The traditional concentration of Protestant theology upon the ethical question of sin and forgiveness has forced into the background not only the problem of the understanding of the world, but often too the social nature of the reality of human existence. This is characteristic of its approach, since society, like the world of nature, goes beyond the narrow circle of the private existence of the individual. It has usually been the themes of a private ethic of personality, and not the objective institutions and "goods" of human action, which have formed the point of reference of theological statements. The centre of gravity in theology lay in problems of individual existence, and was largely isolated from man's relationship to the world of nature, and, especially in the Lutheran tradition, from society. The picture of the problems of individual existence which was developed in the process, and became fixed in tradition, was bound to solidify into abstraction, because the existence of the individual possesses no historical concrete form outside his relationship to the world and his social connections. This abstract picture of the problems of individual existence, which is still an effective force in Protestant tradition, could only have taken on such an indepedent form against the background of the apparent independence of the themes of ethics from those of natural philosophy and metaphics. For it is obvious that man cannot realize his position in the universe as an isolated individual. The natural history of mankind argues overwhelmingly for the priority of society over the individual. Only within the horizon of ethical questions is a different picture possible, because with the rise of an intellectual consideration of ethical problems, the individual in fact became isolated within himself. But on the basis of the isolated individual it is possible to understand neither the functioning of society, as abstract contract theories of the origin of society have attempted to do, nor the relationship of man to the world of nature. The contrary is the case: the emancipation of the individual has always been brought about by way of society and his relationship to the world, and remains firmly dependent upon assumptions rooted in these two spheres. Thus the separation of man's ethical enquiry into his own being and purpose from the themes of a general understanding of reality has its own social and historical assumptions.

This is particularly true, moreover, of the ethical individualism of Protestant piety. There is not space here to describe the social and historical background of Protestant individualism. It must suffice to ask why the dominant form of piety in Protestantism was so little conscious of the social conditions, and the conditions laid down by the understanding of reality as a whole, which underlay its ethical individualism. The reasons are to be sought in the origin of Protestant piety in the history of human thought. They seem to be associated very much with the fact that the ethics of the Middle Ages was an ethics of commandment. By the authority of God who commanded, ethical norms were isolated from the understanding of reality, and from society, and were no longer relative to them. But a belief that they were identical in content with a natural law, whatever its basis, meant that they were no longer arbitrary whims of God who commanded. This syndrome, and the impression that accompanied it, that ethical concerns and propositions were independent of others, could continue to exist as long as the content of ethical obligations could be regarded as generally agreed, either in the field of the traditional Christian ethics of commandment or that of rationalist substitutes for it, down to the Kantian categorical imperative and the idea of values which carry an obligation in themselves, and which need only to be "felt" as such. But the increasing need for a constant renewal of the rational justification for traditional norms is enough to show that there is a progressive decline in the readiness to take their validity for granted. This has virtually not been the case since the second half of the last century. Nietzsche's criticism of morality and the experience of the present century have made an increasing number of people aware of this. In the face of this, the philosophy of values gives the impression of being a last attempt to salvage the taking for granted of ethical values – even at the cost of recognizing their conflicts with one another. But once traditional ethical norms can no longer be taken for granted, the propositions of ethics cease to appear independent of the questions of a general understanding of reality and of social processes. Today the ethical being and purpose of man needs to be expounded once again from first principles, and this is possible only in association with a study of the distinctive nature of man's being as a whole, which in turn cannot be made clear without discussing the position of man in the cosmos.

The retreat not only of theology, but also of the Protestant piety which has been renewed and shaped by revival movements, into the ethical problems of individual existence, and the abandonment of questions concerning the understanding of the world, is becoming more and more obviously a dead end for theological thought. Unless the idea of God is related to the reality of the world, it can no longer be maintained, as is shown by the present dispute about the "death of God". And ultimately the isolation of the themes and concerns of ethics casts doubt upon the actual content of ethical obligations, as norms which are merely imposed from outside. This destroys the basis of the link which is traditional in Protestantism between the promise of forgiveness and a presupposed consciousness of guilt, that is, between the gospel and the law. In a world in which, according to Paul Tillich's acute diagnosis, men are suffering less from feelings of guilt than from the sensation of the meaninglessness of existence, the message of forgiveness is no longer aimed at a clearly defined target. On the one hand the need for forgiveness has disappeared, because the norms which are transgressed are no longer felt to be unconditionally valid, while on the other hand (but in connection with the first) the traditional Christian view that forgiveness is from God seems to exaggerate beyond reason the simple fact that men have somehow or other to sort things out amongst themselves. In view of the relativization in modern industrial society of norms which in the past were absolutely valid, even the gospel of forgiveness no longer lays direct claim to the name of God – whether by usurping it or as a revelation. The concentration of devotion and theology upon a commandment ethic, or upon a forgiveness which, because it is the forgiveness of the transgression of absolute commandments, can be justified only on the basis of the Absolute, leads to increasingly strenuous but futile efforts. To state this does not mean that the problem of ethical existence has become irrelevant to theology. But the concentration of the concerns of ethics entirely upon the individual problems of guilt and forgiveness, and the isolation of ethics from questions of the theoretical understanding of reality, and therefore from the reality of society, must be overcome, and the question of the being and purpose of man must be restored to its place in the wider question of the meaning of existence as a whole.

In this situation theology must become involved in the whole range of philosophical topics. This has happened only rarely in the recent history of theology. The reason may be, as in Catholic theology, its limitation to a particular system of philosophy already adapted to theological needs. Or it may be, as in Protestantism, because of the dominant association between a faith based on revelation, and ethical and existential themes. Almost, the only exception, in the history of modern German Protestant theology, is found in the movements which have arisen out of German idealism. The early influence of idealism can be seen in the first version of Schleiermacher's *Discourses on Religion,* while its offshoots in the present century are represented by Troeltsch and Tillich. But to understand the extent of the task which now faces us, we must go back even further, to the first classical period of Christian theology, to patristics. At that period theology was in competition with the philosophical schools of antiquity; both claimed to provide the basis of true philosophy. This has set a standard for all theological thought, a standard which no theological system can finally satisfy, and in the light of which much that has been presented as theology in the course of history must appear wholly inadequate. And yet this standard alone is capable of giving any idea of the vastness of the task with which Christian theology is faced at the present day, if it is to endure in the intellectual struggle of modern man.

The idea of theology as "true philosophy" is hardly suitable for bringing about a peaceful co-existence between theology and philosophy. It disputes the truth of the conceptions of non-theological philosophy, in the same way as philosophy in the course of history has asserted itself over a wide range by the critical analysis of theological doctrine and tradition. Philosophers here have sometimes opposed to the positive theology generally held in society a "natural" theology, that is one which is in accordance with the nature of the divine and does not rest solely upon human convention. Or else they have mounted a destructive attack upon religion and theology as a whole, or treated it as obsolete. By contrast, when Christian theology was still certain of the universality of its truth, it represented itself as the "natural" theology which philosophy proposed, and attacked in non-Christian philosophies not only the ultimate basis of reality they put forward, but also their claim to give a definitive account of the nature of man and the world. When theology later created an enclave within its own domain for a philosophical system which was still untouched by the Christian revelation, for a *theologia naturalis* which was no longer identical with the theology of revelation, but was distinct from it and purported to prepare the way for it, it was already setting about the renunciation of its own universality. Such a pact with a philosophy based upon non-Christian assumptions, such as that of Aristotle, proclaimed the decline of theology; for either theology is universal, and its thinking corresponds to the one God with whose revelation it is concerned, or else it loses its intellectual integrity. Every attempt to break down the themes of theology into separately defined parts, and every attempt to limit its competence to a partial area of experience or reality, even if this is an event asserted to be the revelation of God and its imparting through Holy Scripture, contradicts what theology has to say of God as the origin of all reality. Thus a pact with a philosophy resting on non-Christian premises, like that of Aristotle, attributing to this philosophy a relative degree of independence in the field of natural knowledge and limiting theology to the sphere of the supernatural truth of revelation, is extremely questionable from the theological point of view.

On the other hand, the idea of a philosophy which as *theologia naturalis* was merely required to prepare the ground for the higher truth of theology remained a hopeless dream of theologians. The tradition of philosophy led it to be concerned as much as Christian theology with the one total truth. The attempt to put philosophical thought to use as a mere preparation for the truths of revelation, unattainable to reason, was consequently bound to be a failure. It was bound to be a challenge to philosophical thought to set itself free from theology. The conflict between theology and philosophy cannot be resolved by according to each their own particular and separate field of operations. The traditional division between natural and supernatural knowledge and themes breaks down against the fact that an inquiry concerning the nature of things must by its very origins regard itself as definitive and exclusive, and incapable of being complemented or superseded by anything different. But neither are philosophy and theology able to treat each other as different perspectives of a single truth, because the question of the way these two distinct perspectives are to be co-ordinated into the one truth is an inevitable one. And it is here that the true concern of philosophy lies. Consequently, there cannot be a "Christian philosophy" as a special form of philosophy on a par with others. It must either be classified and categorized by the philosophy which reflects upon the unity of the truth as a subordinate form of the knowledge of truth, or else it must assert its own right to be considered the "true" philosophy. The conflict between theology and the philosophy which distinguishes itself from theology is unavoidable, so long as philosophy does not itself become theological, or theology remains unable to convince us that it is true philosophy. The conflict between them is inevitable from their nature, because both can be taken seriously only in so far as they lay claim to the whole and undivided truth. But the assertion that the truth about which they disagree is one and the same forms a common ground in their conflict, and should enable each to recognize the arguments of the other side as of value for its own purpose.

The attempt to describe more closely the common theme which is the subject of dispute between theology and philosophy runs into considerable difficulties from the very first. In the metaphysical tradition, the unity of truth is co-ordinated in detail and as a whole with the unity of that which exists. This makes it immediately obvious that even a provisional description of the disputed ground between philosophy and theology is inevitably bound to become entangled in the thorny basic questions of metaphysics, and in the no less thorny issues of the popular rejection at the present day of the subjects and concerns of metaphysics. This is not the place to discuss whether metaphysics can so easily be dismissed or whether the questions and themes of metaphysics which underlie its traditional answers, if not these answers themselves, are implicit in their basic form in the nature of thinking experience itself and thrust themselves inescapably upon anyone who reflects conscientiously upon it. Yet the thesis that metaphysics has come to an end in modern times has been proclaimed as a corollary of the exposition of many very different points of view (Comte,

Dilthey, Heidegger), and this is rather odd. The lack of clarity in the attitude of modern philosophy to the themes of the metaphysical tradition also makes it hard to describe the relationship of philosophy to theology. Such a description was formerly attainable in connection with the metaphysical themes of the unity of that which is and of truth. Of course theology does not have the same general concern with the unity of that which is as metaphysics. The subject of theology is rather the endeavour to conceive of the reality of God. But in spite of every other disagreement about the idea of God, the proposition has so far remained unshaken, that at least God is not thought of as God at all if he is not thought of as the unity which unites all that is. As a result, the involvement of theology in the problems of metaphysics is inevitable. Similarly, the degree to which the theme of theology and philosophy are in dispute between them becomes clear. By considering the being of that which is – the common element in all that is real in all its diverse forms – philosophy is already pursuing the question of the unity which unites all that is, and thereby competes with what theology says about God. On the other hand, when any theology seriously takes up the task of thinking of God, which means thinking of him as the unity which unites all that is, then it is already involved in the question of the relationship between unity and diversity in the constitution of every concrete real existent. In view of the history of Western philosophy, deter-mined as it is by the criticism of the points of view advanced by religion, it is hardly to be expected that in discussing the same body of topics from opposite starting points theology and philosophy should have achieved the same results. Whether or not such an agreement is regarded as desirable may well have important consequences for thought, and not least for the thought of its present day. But for everyday thought they are as far off as a reality as the idylls of eschatology or paradise, and will occur at best on rare occasions as a chance stroke of luck.

Following this provisional description of the disputed common theme of theological and philosophical thought as the unity of truth and of that which is, we must now consider the justification for the criticism of it in the form which has become classical in metaphysics. It is no longer justifiable at the present day to think of the unity of that which is as a totality existent here and now – and in this sense self-existent – and to think of the unity which unites this totality as likewise existent here and now. Consequently, the mere attempt to think of the totality of all that is in definitive form in the unity of a system is at once seen to be a mistake. It contradicts the finitude of human experience and the inconclusiveness of reality, which is a process. Being and time must be considered in their intimate relationship to one another, and the processes which belong to everything that is are never definitively concluded. In particular, the historical reality of human freedom is always related to what exists here and now, but at the same time it has always already gone beyond it. When what exists here and now is represented as a totality complete in itself, the points in which changes in it originate are neglected and disguised. As a result, the idea of everything that is as a totality existing here and now comes to have an ideological function. The gaps and absurdities in what now exists, which call for change in the direction of some other possible totality, are concealed or at least passed over by the illusion of a world which is whole and sound. What exists here and now, taken as a totality – as a system existing here and now in itself – can only be untruth. Instead, what now exists – and that which is in this sense – must be defined as that beyond which questions and thought can always lead. And for this reason it will also seem blasphemous to think of God as an existent being, as the unity who, while he is an existent being himself, unites the world. If God were thought of in this way, it would no longer be as the reality which determines everything, except at the cost of human freedom. The principle of a world complete in what exists here and now, and excluding freedom and change, would be diabolical rather than divine.

Thus although the unity and totality of the real can no longer be regarded as definitively existent, the thought which reflects upon experienced reality, and at the same time upon itself, cannot simply ignore the metaphysical theme of unity. Every step this thought takes implies identity. Of course identity here means only the unity of what is different and non-identical. But the non-identity itself is not considered except in the light of a larger unity, even if this has not yet been clearly formulated. Thus any thinking is allied to unity and totality. This, however, must not simply be conceived of as an already existent unity and totality, nor merely as the abstract unity of the universal, but most be understood as the unity of meaning which simultaneously comprehends and transcends that which is.

The meaning accorded, as the basis of experience, to something which is always extends beyond that in it which exists here and now in experience. In this way our experience apprehends the particular and the individual only through the explicit or implicit anticipation of a totality of meaning which, and which alone, gives meaning to everything. The same is true of every particular unit of meaning in relation to any wider totality of meaning, and ultimately to a totality of meaning which, while it may already constitute all concretely experienced meaning, has not yet been made the subject of definitive inquiry by a process of reflective thought. Such a totality of meaning is not a merely regulative idea of the unity of the whole content of experience. It is rather the whole unit of meaning which in any given case already constitutes the significance of the individual and particular. It cannot therefore be claimed that it is a secondary and extrinsic principle of integration for a primary and prior diversity of experience. Furthermore, a whole unit of meaning, and the totality of meaning, *are not to be confused with the universal*, which rather forms merely the abstract reflection of the totality of concrete relationships of meaning. Finally, the ultimate horizon of a totality of meaning which is always a guide to our experience, but has never been fully discussed and defined by a process of reflective thought, is not to be confused with the idea of the totality of that which is. For meaning always transcends that which is and is experienced as meaningful. Thus while the totality of meaning comprehends that which is in its totality, it transcends what merely is, and may perhaps, for this very reason, be able to unite the fissiparous diversity of that which is.

Thus the basic error of all previous metaphysics is not simply the fact that it tried to think of reality as a whole. The very first steps in thought are always concerned with identity, with wholeness, and therefore cannot persist in a merely negative dialectic. But the harm was done by thinking of the whole of everything real as already existent. The corresponding form of thought was that of the closed system. But systems which put forward a claim to total and final knowledge reveal their untruth, if nowhere else, in the fact that reality as a whole is not yet complete, and is still in the process of becoming. Consequently the totality which thinking experience cannot escape as long as it is concerned with truth, even with regard to the individual and particular, is attainable only as a totality of meaning which apprehends in anticipation, in a still incomplete and contradictory reality, a wholeness of meaning which is not yet realized in all the relationships of meaning within that reality. This anticipatory wholeness of meaning, be it obscure or pellucid, is to be found in the experience of the significant particular.

All religious experience is concerned with such a totality of meaning of existence, by contrast with the incomplete fragmentariness of what exists at any particular time. This is so even where the saving totality of existence is contemplated not in the mode of "not yet" and of promise, but as the archetypal and primeval order proclaimed in myth. Such a sacred order also transcends the present reality. But the characteristic of the experience of mythical thought is that the order of things is reversed. Profane existence and the present world always lag behind the archetypes of the myth. It was the religion of promise which first sought salvation in a future which is still open, instead of in the earliest past that could be imagined.

From its very beginnings, philosophy has looked critically at the totalities of meaning asserted by religious tradition. The origin of philosophy seems to be associated with a discontent at the fact that religious conceptions did not provide what they claimed to provide with regard to the understanding of existence as a whole. The rational constructions of philosophy seem to be concentrated upon trying to find out what seemed more suitable than the particular religious tradition of the time for fulfilling the function of the divine foundation of existence as a whole. Philosophy, with its conjectures, steps into the gaps in religious tradition and rejects its assertions as inadequate to the nature of the divine, and therefore as failing to do justice to its function. It constructs alternatives to the existing solutions provided by religious traditions. Ancient philosophy was concerned in the first instance with the true, that is, with the form of divine origin which, as the cause of all that now exists, legitimates it. This was in accordance with the ancient Greek view of the nature of the divine. By contrast, the criticism of religion in modern philosophy has rejected the idea of a divine origin as superfluous, self-contradictory and the product of human projections, and has turned with increasing definiteness to the search for true atonement, that is, an atonement which overcomes all present suffering and evil, in accordance with the Christian understanding of God, which finds the revelation of the true origin of all things in the first instance in the redemption and reconciliation of the world. Thus the transition to revolutionary practice is a natural consequence of the modern philosophical criticism of Christianity, and continues its basic concern, which it has transformed in an anthropocentric sense. The criticism of Christianity hits the mark only when it accomplishes the main concern of the Christian revelation, the redemption and salvation of man, more effectively than the churches.

The outcome of the rational reconstruction was never as impressive as the critical destruction of the religious tradition. Or rather, the inadequacy of the tradition sometimes appeared only when its philosophical reconstruction collapsed. The history of philosophy shows us that the great systems were amongst the most transitory of its achievements. They fell before the criticism of their philosophical successors even more quickly than religious traditions. This is easy to understand, because each system always formed only a single rational model, whereas the religious traditions remained capable of interpretation by many such models. The more permanent achievement of philosophy should perhaps be sought in the rationalization of the concrete through classification, and also in the analysis of such phenomena as that of movement. Philosophical thought seems in fact to have studied the diversity of that which possesses concrete being not so much for its own sake, as with regard to its place in the system of the totality of that which is. It dealt with the concrete as the criterion and starting-point for an adequate understanding of being as a whole. But whereas the universal constructions which were its primary purpose turned out to be fragile, the examination of the concrete repeatedly prepared the way for the taking over of partial aspects of experienced reality into the field of competence of individual branches of study, the purpose of which was no longer a comprehensive total meaning, but the linking of phenomena as an end in itself.

The elaboration by philosophy of the logic of the concrete also became important for the relationship between philosophy and theology. In the first instance, the theology of early Christianity adopted into the context of its own thinking the phenomena described by the philosophical schools – and with them, philosophical propositions which were often of considerable scope. In this way it set itself up as "true philosophy".[2]

---

[2] The motive for this must be sought in certain peculiarities of the Christian religion, and in particular in its association with a missionary impulse in which faith has a specific and therefore restricted historical point of reference: In the "Gentile" sphere Jesus and the God whom he proclaimed were neither legitimized by inherited tradition, nor could they be taken for granted as implicit in current structures of existence. The second deficiency was the easiest to deal with, as is shown by the appropriation in christology of the themes of death and new life which were characteristic of the ancient mystery religions. But in so doing, Christianity faced all kinds of competition in the Hellenistic world. Wherever the Christian God was felt primarily to be an "alien" God – and even in the period of his undisputed authority in the Christian Middle Ages this was the case, as is shown indeed by the thesis of the "supernaturalness" of the truths of revelation, which was so unfortunate in its results for theology – the requirements of faith were bound to come up against the need for reasons for the deity of this God, and inevitably created a need for philosophy. Consequently,

But the logic of phenomena also forms the battlefield in which the conflict between theology and philosophy was to take place in the post-medieval situation. For the philosophical criticism of Christianity, like that of the world of the Homeric gods in the past, is based upon the logic of phenomena: upon the process of nature as a closed system and its independence of divine intervention, upon the revision of the historical picture given by Christian traditions on the basis of the modern understanding of nature, upon the description of religious phenomena as projections of human subjectivity, upon an anthropology which presents religion as an attitude not essential to man as such and atheism as a condition of human freedom, and finally upon an historical assessment of Christianity which treats its basic ideas as hostile to the world, and in any case betrayed from its earliest days. Christian theology can resist such philosophical criticism only by becoming committed to a discussion of the phenomena to which this criticism appeals: that is, to the phenomena of the processes of nature, of human

---

Christian apologetics, as "true philosophy" – or by presenting the Christian faith itself as true philosophy – constantly sought to conceive of the alien God of the Christian gospel as the creator of the world, and thereby to overcome his strangeness. But there was no final solution to this task, and consequently the need of Christian tradition for philosophy, its need for theology in the sense of a reflective apologetic thought over and above the mere reproduction of a sacred tradition, persisted. In the concept of the creation itself the conflicting factors of the original association between the creator and the creature, and the otherness and separateness of the creator from the world which he had created, remain unreconciled. By undertaking to work out the relationship between them in the concept of the creation, theology was never able to escape the fact that faith in the biblical God as the creator of the world can appeal at best only partially to the testimony of his creation, so that this appeal is subject to dispute and constantly provokes new conflicts. The best theology can do is to appeal to the phenomena which themselves first originated within the sphere of influence of Jewish and Christian religion, or were most fully developed within it: that is, the historicity of man, his personal freedom which breaks the bonds which tie him into the structure of some existent world, and the directional nature of time, the character of all reality as a process. But even here the incompleteness of historical processes has to be taken into account, and with it the questionableness and openness of all judgments concerning reality as a whole and the power which unites it into a totality.

and particularly of religious behaviour and the subjectivity which is expressed in them, and finally of the course of human history and the position of Christianity within it. In such a discussion the description of the phenomena will itself be called into dispute. This does not prevent theology from acknowledging that a large part of the philosophical criticism of the Christian tradition is justified. But it will restrict its relevance. Theology will not accept certain generalizations in the philosophical criticism of religion any more than it will accept certain tendencies of the phenomena described by philosophy to disassociate themselves from every concern and proposition of religion. From these two points of view at least, the integration into itself of philosophical criticism by theology can take place only as a "meta-criticism" of philosophy. But this "meta-criticism" can do justice to the arguments of philosophy only if its own form is that of reflective philosophical thought. It is possible to rebut the philosophical criticism of religious traditions only if the thinking which sets out to vindicate the religious tradition becomes philosophical in its turn, and above all renounces any appeal to authoritative data and sources of any kind.

Unfortunately in the modern period the encounter between theologians and philosophers has often failed to take the form of an open critical process wrestling with the meaning of phenomena. This pure form of encounter was damaged by reservations and prejudices on both sides. Theology often understood philosophical criticism merely as the expression of disbelief, and philosophers often condemned theology in advance as a mode of thought based on authoritarian principles and therefore ultimately inaccessible to rational argument. This meant that on both sides the encounter was not treated seriously enough, for in these circumstances it seemed superfluous to take the objections and conceptions of the other side seriously. Unfortunately, however, the prejudices of both sides were not altogether without foundation. At the beginning of the modern period Christianity, of whatever denomination, appeared much more in the form of a positivism of doctrines of revelation which were beyond rational judgement, than of a "true philosophy". In the Middle Ages, it is true, established Christianity accommodated the educational impulse of philosophy, but, in the face of a criticism which threatened its own foundations, withdrew behind the supposedly secure authority of revelation, of which it was thought the individual could be sure by virtue of an experience of faith which took place beyond any philosophical reflection. Although the Enlightenment theology of the nineteenth century by no means always followed this course, there is sufficient reason for regarding it as characteristic of the attitude of the churches in the modern age. On the other hand, the struggle for emancipation from the pressure of the theological principle of authority and its social effects in church and state made it difficult for an atmosphere to exist in which the points of view which favoured the Christian tradition could receive the same attention and consideration as those which served to destroy it. Theological dogmatism was met by a rationalist dogmatism which proclaimed either sense perception or supposed first principles of reason, or both together, to be the exclusive source of all reliable assertions. The rationality of the experience of faith even today encounters the rationality of a self-assertion which is still seeking emancipation (it is admittedly still provoked by authoritarian ecclesiasticism and theology), and which regards Christian faith and human freedom as being of their nature irreconcilable contraries.

These prejudices and reserves, but also the attitudes which give rise to them, must be broken down, in order to leave the field open on both sides for a critical dialogue between theology and philosophy. If the discussion concerning the significance of individual phenomena and their relevance for the totality of the meaning of human existence is conducted with complete openness on both sides, it will be to the advantage both of theology and philosophy.

Philosophical criticism can help theology to achieve an understanding of the conditions of a credible way of speaking of God, which makes more careful distinctions and is better adapted to man's experience of himself and his world in nature and history. It can also help theology to study in a more impartial way the relevance of the life and ministry of Jesus of Nazareth to mankind and to the whole of reality. Like all other statements which are concerned with the totality of the meaning of existence, theological statements go beyond the antagonisms and absurdities of the world as it now exists, and beyond the fragmentary nature of reality. But the measure of their importance is the extent to which they show themselves capable of taking into account the fragments of reality, and the wholeness to which these fragments point because they lack it. It must do so not merely as a theoretical fiction, but in rational confidence of a future success, a confidence inspiring the attitude of the present moment. The salvation and therefore the wholeness of the world in which the history of God achieves its aim and in which his reality will finally be revealed, can certainly not be shown to exist here and now. But to speak about it is not merely to contemplate an image that contrasts with the world as it now is, in the sense of consolation at the hope of another world above; it is to point forward to a future which is the destiny of this world, and will change it for the better. Such a promise cannot merely be a contrast to the world as it is now. It is a promise because it relates the suffering and the lack of perfection, but also the elements of success and achievement in present existence, to the reconciliation and fulfilment in which both will be overcome. That the salvation which is promised and is already present in Jesus is related to the present world and its phenomena, the salvation of which is of course at issue, is the reason why Christian theology must concern itself with the philosophical criticism directed towards it.

But if philosophy too is to be clearly conscious of the conditions of its own thinking, and of the threat to its own reflection upon its foundations, it cannot simply regard a dialogue with religion and theology as something irrelevant to its own purpose. It is perhaps not by chance that there is a correlation between the breaking down of religious institutions and traditions in modern society and an unmistakable decline in the power and urge to construct comprehensive philosophical systems. In the early centuries of the modern age it may have seemed that philosophy was called to replace theology in the task of finding a comprehensive interpretation of the meaning of reality. But in recent centuries the picture has changed. Philosophy has become more deeply entangled in the problems of subjectivity. It has had to abandon the field of the universally valid knowledge of the positive sciences. Its own activity has by contrast come to be increasingly regarded as subjective and imposing no obligation. It thereby revealed itself as prey to the historical conditioning and transitoriness of the intellectual subjectivity which has become the central theme of philosophy in the modern age. Perhaps the most important achievement of modern philosophy is its emancipation from tutelage to traditional authorities, and this was won in conflict with Christian religion and theology. But the emancipated subjectivity then faces the question of what it is which, in concrete terms, constitutes its own freedom and gives content to its existence. This moreover is a question which is posed as a matter of theoretical reflection, but equally arises as a social problem of civil liberty. There have been repeated attempts to anticipate the issue of the reality which constitutes and makes possible subjective freedom by insisting upon the autonomy of the subject. It was transcendental idealism which took the first steps in this direction, and existentialist philosophy also sought in it a solution for the problems of subjectivity. But it looks as though on the basis of the autonomy of the subject it is possible to achieve only an empty formal freedom, curiously similar to the formal character of the political freedom achieved in bourgeois democracies. It is clear that freedom with a concrete content has not yet been won. The formal principle of subjectivity remains empty of content. As a direct consequence, its content becomes arbitrary. At the same time, in spite of a formal freedom, it becomes subject to the laws of its content, which are alien to it. Philosophical thought which is carried out on this principle is at the mercy of a subjectivism which carries no compelling force of conviction.

And there is no way out of this dilemma by recourse to the sciences, in the hope that some of them, for example sociology, might be able to make more convincing statements about the meaning of existence. A characteristic feature of modern sciences is that they place the phenomena they study at the disposal of the subject – "the" subject, because in principle any person can clothe himself in this formal garment. The individual branches of knowledge were able to separate themselves from the comprehensive inquiry of philosophy into the meaning of existence, and maintain their independence, only because the hidden purpose of the activity of modern science is to place phenomena at the free disposal of the subject. The question of meaning could be excluded, because the task of giving meaning to such knowledge could be left to the free judgment of the subjects who used it and the purposes they prescribed. The freedom of knowledge from value judgments is a condition for its remaining at the disposal of the formal freedom of the subject for any purpose whatsoever. But this is exactly why no individual discipline, its object limited to a restricted field, is capable of constituting subjective freedom on its own account. When this attempt is made, freedom in every sense falls prey to a world of objects, in spite of the fact that these objects were meant to be placed by science at the disposal of the subject and his freedom. This too, is not merely a theoretical problem; mankind can bear witness to the form these dilemmas have taken in a "scientifically" organized society.

The constitution of subjectivity, and its realization in the sense of a freedom which has a content, remains the unresolved theme of modern thought. Anyone who realizes that the principle of autonomy in itself leads only to a formal freedom, and that the basing of freedom on the sciences must lead to the loss of freedom, may perhaps be ready to pay attention once again to the concerns and propositions of religion. Ultimately, some of the themes of modern subjectivity, for example its freedom from the structure of the cosmos and its direct openness to the truth, find their natural home in Christian freedom.

Nevertheless, the Christian religion can once again become relevant to the problem of subjectivity only when the church and theology have abandoned their authoritarian form, from which the subjectivity of the modern age has become emancipated, and which is irreconcilable in any form with its freedom. But without the trappings of the actual form it takes, the Christian tradition reveals the horizon of the totality of the meaning of existence which transcends the world as it exists here and now, but also takes it up and transforms it, and which constitutes subjective freedom in the face of the world and the social system at any time. The decisive factor here is that the structure of meaning proposed by Christianity is open to a future, not yet realized, in which it will be finally fulfilled and which alone will provide a basis for the totality of its structures of meaning. This makes possible a constant revision of the Christian understanding of existence in every detail. It is by this, and by this alone, that every authoritarian function of any of the conceptions of the Christian religion and its institutions is inherently excluded. Only when Christianity displays a constant openness to its possible transformation and "perfectibility" is it capable of constituting human freedom, without destroying it at the same time, as was the case with the authoritarian forms of Christian tradition and its institutions.

These considerations do not lead to any conclusion about the truth of Christianity, but they do have something to say about the conditions under which it can possibly become relevant again to philosophy, with regard to the central problem of philosophy itself, that of subjectivity. The original conception of the unity of meaning of existence is strictly speaking not a possibility for philosophy. It is the basic act of the religious apprehension of the "universe", as the young Schleiermacher said, the apprehension of a totality of meaning of existence which transcends fragmentary reality and so shows the way to freedom. A religious apprehension of this kind is the starting point not only of theology, which interprets it and makes its range explicit, but also of philosophy, which tests the range of the religious experience of meaning with regard to its ability to be integrated with the world of phenomena, sometimes corrects it, and is therefore in competition with the constructive thinking of theology. But philosophy alone is never able to derive this totality of meaning from the subjectivity of thought. Whereas philosophical reflection introduces the element of negativeness, of non-identity and therefore of the movement of thought into the life of the consciousness, it always has a reference to something thought previously, which it may be able to attack and refute, but cannot bring into being itself. Thus it may be that those thinkers who have considered that philosophy depended upon prior religious experience and tradition were right, in spite of the critical attitude to them which seems to be essential to philosophical thought. Philosophical criticism breaks down the authoritarian structure of religious tradition. It forces what has been handed down by tradition to change, when it is incapable of comprehending the present reality of life. This is a challenge to religion and theology, but its nature is such that the challenge gives to each the opportunity of expressing its own essence in a purer and clearer form. Where this is successful, it can only be a gain for philosophical thought, in so far as it is concerned not only with the negative dialectic which shows the limits of the finite and of any construction of meaning here and now, but also with casting light on the horizon of meaning to which this negative dialectic is always implicitly drawn, which is prior to everything posited by the mind as subject, but which enters the world as it now exists only through the act of the freedom of the subject, in order to reveal in it the unity of the truth and to make peace known amongst men.

5

THE SIGNIFICANCE OF CHRISTIANITY
IN THE PHILOSOPHY OF HEGEL

Lecture delivered at the Hegel Congress at Stuttgart on 14 July 1970, and later published in *Archives de Philosophie* 33, 1970 (1971), as well as in the Proceedings of the Stuttgart Congress.

I

ONE OF THE basic conditions of the modern world we live in is the relaxation of the close links which existed in the Middle Ages between the Church and society. If, with some degree of over-simplification, we trace this extraordinarily complex and wide-ranging process, which took place at different rates in various countries, to a single event which sparked it off, we must point to the Reformation, and in the first instance to its unintended consequences for the course of world history. The Western schism, and the religious wars which followed it and crippled the nations of Europe for more than a century, called for the emancipation of the state and its law from the con-troversial claims of the confessional churches. As a result, the tendencies towards the development of a purely secular culture, which reached far back into the Middle Ages, now had room to evolve freely and break away in their turn from the claims to authority of the churches, now separated into different confessions. This led to a breach between the Christianity of the church and the world of modern life which became one of increasing antagonism, because neither of the two sides have been able to abandon their claim to the one and indivisible truth. One side was concerned with emancipation from ecclesiastical tutelage and the removal of ecclesiastical privileges and the other side with the self-assertion of the Christianity of the church against the spirit of the modern age.

This dualism between the Christianity of the church and the world of modern life determined Hegel's awareness of the problem from the years when he was a student of theology at Tübingen. The young Hegel did not think of himself in any sense as an advocate of the maintenance of ecclesiastical Christianity, either in the sense of an orthodoxy which cut itself off from the rest of the world, nor that of the assimilation of religious tradition to the spirit of the Enlightenment. Hegel concentrated upon the issues and concerns of religion, because to him they seemed indispensable for a solution to the problems of modern society. From a very early age, Hegel's understanding of the nature of the modern world was too profound for him to follow the radical French Enlightenment in regarding a break with traditional Christianity as itself an emancipation, in the sense of a liberation of man. As early as the essays published by Nohl under the title "Volksreligion und Christentum" ("Popular Religion and Christianity") Hegel recognized that the problem of society itself was a religious problem. Thus it is pointless, in interpreting the writings of Hegel's youth, to emphasize his concern with society and politics at the expense of his concern with religion, or vice versa. The theme of political emancipation is itself, in its central issue, a religious one. This insight distinguishes Hegel not only from the iconoclastic critics of religion in the French Enlightenment, but also from those who, after the middle of the nineteenth century, made the attempt, still dominant today, to describe the relationship between Christianity and the modern age by means of the concept of secularization. They saw it, that is, as a working out of originally Christian themes, which have, however, lost their religious form in the process. Hegel in fact regarded the religious form itself as indispensable in the interests of social emancipation. When he was still at school at the *Gymnasium* in Stuttgart he expressed this by saying that the "common man" could not participate in the Enlightenment by means of the sciences and arts, but only through religion.[1] As a student of theology in Tübingen he expressed it in the language of Kant's ethical theology: religion gives "morality and its motivating forces a new and nobler impulse".[2] A few years later Hegel came to criticize Kant's conception of morality, and from then on he developed a deeper concept of religion as the self-elevation of man "from finite life to infinite life", i.e. to that "Spirit of the whole" in which everything separated and opposed in life is united.[3] But even religion defined in this way remained for Hegel associated with the themes of politics. Thus in the *Philosophy of Right* we read that religion is for the state "an integrating factor . . . in the depths of men's minds".[4]

> The content of religion is absolute truth, and consequently the religious is the most sublime of all dispositions . . . It is in being thus related to religion that state, laws and duties all alike acquire for consciousness their supreme confirmation and their supreme obligatoriness, because even the state, laws and duties are in their actuality something determinate which passes over into a higher sphere and so into that on which it is grounded.[5]

Thus even in the *Philosophy of Right* Hegel regarded the reality of the state as a finite and limited reality, although for him the state was in principle – albeit in the sense of an inquiry which dominates his early writings – "the divine will, in the sense that it is mind present upon earth, unfolding itself to be the actual shape and organization of a world".[6] The finite and limited nature of the ethical reality of the state is the basis of the necessity of religion for the state. Here the relationship of religion to the state is not that of giving it a higher legitimation

---

[1] *Dokumente zu Hegels Entwicklung*, ed. J. Hoffmeister, 1936, p. 37.

[2] *Theologische Jugendschriften*, ed. H. Nohl, 1907, p. 5.

[3] Nohl, p. 347; ET *Early Theological Writings*, trs. T. M. Knox, 1948 (reissued 1961), pp. 311f.

[4] *Grundlinien der Philosophie des Rechts*, ed. J. Hoffmeister (*Werke* 6, PhB 124a), 4th ed., 1955, §270, p. 225; ET *Hegel's Philosophy of Right*, trs. T. M. Knox, 1942, §270, p. 168; cf. *Hegels Vorlesungen über die Philosophie der Religion*, ed. P. Marheineke, *Jubiläumsausgabe der sämtliche Werke* 15, 1928, p. 116; ET *Lectures on the Philosophy of Religion*, trs. E. B. Speirs and J. B. Sanderson, 1895, Vol. I, pp. 102f.

[5] *Philosophie des Rechts*, §270, pp. 221f.; ET pp. 165f.

[6] *Ibid.*, p. 222; ET, p. 166.

and justification. It can also have a critical significance, as is recognized in Hegel's comments on those states in which the Christian principle of freedom has not yet become fully effective. But in one way or another the need for religion derives from the experience of the limits of political reality, and in this sense Hegel was still able in 1817 to write in his *Encyclopedia* that Kant was right to regard the religious self-elevation to faith in God as "proceeding from the practical Reason".[7] "Genuine religion and genuine religiosity only issue from the moral life: religion is that life rising to think, i.e. becoming aware of the free universality of its concrete essence", while the ethical life itself is none other than "the divine spirit as indwelling in self-consciousness, as it is actually present in a nation and its individual members" (ibid.). But for Hegel the religious elevation to God is no longer, as for Kant, a mere consequence or a "postulate" (ibid.) from a morality which is self-subsistent. Rather, "the truly moral life is . . . a sequel of religion", as we read in the third edition of the *Encyclopedia* in 1830, in the same context. Consequently, although the religious elevation has its "starting point" in the sphere of morality – and for Hegel this always means in concrete social life – the theme of religion as "the consciousness of absolute truth" has its basis in itself, and is by no means justified solely by its practical relevance for ethics and public morality. In the eyes of Hegel, in his mature years, religion is of fundamental significance for the state and society for the very reason that it does not need first of all to be justified by its outward usefulness, but has "absolute truth as its content". The moral life of society and the state are, according to the *Encylopedia*, so dependent upon the religious life of the people that Hegel can say: "So long as true religion did not spring up in the world and hold sway in political life, so long the genuine principle of the state had not come into actuality." Plato did not see that this was the case because he

---

[7] *Enzyklopädie der Philosophischen Wissenschaften im Grundriss*, ed. J. Hoffmeister (*Werke* 5, PhB 33), 1930, §552, pp. 463, 470; ET *Hegel's Philosophy of Mind (Part III of the Encyclopaedia of Philosophical Sciences)*, trs. A. V. Miller, 1971, § 552, pp. 282f., 290.

did not yet recognize the subjective disposition as the focus of religion and perceive its political significance, just as his state as he conceived it was still "wanting in subjective liberty". Subjective freedom, and therefore the subjectivity of the moral disposition as the vehicle of the political relevance of religion, was first achieved in the course of world history, according to the mature Hegel, by Christianity. In Hegel's early writing a different view appears. In his early essay upon "Popular Religion and Christianity" Hegel says of the popular religion which he had in mind, in contrast to the existing forms of Christianity, that it "goes hand in hand with freedom".[8] In elaborating this ideal Hegel made use not of Christianity, but of the example of Greek religion. Later, however, Hegel emphasized the limitations of freedom in ancient Greece, and its dependence upon external circumstances, particularly upon the accident of birth and the good fortune of being preserved from slavery. In his Berlin introduction to the *History of Philosophy* (1820) Hegel writes that the Greeks and Romans did not know "that man, as man, is free". Only "in the Christian religion did the teaching arise, that before God all men are free, that Christ set men free, set men free equally in the sight of God, for Christian liberty. These provisions make freedom independent of birth, class, education, etc."[9] Hegel also calls this freedom which came into the world with Christianity "the principle of absolute Freedom in God";[10] for this subjective freedom, with its certainty which is independent of the external circumstances of life, is based upon the unity of man with God revealed through Christ.[11] Because the freedom revealed by Christianity is based upon man's participation in

[8] Nohl, p. 27.

[9] *Vorlesungen über die Geschichte der Philosophie*: I: *System und Geschichte der Philosophie*, ed. J. Hoffmeister Werke 15a (PhB 166), 1940, p. 63; cf. ET *Lectures on the History of Philosophy*, trs. E. S. Haldane and F. H. Simson, Vol. I, 1892, p. 49; cf. *Philosophie der Geschichte*, ed. F. Brunstad (Reclam), 1961, pp. 339, 459; ET *Philosophy of History*, trs. J. Sibree, 1899, pp. 347f.

[10] *Philosophie der Geschichte*, p. 459; ET, p. 347. Freedom in this sense can exist only "where the individuality becomes known as positive in the divine being" (*ibid.*, p. 101).

[11] *Geschichte der Philosophie* I, pp. 245f., ET, Vol. I, p. 105.

God, and is universal, in that the one God is the God of all men, the universal freedom of man as man and the Christian dogma of the incarnation are for Hegel intimately related. Hegel came to pass a positive judgment upon the christological dogma, which he did not see like Kant as an illustration of a general principle of reason, but as the accurate expression of the turning point in the course of world history from which all history before and after is dated. This positive judgment is associated with the realization that christological dogma is linked with the history of freedom. This realization is not yet to be found in Hegel's early theological writings. We find it first in the *Phenomenology of Mind*. It is hinted at, still obscurely and enigmatically, in the famous chapter concerning the "unhappy consciousness", which is aware of the abstract nature of Stoic and Sceptic freedom, and realizes that it cannot possess its freedom and truth independently of the conditions of the world. This consciousness is an unhappy one in that it realizes it is isolated from what could be its nature and its truth. In the study of Hegel, the view going back to left-wing Hegelianism, that this concept of the unhappy consciousness describes Christianity with its belief in another world, has oddly enough been held until the present day.[12] The criticism of religion on the part of the Hegelian left saw in the phenomenon of the unhappy consciousness, which thinks of its own true being as something outside itself and separate from itself, the model of religion in general. But for Hegel the unhappy consciousness is a historical stage in the development of mind, associated in its early forms with the Jewish religion, and also later with the spirit of the Roman Imperial period[13] and which at least in principle

[12] E.g. G. Lukacs, *Der junge Hegel und die Probleme der kapitalistischen Gesellschaft* (1948), 1954, pp. 546f.; also A. Kojève, *Hegel*, 1958, pp. 55f., 62ff., 65 etc. R. Haym already saw in the unhappy consciousness "a characteristic of the ecclesiastical ethic of medieval Christianity" (*Hegel und seine Zeit*, 1857, p. 238). On the other hand J. Hyppolite, *La phénoménologie de l'esprit* I, 1939, pp. 176–92, pointed to the connection between the "unhappy consciousness" in Hegel and the Jewish religion (p. 178 n. 24).

[13] *Philosophie der Religion*, *Werke* 16, pp. 185ff., 273ff., ET Vol. II, pp. 320ff., Vol. III, pp. 62ff.; *Philosophie der Geschichte*, pp. 440 and 442ff., ET,

was overcome by Christianity. For the principle of Christianity is not in fact the duality and separation between the divine and the human, but the *reconciliation*[14] of this opposition in the unity of God and man. The unhappy consciousness persists in Christianity only in so far as "the simple content of Absolute Religion", that is, "the incarnation of the Divine Being",[15] is seen in the first instance solely in the individual figure of Jesus, and thought of as a special characteristic of his person, but not yet understood in its universal scope; ". . . The whole sequel of History is occupied with the realization of this concrete freedom. [In the church of early period and the Middle Ages] the light of Infinite Freedom . . . has not yet penetrated secular existence with its rays."[16] The "religious principle which dwells in the heart of man" must be produced "under the form of Secular Freedom".[17] In Hegel's view the decisive step in this direction

---

pp. 332ff., where by contrast to the Roman world the positive significance of the Jewish experience of infinite pain is described. For a different view, Nohl, pp. 260 and 373; ET *Early Theological Writings*, pp. 203ff. (the second passage is not translated), where Mosaic religion is described as "a religion from and for unhappiness, not for happiness which wants a joyful game; which takes God too seriously . . . a religion of unhappiness, for unhappiness is present in separation; we feel ourselves objects and fly to him who decides our destiny; in happiness this separation has disappeared."

[14] The atonement as the overcoming of the unhappy consciousness is discussed on pp. 160 and 163 of *Phenomenologie des Geistes* (ed. Hoffmeister, *Werke* 2 [PhB 114], 1928); ET *The Phenomenology of Mind*, trs. J. B. Baillie, 1931, pp. 253, 255. The later references to the unhappy consciousness, esp. pp. 523ff. and 533, (ET, pp. 752ff., 765ff.), also show that while this consciousness forms the starting point for Christianity ("the common birth pangs at its production", p. 525; ET, p. 755), it is distinct from it. The allusions to Christian themes (e.g. p. 166 to the incarnation, p. 169 to the idea of the mediator; ET, pp. 258, 261) occur in the subsequent chapter only in the sense that "the content has the characteristic of being produced from a consciousness . . . for which it yearns, a content wherein the spirit can never be satiated nor find rest because the content is not yet its own content inherently and essentially, or in the sense of being its substance" (p. 533; ET, pp. 765f.), although the content of revealed religion has "in part been met with already" (p. 533; ET, p. 765).

[15] *Ibid.*, p. 527; ET, p. 758.

[16] *Philosophie der Geschichte*, p. 457; ET, p. 345; cf. *Vorlesungen über die Philosophie der Religion*, *Werke* 16, pp. 145f.; 253ff., etc., ET Vol. II, pp. 276f.; Vol. III, pp. 40ff., etc.

[17] *Philosophie der Geschichte*, p. 461; ET, p. 348.

was taken by the Reformation. Hegel recognized with astonishing accuracy the connection in Luther between belief in justification and Christian freedom; because the believer abandons all righteousness of his own, he attains in faith to participation in Christ and in his righteousness, and therefore to participation in the righteousness of God. In Hegel's words, "the subjective spirit gains emancipation in the Truth, abnegates its particularity and comes to itself in realizing the truth of its being".[18] By giving up his own finitude and particularity man achieves participation in God. What before that was something peculiar to Christ has now become universal through faith in him: the union of man with God, and with it the freedom from all external obligation and authority.

In the rational autonomy of the enlightened mind and in the political freedom of the French Revolution Hegel saw the effects of the basic Reformation idea of Christian freedom. He did not overlook the fact that in Luther freedom in God was still tied to an overriding religious authority, whereas for the Enlightenment only the insight and conviction of the individual was considered valid.[19] But the transition from the Reformation idea of freedom to the rational and secular freedom of the Enlightenment seemed to Hegel to be an intrinsically necessary step. The Reformation principle that the faith of the individual was independent of all human authority was bound to lead to the autonomy of reason in the Enlightenment. The Christian freedom of the Reformation did not achieve its realization on a universal scale until the Enlightenment and the political freedom

[18] *Ibid.*, p. 558; ET p. 433.

[19] "Luther had secured to mankind Spiritual Freedom and the Reconciliation [of the Objective and Subjective] in the concrete: he triumphantly established the position that man's eternal destiny must be wrought out in himself. But the *import* of that which is to take place in him – what truth is to become vital in him – was taken for granted by Luther as something already given, something revealed by religion. *Now* the principle was set up that this import must be capable of rational investigation – something of which I can gain an inward conviction, and that to this basis of inward demonstration every dogma must be referred." (*Ibid.*, p. 587; ET p. 460). Cf., with further references, K. Löwith, *Hegels Aufhebung der christlichen Religion, Hegel-Studien* Beiheft I, 1964, pp. 193–236, esp. pp. 222f.

which came from it. Hegel was also quite clear, however, that the process by which the Reformation idea of freedom came to have this effect did not take the form of a straight line, but followed a circuitous route of its own. It was the schism in the church which made possible this emancipation of the state from the religious authority of the churches, and this emancipation in its turn became the basis of the freedom of thought which established its independence of "particular" churches, and established also the freedom of religion itself – in the sense of tolerance of other denominations. Thus in the *Philosophy of Right* Hegel was even able to interpret the schism in the church as a necessary condition of the realization of Christian freedom:

> So far from its being or having been a misfortune for the state that the church is disunited, it is only as a result of that discussion that the state has been able to reach its appointed end as a self-consciously rational organization. Moreover, this discussion is the best piece of good fortune which could have befallen either the church or thought so far as the freedom and rationality of either is concerned.[20]

This was the roundabout way in which the intellectual and political freedom of the modern age was derived from Christianity. From the point of view of a modern ecumenical awareness, it is not of course so easy to regard it as so unreservedly necessary and fortunate in every respect. The full weight of this historical assertion is seen, however, only in the further thesis that the process was by no means simply the accidental historical condition for the first steps towards a reality which from then on supplied its own justification. According to Hegel, the true substance of the freedom of a state based on ethical principles also lies in the Christian "freedom in God".[21] In view of the numerous tensions between the spirit of the modern age and traditional Christianity, this assertion is far from self-evident. But it is only this idea which enables Hegel to go beyond the theories which interpret the modern age as one of emancipation from its Christian origins. It was in the

---

[20] *Philosophie des Rechts*, § 270, pp. 232f.; ET *Philosophy of Rights*, § 270, p. 174.

[21] See n. 10 above.

Phenomenology of Mind that Hegel laid the basis of the permanent link between the intellectual freedom of the Enlightenment and the absolute content preserved in religious faith. The "pure insight" of the Enlightenment, by adopting a negative attitude to the context of faith, and not identifying itself with the content of faith, becomes self-estranged in it and becomes "untruth and unreason".[22]

The criticism of the Enlightenment is right to point to the finitude of the conceptions of faith,[23] but because it rejects every particular characteristic "i.e. every content and filling" as a "finite fact . . . a human entity and a mental presentation, absolute being on its view turns out to be a mere vacuum, to which can be attributed no characteristics, no predicates at all",[24] and as a result the enlightened criticism of faith lapses into "sheer insipidity" and the contradiction of claiming to know "nothing but finitude, taking this, moreover, to be the truth, and thinking this knowledge about finitude as the truth to be the highest knowledge available".[25] For Hegel it was of lesser importance, whether the criticism of religion which emptied the idea of God of meaning left it as an empty general term, emphasizing only man's ignorance of God, or whether it rejected the idea of God as a whole. In both cases this amounted to "indifference towards religion, which is either left unquestioned and let alone, or is ultimately attacked and opposed". Hegel commented: "That is the course followed by shallow spirits."[26] Because reason reduced knowledge to the

---

[22] *Phänomenologie des Geistes*, ed. Hoffmeister, p. 389; cf. pp. 401f.; ET p. 565; cf. pp. 581ff.

[23] *Ibid.*, p. 406; cf. p. 393; ET p. 588; cf. p. 569.

[24] *Ibid.*, p. 397; ET, p. 576.

[25] *Ibid.*, p. 400; ET, p. 580. Cf. *Philosophie der Religion*, Werke 16, pp. 32f.; ET Vol. II, pp. 154f.

[26] *Philosophie der Religion*, Werke 15, p. 67, cf. pp. 202f., esp. 203; ET Vol. I, p. 50, cf. pp. 191f., esp. 192: "From this point of view, on the contrary, which has no content in it, no religion whatever is possible, for it is I who am the affirmative, while the Idea which has absolute Being must in religion be established purely through itself and not through me. Here, therefore, there can be no religion, any more than from the standpoint of sensuous consciousness".

knowledge of finite objects, and the Divine Being perceived by faith was broken down into its finite elements, the modern consciousness of the freedom of the pure understanding came to have a remarkable similarity to the unhappy consciousness of the ancient world. It suffers from "the tragic fate that befalls certainty of self which aims at being absolute, at being self-sufficient". This tragic fate of the pure insight lies in the fact that with the negation of the substantial truth which sustains its own being as such, the insight itself collapses:

It is consciousness of the loss of everything of significance in this certainty of itself, and of the loss even of this knowledge or certainty of self – the loss of substance as well as of self; it is the bitter pain which finds expression in the cruel words, "God is dead."[27]

Hegel's famous and often misunderstood saying concerning the death of God is a formulation of the outcome for Christianity of the rationalist criticism of the Enlightenment. It represents what happens when a subjective freedom which regards itself as free understanding, breaks away from its historical origins in Christian "freedom in God". For Hegel the death of God is a necessary factor in the actualization of Christianity in subjective freedom, because in the first instance this subjective freedom is in direct rebellion against all authority and tradition. But at the same time the death of God signals the end of a conception of God thought of as an abstract other reality. The death of the mediator "implies at the same time the death of the abstraction of Divine Being which is not yet affirmed as a self"[28] and in which, therefore, the unity of God and man in the idea of the incarnation is not yet conceived of in its full scope, and God is thought of instead in the exclusive opposition to man and the world which finds its expression in the unhappy consciousness. Thus for Hegel the abstract dualism of an infinite which is

[27] *Phänomenologie des Geistes*, p. 523, cf. p. 546; ET, pp. 752f., cf. p. 781. The parallels between the present day and the "period of the Roman Empire" are also found – and explicitly mentioned – in *Philosophie der Religion, Werke* 16, pp. 196 and 354f.; ET Vol. II, p. 333 and Vol. III, p. 150. The expression "death of God" first appears in Hegel in 1803 in his *Abhandlung über Glauben und Wissen*, (Werke 1, PhB 62b), 1928, pp. 123f.
[28] *Phänomenologie des Geistes*, p. 546; ET, pp. 752f.

simply opposed to the finite (and therefore finite itself) is obsolete. But Hegel's thought could not remain satisfied with the affirmation of the death of Gód, because the death of God must also mean the loss of self-consciousness and the subjective freedom that comes with it. The recognition that the subjective freedom of the modern consciousness cannot be maintained without God leads him to revise the one-sided nature of the criticism of religion in the Enlightenment. He does not try to reverse what is justifiable in this criticism. But he restores the concrete content of religion by overcoming the false opposition of the infinite and the finite, and working out to a conclusion the unity of finite and infinite in the central Christian idea of the incarnation, and therefore in the principle of subjective freedom itself.

Thus for Hegel the principle of subjective freedom is the reason why one cannot, in the name of this freedom, abandon the Christian religion in a process of "secularization". For the same reason, in his *Encylopedia* Hegel resists the separation of the state and religion: the modern state cannot be an *ethical* state in the sense of the realization of subjective freedom without the basis of this subjective freedom in the Christian religion. Glancing aside at the French Revolution, Hegel says:

It is nothing but a modern folly to try to alter a corrupt moral organization by altering its political constitution and code of laws without changing the religion – to make a revolution without having made a reformation.

And again:

It has been the monstrous blunder of our times to try to look upon these inseparables as separable from one another, and even as mutually indifferent. The view taken of the relationship of religion to the state has been that, whereas the state had an independent existence of its own, springing from some force and power, religion was a later addition, something desirable perhaps for strengthening the political bulwarks, but purely subjective in individuals: – or it may be, religion is treated as something without effect on the moral life of the state, i.e. its reasonable law and constitution which are based on a ground of their own.[29]

This is a "monstrous blunder", because the state requires the

[29] *Enzyklopädie* § 552, pp. 469 (*Zusatz*, 3 August 1830) and 465; ET, *Philosophy of Mind*, § 552, pp. 287 and 284.

awareness of absolute truth which only religion can provide as the basis for its institutions and the attitude of mind which sustains it. This of course does not mean that the state can or ought once again to be bound to the religious authority of a church.[30] Rather, the church itself gave rise both to the idea of freedom in the Reformation, and the principle which makes the state, precisely because it is a Christian state, independent of particular churches.[31] But this autonomy of the states as a *general* basis of the realization of Christian freedom with regard to "particular churches" must not be confused with a complete separation between the state and religion, which in Hegel's view could only lead to the destruction of the state.

Of course if this autonomy of the ethical state with regard to particular churches is not to be understood in the sense of a complete separation between the state and religion, but as the apprehension of the rational *general validity* of the Christian idea of freedom, as opposed to the exclusiveness of confessional churches, it requires a corresponding *awareness* of this rational universality of Christianity. We will not go far wrong in supposing that Hegel saw in this the function of *philosophy* in the modern state. Indications of this are the fact that in opposition to the church's principle of authority Hegel attributes to "science", together with the ethically based state, the form of "universality of thought", the "objective truth and rationality" which the state has a duty to "protect" against the subjectivity of mere opinion.[32]

If philosophy shares with the state the form of the universality of thought, it contains in itself at the same time the substantial content of religion, its truth, which Hegel considered the theology of his time was abandoning. Under the pressure of the intellectual criticism of the Enlightenment, theology had withdrawn into the subjectivity of emotion, and had abandoned all

---

[30] On "theocracy" Hegel's view was: "There freedom as subjective, moral freedom . . . is completely lost" (*Geschichte der Philosophie* I, p. 200; not in ET).

[31] *Philosophie des Rechts* § 270, pp. 232f.; ET, pp. 173f.

[32] *Ibid.*, pp. 228f.; ET, pp. 170f.

content to the critics.[33] In his preface to his *Philosophy of Right* Hegel lamented that this contraction of religion to mere subjectivity corresponded to the fact that "the ethical world is Godless".[34] This withdrawal into inward piety, together with the abandonment of the field of objective truth, left social institutions godless as well. Hegel recognized the connection between this withdrawal into a purely inward religion in the face of the Enlightenment, and pietism. He ruthlessly unmasked the futility of the religious subjectivity found in pietist religion: "On this side of the empty essence of God there thus stands a finitude which is free on its own account and has become independent, which has an absolute value in itself."[35] Hegel was surprised that from this point of view "objectivity is ascribed to God at all", and he described as more logical the materialism which takes the empty subjectivity of pious emotion at its word, and draws from it the consequence of atheism.[36] Thus the rise in theology itself of a Christian atheism would have been regarded by Hegel as merely a confirmation of his views, and also of a confirmation of his contempt for the

[33] Hegel in his preface to the second edition of his *Enzyklopädie*, 1827, pp. 14f. (Not translated, but cf. *The Logic of Hegel*, trs. W. Wallace, 1892 [translation of the first part of the *Enzyklopädie*,] pp. xviiiff., where this preface is summarized.) See also *Philosophie der Religion*, *Werke* 15, p. 33; ET Vol. I, p. 15: "Religion has become devoid of knowledge, and has shrivelled up into simple feeling, into the countless or empty elevation of the spiritual to the Eternal. It can, however, affirm nothing regarding the Eternal, for all that could be regarded as Knowledge would be a drawing down of the Eternal into the sphere of the finite, and of finite connections of things." Theology has "as little content as possible, has cleared the ground of dogma and has been reduced to a minimum" (*Geschichte der Philosophie*, Introduction, p. 198). Thus the idea of the reason in the Enlightenment "empties feeling, heaven, and the knowing mind, and the religious content accordingly takes refuge in the Notion" (*Philosophie der Religion*, *Werke* 16, pp. 351f.; ET Vol. III, pp. 146f.).

[34] *Philosophie des Rechts*, p. 7; ET, p. 4.

[35] *Philosophie der Religion*, *Werke* 16, pp. 346f.; ET, Vol. III, p. 141.

[36] *Ibid.*, *Werke* 15, p. 68; ET Vol. I, p. 51: "God would thus be an historical product of weakness, of fear, of joy, or of interested hopes, cupidity, and lust of power. What has its root only in my feelings is only for me; it is mine, but not its own; it has no independent existence in and for itself." Thus one must show "that God is not rooted in feeling merely, is not merely my God".

readiness of theology to abandon the content of religion in order to accommodate rationalist criticism.

> The fundamental doctrines of Christianity have for the most part disappeared from Dogmatics. At the present time it is philosophy which is not only orthodox, but orthodox *par excellence*; and it is it which maintains and preserves the principles which have always held good, the fundamental truths of Christianity.[37]

For by overcoming abstract rationalist thought, philosophy was capable of showing the limits of the Enlightenment criticism of religion, and of reformulating the objective truth of Christianity in a new way, which could be shown to be superior to the rationalist criticism of the Enlightenment. In the face of the criticism of the Enlightenment, the truth of religion could not be saved except in the field of the universality of thought. Here it is the task of philosophy in Hegel's sense to formulate the general validity of the Christian religion for the state as well. Thus as Hegel saw it, in the situation of the modern mind produced by the Enlightenment, philosophy has a task on the scale of world history. But in his later years Hegel came to realize that philosophy of itself could not effectively claim to embody the general validity of the Christian religion altogether, by contrast to particular churches; for the reconciliation in philosophical thought is itself "merely a partial one without outward universality",[38] because it is limited to the esoteric circle of those who practise philosophy. The fate of Hegelian philosophy itself provides an example which strongly reinforces this remark; for philosophy clearly lacks external universality even amongst those who practise philosophy. By contrast, religion, as a result of its institutional links, is the form which, as Hegel says, is the absolute truth of all men. How far it was possible for Hegel to approach through the medium of philosophical thought the goal of his youth, the goal of a reform of society by means of a reform of religion, must be decided not least by examining the relationship of his philosophy to religion as it actually exists, and to the way it regards itself.

[37] *Ibid., Werke* 16, p. 207; ET Vol. II, p. 345.
[38] *Ibid., Werke* 16, p. 356: ET Vol. III, p. 151.

II

One might suppose that Christian theology would have had sufficient reason to welcome Hegel's philosophy as a means of rescuing itself from its difficult situation, as a liberation from the attacks of rationalist criticism upon the substance of Christian faith and from the pressure to seek refuge from these attacks in an inward piety without content. Hardly any of the great thinkers of the modern age have done as much as Hegel to set the Christian religion back upon the throne from which the Enlightenment had removed it. And he did this not like Kant, by basing it upon another extrinsic principle, but on the basis of the intrinsic rights of religion and the Christian revelation itself. It is quite clear that one of Hegel's greatest disappointments was that with some exceptions theologians did not take the opportunity offered by his thought, but regarded the refuge of an inward piety, to which they had fled from the attacks of the Enlightenment, as the Promised Land itself. They failed to take possession of the field of universal truth, on which alone the idea of God can endure. In his preface to the third edition of the *Encyclopedia* in 1830, Hegel speaks with perceptible bitterness of this pact between religious faith and its most determined enemies, and notes with distress how because of this his own philosophical commitment ceased to have any function:

The profound and rich content of the greatest, the absolute, concern of human nature has been allowed to wither away, and religious faith, both in its worshipping and its reflective forms, has come to find its highest fulfilment without content. As a result, philosophy has come to be a casual and subjective requirement. In both aspects of religious faith, these absolute concerns have been reduced to such a form – by the reasonings of those who defend them – that they no longer have any need of philosophy to satisfy these concerns. In fact it is regarded, and rightly, as having a damaging effect on this new kind of satisfaction, this narrowly restricted fulfilment.[39]

[39] *Enzyklopädie*, p. 26. (Not translated; this preface summarized in *The Logic of Hegel*, pp. xxivff.) As the continuation shows, the often noted and criticized withdrawal of the later Hegel to pure knowledge and esoteric theory is closely related to this experience.

How can we explain why the Christian religion and theology treated Hegel with so much mistrust and reserve? Even Karl Barth asks in astonishment (though not without ironically disassociating himself from the nineteenth century as a whole, since he believed his theology had gone beyond the outlook of that century): "Why did Hegel not become for the Protestant world something similar to what Thomas Aquinas was for Roman Catholicism?"[40] It is not usually possible to give an exhaustive answer to questions of this kind. Here too, we must be satisfied with listing a number of points.

The most effective theological charge against Hegel's philosophy is unquestionably the suspicion that its idea of God was *pantheistic*. There always seemed to be some cause for this suspicion, because of the close association of the young Hegel with Schelling, who in his early period had made no secret of his sympathies for the philosophy of Spinoza as held by Lessing. Hegel's energetic attack upon the abstract opposition between the finite and infinite, and his concept of the truly infinite, which the finite contains in itself as a "moment",[41] might on a superficial understanding give rise to the same suspicion. One of the first who categorized Hegel's philosophy as pantheist was Friedrich-August G. Tholuck (1799–1877), who was later very influential as a revivalist theologian, and who as early as 1823, in a romantic treatise on "The Doctrine of Sin and the Atoner", and then in 1825 in his "Florilegium of Western Mysticism" compared idealist philosophy to the pantheist mysticism of Islam with which he was familiar from his orientalist studies. In the preface to the second edition of his *Encyclopedia* (1827)

[40] K. Barth, *Die Protestantische Theologie im 19. Jahrhundert* (1946), 2nd ed. 1952, p. 343; ET *Protestant Theology in the Nineteenth Century*, complete ed. 1972, p. 384.

[41] *Wissenschaft der Logik*, ed. G. Lasson, Vol. I (*Werke* 3, PhB 56), 1932, p. 139; ET by A. V. Miller, *The Science of Logic*, 1969, p. 136. On a similar expression in the lectures on the history of philosophy (*Geschichte der Philosophie*, p. 414), W. Lütgert (*Die Religion des deutschen Idealismus und ihr Ende* III, 1925, p. 93) remarks: "This is clear enough", i.e. as a confirmation of the suspicion of pantheism. The fact that in the quotation Hegel carefully distinguishes the process within the Trinity from the world process escaped Lütgert's notice.

Hegel defended himself against the charge of pantheism, actually naming Tholuck, and elsewhere repeatedly and explicitly defended his philosophy against this label.[42] This did not prevent the obstinate persistence of the prejudice against Hegel's philosophy on the grounds that it was pantheist. Thus in 1925, in the third volume of his widely read work on the religion of German Idealism and its downfall, Wilhelm Lütgert said of Hegel's controversy with Tholuck: "He never took seriously or really understood the charge of pantheism made against him. He dismissed it" (p. 92). For Lütgert, a sufficient indication of Hegel's pantheism was the statement that Hegel's dominant concern lay in the "overcoming of belief in a God above and beyond the world". That the suspicion of pantheism could harden into a prejudice in this way is largely explained by the fact that from the time of D. F. Strauss onwards the Hegelian left wing, where it did not reject the idea of God altogether, more or less openly professed pantheism.[43] For the theological opponents both of Hegelianism and of speculative theism, this served to confirm their suspicions against Hegel. When one notes that even Dilthey interpreted Hegel in the sense of a "mystical pantheism",[44] which conflicted with his own sympathies, it is not surprising that in spite of the energetic rebuttal by Hegel scholars such as T. H. Haering[45] this prejudice has persisted down to the present day.[46] Little is done to clear the misunderstanding by the use of the more cautious term "panentheism",[47] for the concept of a panentheism is not far from the conception that finite things are contained in God.

[42] *Enzyklopädie* (2nd and 3rd eds.) § 573; ET *The Philosophy of Mind,* § 573, pp. 302ff.; summarized in *The Logic of Hegel,* pp. xviiiff.

[43] D. F. Strauss, *Die christliche Glaubenslehre* I, 1840, pp. 496 and 512; the substance is found in the "Concluding Dissertation" in *Das Leben Jesu* II, 1836, pp. 734f.; ET *The Life of Jesus,* trs. George Eliot, 1846, Vol. III, pp. 432ff.

[44] W. Dilthey, *Die Jugendgeschichte Hegels,* in *Gesammelte Werke* IV, 1921, esp. pp. 36ff., 51ff.

[45] T. Haering, *Hegel* I, 1929, pp. 463–5 and 547ff.

[46] See the summary in I.Iljin, *Hegels Philosophie als kontemplative Gotteslehre,* 1946, pp. 402f.

[47] H. Küng, *Menschwerdung Gottes,* 1970, pp. 170f., 339ff.

But while Hegel sometimes speaks of a unity or identity of the finite with the infinite or absolute[48] – something which he acknowledged was liable to misunderstanding[49] – this is always a *negative* unity, an identity mediated by the negation and superseding of the finite,[50] which consequently cannot properly be thought of as being contained in God. The opposite interpretation, which ascribes to him an acosmic position, according to which the finite is really nothing and God is everything, can appeal more successfully to Hegel. For a "pantheism" in this sense, in which the divine all is mediated through the nothingness of the finite, one can quote for example a passage in the *Science of Logic* in which Hegel attacks the usual form of the proofs of God:

> In ordinary inference, the *being* of the finite appears as ground of the absolute; because the finite is, therefore the absolute is. But the truth is that the absolute is, because the finite is the inherently self-contradictory opposition, because it is *not*. . . . The non-being of the finite is the being of the absolute.[51]

[48] In his early writings (*Werke* I, PhB 62ab, 1928), *Über die Differenz des Fichteschen und Schellingschen Systems der Philosophie*, p. 90, and *Glauben und Wissen*, p. 12. See also *Phänomenologie des Geistes*, p. 538; ET, p. 772. A few pages later we read that "implicitly and inherently" the divine Being and human nature are "not separate" (p. 540; ET, p. 775). Also p. 529; ET p. 760: "The divine nature is the same as the human, and it is this unity which is intuitively apprehended" (i.e. in the incarnation of the divine being). Cf. also *Wissenschaft der Logik* I, p. 133 (and also p. 138), ET pp. 130 and 136; *Philosophie der Religion*, *Werke* 15, pp. 87 and 121; ET Vol. I, pp. 70f., 108.

[49] As early as the *Phänomenologie des Geistes*, Hegel calls it "an unspiritual mode of expression" to say "that inherently . . . the Divine Being is the same as nature in its entire extent" (p. 542; ET p. 776; cf. also the distinction between what the unhappy consciousness is "implicitly" and what it is "for itself", p. 171; ET p. 267; and also pp. 386f. and 525f., ET pp. 562f. and 755f.). Similarly Hegel attacks in his *Enzyklopädie* (§ 573, pp. 486ff.; ET *Philosophy of Mind*, § 573, pp. 304ff.) the misinterpretation of his concept of identity. See also *Philosophie der Religion*, *Werke* 15, pp. 111ff.; ET Vol. I, pp. 97ff.

[50] Cf. *Wissenschaft der Logik* I, p. 132; ET pp. 133f.; *Philosophie der Religion*, *Werke* 15, pp. 82, 227, cf. 210; *Werke* 16, 280f., cf. 283, 286, 222; ET Vol. I, pp. 65f., 216f., 199f.; Vol. III, pp. 69f., cf. pp. 73f., 76f., 5.

[51] *Wissenschaft der Logik* II (*Werke* 4, PhB 57), 1923, p. 62; ET *The Science of Logic*, p. 443.

It is easy to see why it is possible to say of such statements: "There is no room in this system for a finite life which develops in a pure and undisturbed harmony with God and itself . . ."[52] Here Hegel might be supposed to be holding the acosmic view which he himself attributed to Spinoza.[53] But this would be to overlook the fact that the *Phenomenology of Mind* had already explicitly opposed the idea that "the Divine Being is the same as nature in its entire extent".[54] By contrast to Spinoza, in Hegel's philosophy of the subject the Absolute attains to itself in its *otherness*, and the world derives from the free choice on the part of the Idea of its otherness, which is thus vindicated as such.[55]

The interpretation of Hegel's idea of God as pantheist has been based since the time of D. F. Strauss on the fact that in Hegel's speculative doctrine of the Trinity, as in Schelling, "the Son is not a being above and beyond the world, but can only be the world or the finite consciousness itself".[56] There are unambiguous statements by Hegel which contradict this view, and distinguish between, on the one hand, the encounter within the Godhead as a "playing of love with itself, in which it does not get to be otherness or Other-Being in any serious sense, not actually reach a condition of separation and division", and, on the other hand, free positing of this otherness as a distinct element, as a world, in which "difference gets its rights, the right of being different".[57] The distinction between the im-

---

[52] J. Müller, *Die christliche Lehre von der Sünde* (1838, 3rd ed. 1849, I, p. 549).

[53] Iljin, *op. cit.*, pp. 194ff. interprets Hegel's philosophy in this way as "pantheism" of the unique reality of God (cf. Preface to second edition of the *Enzyklopädie*, p. 12, and § 50, n.; ET *The Logic of Hegel*, § 50 n.).

[54] *Phänomenologie des Geistes*, pp. 541ff.; ET p. 776.

[55] *Enzyklopädie*, (ET *The Logic of Hegel*) § 244.

[56] D. F. Strauss, *Die christliche Glaubenslehre* I, 1840, p. 490. Strauss describes in these terms the view of the early Schelling, and then continues to state that Hegel's view "agrees with it".

[57] *Philosophie der Religion*, *Werke* 16, pp. 248 and 250; ET Vol. III, pp. 35 and 37. Hegel goes on to refute explicitly "an incorrect conception . . . that the eternal Son of the Father, the Godhead who exists objectively for himself, is the same as the world and that we are to understand by the former nothing more than what we mean by the latter" (16, pp. 251f.; ET Vol. III, p. 39).

manent Trinity, that is, the emanation of the Son from the Father, and the creation of the world, does not in fact occur for the first time in the *Lectures on the Philosophy of Religion*, which Strauss described as displaying "excessive subservience to the religious conception"[58] but is found as early as the *Phenomenology of Mind*, which Strauss described as Hegel's "fundamental work".[59] If this explicit distinction on Hegel's part is taken into account, it is impossible to deny that Hegel distinguished between the movement of God within the Trinity and the world process. The only charge that can rightly be made against Hegel on this issue is that he derives the coming into being of the world with *logical* necessity from the inner life of the divine Trinity, that is, with the necessity which entails that the otherness posited within God must assert itself, that is, assert its diversity. While in this context the freedom of the divine act of creation is not taken into account in Hegel, it must be remembered that for Hegel freedom and necessity are not mutually exclusive,[60] and Hegel cannot be accused of thinking of the world in a Neo-Platonic way as an emanation from the being of God. For Hegel consistently distinguished the concept of creation from that of a mere emanation, and he sees the basis of this distinction as lying in the fact that God is thought of as a subject, as was already the case in Israelite religion.[61] The world cannot simply emanate from an Absolute

[58] D. F. Strauss, *Die christliche Glaubenslehre* I, 1840, p. 493.

[59] *Ibid.*, p. 512. In his work on the *Differenz des Fichteschen und Schellingschen Systems der Philosophie* (1801), Hegel seems not yet to have made this distinction between the process within the Trinity and the world process; this can only be deduced indirectly from Hegel's statement that the original identity of the Absolute extending into time and space and the Absolute returning within itself from this exclusivity "must unite both in the apprehension of the Absolute become objective to itself in completed totality – in the apprehension of the eternal (!) incarnation of God, of the testimony of the word from the beginning" (p. 90). The trinitarian begetting of the Son and the incarnation do seem in fact to be the same here.

[60] *Wissenschaft der Logik* II, p. 183, ET p. 553; cf. p. 216 (ET p. 580), where "freedom" is called "the truth of necessity" which has its form in the concept, i.e. in the subject (pp. 218f.; ET p. 582). This view is found as early as the *Differenz des Fichteschen . . . Systems*, pp. 86f.

[61] *Philosophie der Religion*, Werke 16, p. 52; ET Vol. II, p. 177.

which is thought of as a subject; nor can the absolute idea simply be thought of as *passing over* into its reflection in the natural world, but only as freely bringing into being a natural world. The expression which Hegel uses in his *Encyclopedia* as he turns from logic to natural philosophy, and which is often seen as the result of confusion, and a deliberate mystification, follows logically from the idea of the Absolute as a subject:

Enjoying however an absolute liberty, the idea does not merely pass over into life, or as finite cognition allow life to show in it: in its own absolute truth it resolves to let the "moment" of its particularity, or of the first characteristic and other-being, the immediate idea, as its reflected image, go forth freely as Nature.[62]

Here Hegel is not, as has been supposed, making a violent and desperate attempt to bridge the gap between the merely conceptual definitions of logic and the concrete facts of a nature which possesses material existence.[63] It is clear here that Hegel's logic of the concept is meant to be taken in all seriousness as a logic of the subject, and indeed of the absolute subject, God. Thus it is difficult to understand how anyone could overlook the idea of the personality of God in Hegel. For after Hegel had declared in the preface to the *Phenomenology of Mind*, "everything depends on grasping and expressing the ultimate truth not as Substance but as Subject as well",[64] in his *Science of Logic* he explicitly distinguished personality as the logical impulse of the being of the subject, that is, in so far as the concrete concept of the self is essentially something individual.[65] In the same way, in the Berlin introduction to the *History of Philosophy*, Hegel said of the "definition of the subjectivity of

[62] *Enzyklopädie* (ET *The Logic of Hegel*) § 244. Here the self-revelation of the Idea is described as the form of the logical process characteristic of the logic of the subject, and it is distinguished from the external *transition* from one determination to another which is characteristic of the logic of being, and from the *illusion* of a determination in the "other" which appertains to it, which is characteristic of the logic of essence.

[63] Marx, as early as the philosophical and economic manuscripts of 1844 (MEGA, suppl. Vol. I, Berlin, 1968, pp. 585f.).

[64] *Phänomenologie des Geistes*, pp. 19ff.; ET pp. 8off.

[65] *Wissenschaft der Logik* II, pp. 220f., cf. p. 484 and 502; ET pp. 583, 824 and 840f.

the highest idea, the personality of God" that, by contrast to the idea of God held by the Greeks, it was "a much richer concept".[66] In his *Lectures on the Philosophy of Religion*, Hegel also emphasized the trinitarian three-personal nature of God as a factor in the idea of God, though only as a factor: here as elsewhere he emphasizes at the same time the abstract nature of personality, in so far as it is "a rigid, reserved, independent, self-centred existence".[67] Thus in the *Philosophy of Right* personality appears as a category of abstract right, as the consciousness of itself which the subject has "as a completely abstract ego".[68] But the truth of the person does not lie in this abstract individualization, for :

It is . . . the nature or character of what we mean by person or subject to abolish its isolation, its separateness. . . . In friendship and love I give up my abstract personality, and in this way win it back as concrete personality.[69]

Depending upon whether personality in this sense is conceived of as abstract or as concrete, it is regarded by Hegel either as "a vanishing moment . . . in the absolute Idea" (ibid.) both in its relationship within the Trinity and in the relationship of the absolute subject to the world – or, when it is conceived of as concrete, as its true form. In the *Spirit of Christianity and its Fate*, we read of the abstract personality, that in spite of the difference between his personality and the Jewish character, Jesus "equally vigorously annuls all divine personality, divine individuality, in talking to his friends; with them he will simply be one, and they in him are to be one."[70] Even the later Hegel could say of this abstract personality: "in the divine unity personality is held to be cancelled",[71] that is, in so far as the abstract self-identity is overcome in the process of the divine

---

[66] *Geschichte der Philosophie* (Berlin introduction, *System und Geschichte der Philosophie*, ed. Hoffmeister, *Werke* 15a [PhB 166], 1944), p. 67.

[67] *Philosophie der Religion*, *Werke* 16, pp. 238f.; ET Vol. II, p. 24.

[68] *Philosophie des Rechts* (ET *Philosophy of Right*) § 35.

[69] *Philosophie der Religion*, *Werke* 16, p. 239; ET Vol. III, pp. 24f.; cf. *Wissenschaft der Logik* II, p. 484; ET p. 824.

[70] *Theologische Jugendschriften*, ed. H. Nohl, p. 315; ET *Early Theological Writings*, p. 269.

[71] *Philosophie der Religion*, *Werke* 16, p. 239; ET Vol. III, p. 25.

life. In this way Hegel takes due account of the criticism made by Spinoza and Fichte of the idea of the personality of God as a category irreconcilable with his eternity. On the other hand, he refutes this criticism by the idea that the truth of personality lies in "the winning back of personality by the act of absorption, by the being absorbed into the other".[72] The statement in the Berlin introduction to *The History of Philosophy* concerning the richness of the idea of the personality of God (cf. n. 66 above) must be taken in this sense, and so perhaps also must the "Addition" to §35 of the *Philosophy of Right*, which describes personality as "the sublime" – by contrast to the abstract character of the personality which is set forth in the paragraph itself – and continues: "One may define believing in God how one will, but if personality is not there, the definition is inadequate."[73] The fact that Hegel treated personality in the sense of abstract individuality as no more than a "vanishing moment" (see n. 69 above) of the idea of God, and that by contrast it is easy to overlook his first steps towards a concept of concrete personality, which went further than this, is not sufficient to explain why the view that Hegel denied the personality of God hardened into a firm prejudice. As in the case of the charge of pantheism, in this prejudice the right wing criticism of philosophical theism and revivalist theology once again agreed with the interpretation of Hegel by his "left wing" disciples. Thus D. F. Strauss believed that Hegel's view could be summed up as follows: Only "by means of man constituted by the same, and in him, would the Absolute achieve self-consciousness and personality".[74] This is an interpretation which, however influential it has become, cannot claim to be justified by Hegel's own statements. Its premiss lies in another misinterpretation on the part of Strauss, that is, his misrepresentation of Hegel's distinction between the process within the Trinity and the process of the world: if, as Strauss thought, the eternal Son

[72] *Ibid.*

[73] *Philosophie des Rechts*, p. 234; cf. p. 416 on § 151 (not in ET). On the whole theme cf. also Falk Wagner, *Die Persönlichkeit Gottes bei Fichte und Hegel* (thesis, typed), Munich, 1969.

[74] D. F. Strauss, *Die christliche Glaubenslehre* I, 1840, p. 521.

were for Hegel really identical with the world process, then of course the statements in the *Lectures on the Philosophy of Religion* concerning the relationship between the persons within the Trinity could be applied to the relationship of the absolute subject to the world process, and one could draw with Strauss the conclusion that the absolute subject first achieves self-consciousness and personality in human subjects. But if there is a distinction between the life within the godhead and the world process, then in Hegel the Absolute is already thought of as a person and a subject in itself. Yet an irremediable ambiguity remains here, because for Hegel the distinction between the Absolute and the world, as the essence of the finite, cannot be the last word. The truly infinite cannot be thought of only as the opposite of the finite; it must also transcend this opposition, and be the unity of itself and the Other to which it gives rise. In Hegel this idea appears in the form of the idea we have mentioned, that the bringing into being of the world necessarily belongs to the nature of the Absolute. But then the conclusion is unavoidable that not until the world is brought into being does the Absolute attain to its own nature as absolute subject. Here of course the self-consciousness and personality of the absolute are not yet identical with that of man, as Strauss supposed. But the Absolute realizes itself as a subject only in the bringing into being of the world and of man, and in the encounter with man.

The idea that God necessarily brings the world into being, and that – in Hegel's own words – "the positing of Nature necessarily belongs to the notion or conception of spiritual life",[75] did not become the main stumbling block for Christian theology without a most serious reason. But it seems to underlie all other theological objections to Hegel's philosophy. The misinterpretation of Hegel's philosophy of the Absolute as pantheism, and a denial of the personality of God, neither of which can be verified in the text of his writings, can only be understood as the supposed consequences, imputed to Hegel, of this single assertion, the necessity from the nature of the godhead

[75] *Philosophie der Religion, Werke* 16, p. 51; ET Vol. II, p. 176.

of the creation of the world. Tholuck's friend, the Halle dogmatic theologian Julius Müller, who had a better philosophical training and who made more cautious and subtle distinctions, saw this as the true weakness of Hegel's philosophy, that is, "that this system conceived of the nature of the Spirit in a one-sided way as *thought*, while this thought is understood as a necessary process".[76] As a result "the world becomes the self-realization of God ... and the ethical constitution of human life becomes a factor in this process".[77] The ultimate consequence of this view, he states, is "to recognize evil as an integral factor in the Idea itself".[78] With this last point, Müller certainly hit upon an inconsistency in Hegel's statements. Müller also knew that Hegel distinguished between the immanent self-differentiation of God and the bestowal of the independent existence upon the elements in it, in the world process.[79] But the assertion that the transition from the Absolute to the independent existence of the factor of otherness, and therefore to the world, was a reasonable one, was decisive in persuading him that the world was conceived of as a necessary factor in the self-realization of God, and that therefore Strauss's interpretation of Hegel was justified, at least with regard to the tendency of Hegel's arguments. In this sense, Müller too speaks of Hegel's "logical pantheism",[80] and expresses the view that the Absolute, thought of in this way, is "only the necessary principle of the world, which by means of the world process brings about its own absoluteness, the absolute unity of the world".[81] But neither "the knowledge of God as a personal being nor any kind of knowledge of God at all can co-exist"

[76] J. Müller, *Die christliche Lehre von der Sünde* (1838), 3rd ed. 1849, Vol. I, p. 552.

[77] *Ibid.*, Vol. I, p. 169; cf. Vol. II, p. 195: "Actualization by making himself finite."

[78] *Ibid.*, Vol. I, p. 552, cf. pp. 540f. Müller seems to have in mind in particular § 139 of the *Philosophy of Right* when he says on p. 554 that when Hegel is explicitly discussing the concept of evil, he ascribes it to God "with harsh necessity". But cf. also *Philosophie der Religion*, *Werke* 16, pp. 259f., 270; ET Vol. III, pp. 47f., 59.

[79] Müller, Vol. I, p. 541.   [80] *Ibid.*, Vol. II, p. 241.

[81] *Ibid.*, Vol. I, p. 6.

with such a concept of the Absolute.[82] Thus from Hegel's
assertion of the logical necessity of the creation of the world
and the coming into being of evil as the self-assertion of finiteness, *the consequence is drawn* that in spite of all the distinctions
which Hegel makes, the world must belong to the process of
the self-realization of God, and that therefore Hegel's system is
pantheist. Consequently, it is possible to do justice neither to the
divine personality, God's freedom with regard to the world,
nor to the personality and freedom of man. For both fall victim
to the logical necessity with which the divine Idea passes over
into the world process and the latter is taken back into God.
These were essentially the same theses, in which pantheism,
the elimination of the free self-consciousness and personality of
God, and the elimination of the freedom of man and therefore
also of sin, are inextricably linked, as Tholuck had already put
forward in 1823.[83] But Müller derived them from the logical
necessity which united God and the world,[84] and described
them as consequences of this basic thesis, even in the face of
explicit views expressed by Hegel. It is clear that Müller's
charges arise less from individual misunderstandings to which
particular expressions used by Hegel had given rise, than as a
coherent polemic construction, the starting point of which lies
in the assertion by Hegel that the world was necessarily created
by God, and which attributes to Hegel the real or supposed
consequences of this thesis, regardless of his own utterances.
Only when one recalls that the charges made against Hegel
consist of a set of logical deductions from a polemic construction, is it possible to make any sense of the crass ignorance with
which, for example, W. Lütgert was able to state that Hegel
"came into conflict with the simplest utterances of religious
devotion, with every Our Father, and never seriously tried to
understand why the prayer of Christianity begins with the
words: 'Our Father, who art in Heaven.' His God remained

[82] *Ibid.*, Vol. II, p. 159; Vol. I, p. 169.
[83] A. G. Tholuck, *Guido und Julius. Die Lehre von der Sünde und dem Versöhner oder Die wahre Weihe des Zweiflers*, 1823, pp. 26off., cf. p. 231.
[84] The same judgment was expressed later by R. Haym, *Hegel und seine Zeit*, 1857, p. 411.

Thought, Idea, and Reason; but he was Will, and therefore not Person, least of all Spirit."[85]

In view of such obviously perverse logical deductions, the question arises whether the theological critics of Hegel would not have done better to examine the conditions of the freedom and subjectivity of the Absolute which Hegel himself laid down. What is their relationship to the necessity with which, according to Hegel, the positing of nature falls within the concept of the life of the Spirit? If necessity is understood in the sense of Hegel's concept of absolute necessity, then the constitution of nature in the sense in which the term is used here cannot consist of a compulsion imposed from outside. In Hegel's *Science of Logic*, the category of necessity is dealt with in the passage which discusses the concept of reality, and absolute necessity is nothing other than the real itself in its absoluteness: "That which is simply necessary only *is* because it *is*; it has neither condition nor ground."[86] In this simplicity of its being it is one with the contingent. "But this *contingency* is rather absolute [i.e. having no condition outside itself] necessity."[87] The real is substance in this self-identity. But it possesses "the inner identity"[88] which constitutes its absolute necessity, not in itself, in so far as it differs from other substances, but in its unity with the Other from which it is distinct. Here contingency and necessity are once again separate; for in their simply reality, the different substances appear in themselves as contingent, and they possess their necessity, which is nevertheless proper and intrinsic to them as substances, only in the identity which unites them. This unity is the power and force of causal relationships between substances, and its "unveiling" is the point at

---

[85] W. Lütgert, *Die Religion des deutschen Idealismus und ihr Ende* III, 1925, p. 92.

[86] *Wissenschaft der Logik* II, p. 182; ET p. 552.

[87] *Ibid.*, p. 183; ET p. 553. This concept of absolute necessity must be understood of the Absolute as *ens necessarium*, in contrast to the non-independence and in this sense contingency of things in the world, and thus must be distinguished from every externally imposed necessity, which Hegel seeks rather to conceive anew on the basis of the idea of absolute necessity. Perhaps one may recall here Luther's *necessitas immutabilitatis* which in God is always one with the highest freedom. [88] *Ibid.*, p. 203; ET p. 570.

which necessity turns into freedom.[89] The self-identity of the
real, which constitutes its absolute necessity, therefore transcends substances which are individual and to this extent finite:
it is their universal, which however exists only as what is
definite and individual[90] – i.e. it is subject as existent concept.

But none of this has yet any bearing upon *divine* freedom, and
the question does not yet arise whether and in what way it
takes place through a necessity of the life of God as Mind. For
the identity which is conceived of as the universal which unites
all finite substances, and in which these have both their
necessity and their freedom, cannot be identical with the freedom from which the finite substances came into being at the
first. Thus this creative freedom does not derive from a universality of the concept, in however concrete a form it may be
conceived, and however much it may be supposed to embrace
everything particular and individual. On the contrary, the
creative freedom of God only becomes the ultimate horizon
of the universal which unites the finite "substances", by bringing into being a finite diversity. Thus as freedom it is also love,
and in this way it attains its own historical being, the specific
and definite divine attributes, which come into being only
when absolute freedom acts. But in Hegel the divine freedom
is determined by the logical nature of the concept, its inherent
co-ordination of universal, particular and individual. This
freedom is thought of as the identity of the concept itself, and
not the other way round, as if this identity were thought of as
the achievement of creative freedom, and therefore as contingent. Hegel understood the concept, or more exactly the
"true, infinite universal" as "creative power", which different-
iates and defines itself in its own impulses, thereby realizing

[89] *Ibid.*, p. 204; ET p. 571: "Necessity does not become *freedom* by
vanishing, but only because its still *inner* identity is *manifested.* . . . Con-
versely, at the same time, contingency becomes freedom, for the sides of
necessity, which have this shape of independent, free actualities, not
reflecting themselves in one another, are now *posited as an identity,* so that
these totalities of reflection-into-self in their difference are now also *reflected
as identical.*
[90] *Ibid.*, pp. 204f.; ET p. 571.

itself.[91] But are concept and subject really identical? It is of course not easy to refute Hegel in this respect, without saying what is meaningless and unthinkable; for how can the subject of freedom be thought of if it is not concept itself? Subjective freedom can only be meaningfully distinguished from the concept – which however can only take place in thought – if the concept is not the highest form of thought. Moreover, to refute this argument is to oppose not only Hegel, but also the theologians' traditional doctrine of God. For as long as the freedom of God is thought of as a faculty of a divine being, who is asserted to be free, but who is himself the basis of the act of freedom, then the act of God's freedom is bound to appear either as something additional and external to his being, or as an expression of his being itself, his power, and thus as a manifestation of his self-identity, that is, as a necessity inherent in it. The traditional theological doctrine of God has no solution to this dilemma. Hegel shares with it the acceptance of an absolute being which already exists before the act of divine freedom. As the "free power" of the universal[92] it is prior to the act of freedom itself. Hegel here follows theological tradition, as he does in his derivation of the Trinity from the concept of Mind in which he was already preceded by Anselm of Canterbury. One can scarcely reproach Hegel for taking the doctrine of God held in theology in a more strictly literal sense than it did itself, by trying to think of the freedom of God as the expression of his being, which was supposedly prior to its freedom, so that freedom was a manifestation of God's being. One may be justified in feeling unhappy at this, but the reproach must be directed in the first instance not towards Hegel, but to the insoluble problem which exists here in the traditional doctrine of God, and which he did not succeed in removing. Of course in the intellectually more rigorous formulation of Hegel, it is more noticeable than elsewhere. Hegel rightly resisted the abstract dualism implicit in the idea of a God who was simply opposed to everything finite, seeing this as effectively making the Absolute finite. He does not seem to have noticed

[91] *Ibid.*, pp. 244f.; ET p. 605.   [92] *Ibid.*, p. 242; ET p. 603.

that the concept of a being as the faculty and "power" under-lying this freedom itself made the Absolute finite. But his critics from the ranks of philosophical theism and revivalist theology, who considered that Hegel restricted the freedom of God and of man, did not succeed any better. They maintained the irrational acceptance of a divine being and acts of freedom which were added to him from outside. The only serious alternative to the mode of conception which Hegel applied to the concept of freedom is to understand the nature of God itself on the basis of the absolute future of freedom,[93] instead of thinking of it the other way round, as underlying his faculty of freedom. It is only possible to think of freedom as the absolute future of freedom, if it is not to be subject to the necessity of the nature of a prior being.

Hegel's theological critics were certainly not wrong in supposing that this very idea of freedom – the central idea in Hegel's thought – was not expressed in conceptual form without something being overlooked, with regard both to the freedom of God and the freedom of man. That the freedom of God and the freedom of man affect each other so that the way in which one is conceived is not without consequences for the other, is something that was impressed upon the thinking mind no later than the thirteenth century, with the conflict between Christian theology and the ideas in the Latin versions of Averroes. In Hegel's concept of the freedom both of God and of man, the element which fails to achieve adequate expression is its contingency,[94] in the sense of something that happens on the basis of the future alone, and the impossibility of deriving it from anything that already exists, even from what the person who makes the act of will already is in himself. Associated with this element of contingency, there is also the pluralism of the

[93] Here absolute future belongs to the essence of Freedom, because absolute freedom cannot have any future outside itself and is therefore its own future.

[94] This contingency of freedom forms the element of truth in the insistence of Hegel's critics on the formal freedom on which, as abstract, he places a low value. It is in the idea of concrete freedom that this element of con-tingency in the act of freedom must be maintained.

individual realization of freedom, as well as the independence of historical fact with regard to the logical form of the concept, and the fact that all past and present existence is not yet a closed entity, but is dependent upon a future which still remains open, and which is consequently the indispensable horizon for the understanding of present reality. All this leads to the central question, whether mind and thought really find their highest form in the concept, and in the idea as the concept brought to reality; and whether the concept is itself a subject, and subjective freedom is no more than a concept. When Hegel calls the concrete universal of the concept "the free power" and then defines this free power of the concept as the freedom of love,[95] then the leap in thought and the gap it leaves unfilled is unmistakable, and something which has not been supplied in the argument is forced into verbal juxtaposition. For the freedom of love cannot be conceptually anticipated; it transcends all prior identities. The identity which it brings about itself is the expression of it, but is never yet its full concept, so that it can never be embraced and comprehended in the concept. Here, every concept remains no more than an anticipatory concept.[96]

[95] *Wissenschaft der Logik* II, p. 242; ET p. 603.

[96] The demoting of the concept to an anticipatory concept does not represent merely a formal antithesis to be advanced against Hegel's thought. Rather, the Hegelian categories of thought are seen in themselves to be anticipatory in their dialectic nature. Thus the argument of the *Science of Logic* shows that the logical categories formulate the content of the idea of absolute knowledge or of truth as the identity of subject and object, which is reached at the end of the *Phenomenology of Mind*, but cannot fully embrace it and so transcend it. In the way in which absolute knowledge is manifested directly – as being – it has not yet taken on a form adequate to it, and this inadequacy is clear upon consideration of what was actually "posited" in the original category. The way thus remains open for a new formulation of absolute knowledge, which in its turn would upon consideration reveal that what was posited in it was merely anticipatory, and to be transcended. This anticipatory character of the logical categories, the beginning of which in being is already "inherently" the concept (*Enzyklopädie* [ET *The Logic of Hegel*] § 238, cf. § 84), was not a problem to Hegel only because this beginning, together with the "return to the ground" which followed it, seemed to him, on the basis of the speculative idea, to be "its self-determination" (§ 238). Regardless, however, of this self-interpretation on Hegel's

The autonomy of freedom, of the future, of individuality and of the historical fact, and thereby of Spirit itself with regard to the concept, which in its highest form is no more than an element of the life of the Spirit, has as its consequence that there must be some reserve with regard to the elevation of religious conceptions to the level of the concept, as proclaimed by Hegel. The historically contingent, which forms the content of the religious conception of Christianity at least, cannot be analysed without further ado in terms of the identity of the concept. The same is true of the content of history, which presents something different to each succeeding age, and will have a different meaning for a future which is still to come from that which it has for the present day. Thus Hegel's polemic against endeavours to clarify the historical origins of Christianity fell short of the mark. On the other hand, the very fact that the allusive language of religious conceptions is provisional is its primary and lasting justification, if reality as a whole is not yet a closed entity and its logical nature is not unaffected by the contingent events of the historical future. That religious conceptions make ultimately valid statements in the form of allusion, is one reason, and not the least, why religious traditions are able to leave room for the freedom of the individual and thereby to fulfil the political function for the subjective consciousness which Hegel attributed particularly to Christianity. But in the traditional dogmatic form of religious

---

part, the condition of which is that the reflective course taken by logic towards the absolute idea can actually have a conclusion, the anticipatory structure of the logical categories is obvious in his logic, and to this extent the thinking of these categories itself is relative to the future of its truth, from which it is derived and which it anticipates. The same is also true of the absolute idea, if its truth is not yet attained by its formulation in logical terms, but only with its development by way of the philosophy of nature and of the mind, and on to the philosophy of religion. Here the logical categories are seen to be an anticipatory concept of the truth which is in fact the theme of the history of religion. They were not of course developed by Hegel himself explicitly in this way, but can be seen to be such only by a reflection which makes critical use of the implications of the posited categories and the procedure used to develop them even against the way Hegel understood himself.

conceptions, in Christianity above all, this provisional nature, the way they convey meaning by means of allusion, is given little or no expression. For this reason we must agree with Hegel that the criticism made by the Enlightenment of the traditional conceptions of Christian faith can be dealt with only when its truth is set free from the narrow restrictions of its traditional dogmatic form. This does not mean that the conceptions of faith must be transformed into concept in the sense of Hegelian logic. We need scarcely mention that the conceptions of faith ought or could be reduced to *their own* concept, to the concept of their own logic. The ultimate validity of the claim to reduce the ideas of faith to their concept becomes questionable when it is realized how little the form of the concept is capable of doing justice to experienced reality. To realize this is to anticipate a new form of thought which corresponds better to historical reality than the Hegelian concept, a thought the truth of which includes reflection upon its own provisional nature, as well as the bearing upon it of contingency and the future, with their implications for freedom. But Hegel is surely right in the assertion that now the criticism of the Enlightenment has destroyed the principle of authority, and it is obvious that the subjectivism of religious experience of a religion based solely upon the decision of faith, taken as the ultimate basis of the certainty of faith, brings ruin to the truth of religion. This truth can attain intrinsic certainty only on the basis of the general truth of free and unrestricted thought. The criticism of Hegel's restriction of philosophical thought to the concept of the "concept" should no longer prevent Christian thought from recognizing and seizing upon the possibility which Hegel's thought provides for a new and positive definition of the relationship between Christianity and the modern age. This possibility is associated with the fact that Christian faith is being understood with a new rigorousness and exclusiveness, as the religion of freedom. A summary of the criticism to be applied to Hegel's thought might be that the experience of freedom must be thought out much more deeply than it has been in Hegel. If this happens, the criticism will be moving in the direction that Hegel himself pointed out.

6

CHRISTIANITY AS THE LEGITIMACY OF THE MODERN AGE

Thoughts on a book by Hans Blumenberg

First published in *Radius*, 1968, 3, pp. 40ff.

IN OUR PRESENT world, Christianity can no longer be taken for granted. Many people nowadays feel that the Christian churches are the relics of a past which has otherwise vanished without trace. Has the modern age broken away again from Christianity, or is the Christian heritage in some hidden way still a constituent element in the way of life, which seems so completely secular, of the so-called Western world, either as the hidden capital on which it is living in spite of all the secularization it puts on display, or as the factor which makes this secular life itself a possibility? It depends on the answer to this question whether, as a modern man, one can still be a Christian without having a split personality, and whether, as a Christian, one can still be a modern man without losing one's Christian integrity. The modern age came into being out of a world in which Christianity was dominant, and therefore its relationship, and particularly that of its early stages, to Christianity is not merely a matter of historical interest. For Christians at least it is directly relevant to the possibility of achieving an understanding of themselves at the present time, that is, of retaining the Christian faith at the present day. If the modern age must be understood as a kind of rebellion against its Christian prehistory, then it would be an almost impossible task honestly to be a Christian against the background of life as it is lived in the modern world. At best Christian faith would be possible only as a constant contradiction to the principles of the modern form of life and awareness, and would therefore constantly be in danger of being compromised by accommodating itself too far to the spirit of this modern world.

The question of the relationship of the modern age to the Christian heritage has been answered in very different ways. Thus Romano Guardini has summed up the modern age by the term "secularization", signifying a period of decline from Christian faith.[1] He hopes for a renewal of Christianity only at the end of the modern age, which he proclaimed after the end of the Second World War as the result of the catastrophes which war has brought about in the present century. But the experience of the post-war period has shown that the revival of religion in the early post-war years was no more than an episode, while the basic intellectual and social decisions which created the modern age have once again displayed their normative power for the life of the modern world.

By contrast to Guardini, Friedrich Gogarten attempted to justify the worldliness of the modern age as itself a product of Christian faith.[2] The biblical faith in the one transcendent God, he claimed, desacralized the world, and the adoption as a son of God which man received through the one Son of God meant that this world was given to him as a heritage. Because man, who owes his sonship to God, possesses his salvation, his wholeness, in faith in God the Father, he no longer needs to seek it from the world, but can take the world in a secular way and leave open the question of its totality. From this worldliness, Gogarten distinguishes a secularism which answers the question of salvation, which is a matter of faith, in terms of a man's relationship to the world, either in an ideological or nihilistic form. Gogarten's conception has made possible for modern Christians a new way of accepting in a positive way their existence as modern men. But it is doubtful whether Christian faith exists in such independent isolation of the understanding

---

[1] Romano Guardini, *Das Ende der Neuzeit, Ein Versuch zur Orientierung,*1951.

[2] Friedrich Gogarten, *Verhängnis und Hoffnung der Neuzeit. Die Säkularisierung als theologisches Problem,* 1953.

of the world as it seems to do in Gogarten. In Gogarten, its independence derives from the authority of the word of God. But doubt was cast on this very readiness to bow to traditional authorities from the beginning of the modern age, and it was completely demolished by the modern understanding of the world. How can one affirm the secularization of the modern age and yet still rely upon an authority which calls for faith and provides its basis?

In the first instance, the reaction against traditional authorities at the beginning of the modern age was a reaction against the traditional Christianity of church doctrine, which from the sixteenth century on had taken the form of mutually conflicting denominational variants. A theological understanding of the emancipation of man in the modern age from all heteronomous traditions – which is the real meaning of the worldliness of the modern age – has to work out its attitude above all to this reaction of the modern age against the Christian tradition. Can the criticism of the claim of the Christian tradition to possess authority, a criticism maintained in the name of the autonomy of human reason and experience, be understood in its turn as the working out of Christian elements?

The critical relationship of the modern age to Christianity forms the heart of Hans Blumenberg's book *Die Legitimät der Neuzeit* – "The legitimacy of the modern age".[3] The very title is aimed at the widespread thesis of the secularization of Christian themes in the modern age; for this "expropriation model" (p. 21) burdens the modern age with the stigma of illegitimacy (p. 20). If the modern age really owes what C. F. von Weizsäcker called its "uncanny success" largely to its Christian background, then the immediate conclusion is: "The degree of success determines the size of the wrong done by its having forgotten its true presuppositions" (pp. 72f.). Blumenberg attacks this subordinate role which is apparently characteristic of the category of secularization, in the name of the self-assertion of reason. In the struggle against the category of secularization, he holds, nothing less is at stake than the self-

[3] Hans Blumenberg, *Die Legitimität der Neuzeit*, 1966.

awareness of the modern age, with its claim to possess something new by contrast to the final validity asserted by Christianity (pp. 5of.).

To assert and give a basis for the legitimacy of the ideas one possesses is the elementary endeavour in history of anything which is new or claims to be new; to resist this legitimacy and to disturb or put a brake on the self-consciousness that results from it is the technique employed by the defence of the existing order (p. 46).

To this extent, Blumenberg speaks of "secularization as the final theologumenon . . ., which seeks to impose upon the heirs of theology a guilty conscience for the entry into the world of original sin" (p. 73). Consequently, the historical question of the origins of the modern age cannot simply be ignored, and a different model must be constructed in opposition to that of secularization: that the modern age came into being as a "counter-proposal" (p. 143) on the part of the self-assertion of humanity against a "theological absolutism" which had become intolerable. Even for Blumenberg, however, this "gap between two eras" does not represent a total discontinuity; nevertheless:

The continuity of history across this gap between two eras does not lie in the persistence of an ideal substance, but in the legacy of unsolved problems, in the taking over of the function of knowing once again what had already once been known (p. 35).

Christianity left behind it "a mass of unsatisfied, disappointed and urgently pressing expectations and claims" (p. 71). Modern thought had to face this challenge by filling the gaps left by the theological answers which it had become impossible to accept, just as early Christianity had been unable to escape the "pressure of the problem" posed by the unanswered questions, alien to the nature of Christianity, of antiquity (pp. 42f.).

Blumenberg sets out to demonstrate his thesis by examining the continuity of these problems from late antiquity down to the early modern age. He takes as his guide the theme of theodicy. Amongst the questions which the philosophy of the ancient world left to be solved by Christianity was that of the origin of evil in the world. Within the framework of the ancient religious belief in the cosmos, this question did not at first take explicit form. But Neo-Platonism already saw the world as a unique mistake in its ideal model. Gnosticism thought of the world in an even more radical way as hostile to God, and therefore saw redemption as a liberation from the world. According to Blumenberg, this gnostic dualism corresponded to the "consciousness that the world deserves destruction" (p. 83, cf. pp. 28ff.), which he supposes was characteristic of the primitive Christian expectation of an imminent end. But the consequence of the delay of the expected parousia was that as Christians once again became involved in the world, they had to take up again the unsolved problem of ancient cosmology, the question of the origin of evil in the world. It was impossible for Christian thought to tolerate the idea "that this world was meant to be the prison of the wicked, and yet was not utterly destroyed by the power of the God who according to his revelation had resolved upon redemption" (p. 84). The Christian answer to this question, the classical form of which Blumenberg finds in Augustine, was to place upon man, that is upon human freedom, the responsibility for sin and therefore for evil in the world. The weakness in this argument clearly lies in the fact that it was now possible for freedom itself to appear as an evil. The question of the creator of human freedom, and above all the Augustinian doctrine of predestination, was again to place upon God the ultimate responsibility for evil in the world. As a result, gnostic dualism returned in the form of the hidden God and his incomprehensible sovereignty. The extreme expression of Augustinian ideas in late medieval voluntarism provoked the self-assertion of man aginst this "theological absolutism" (pp. 143f.). The break down in the late Middle Ages of the conceptions of the inviolable order of the universe, and the corresponding conception of divine providence, confronted man with the unrelieved arbitrariness of the divine caprice. In the face of this absolutism of grace, "the way out of the world into transcendence . . . was no longer an alternative chosen by man himself, and as a direct result lost its human relevance and historical effectiveness" (p. 111, cf. p. 90). For subjection to the power of God alone is "not yet a sufficient condition of salvation" (p.111). Consequently, the human self-assertion of reason had to abandon the system of medieval theology and rebel against theological absolutism.

By its attempt to represent the interest of God, and of God alone, theology left the interest of man to look after itself, and allowed his concern for his own affairs to become absolute – that is, to take the place of the attraction which theology had for him (p. 165).

The principal means of this self-assertion was hypothesis as a form of thought and the association implicit in it of science and the overcoming by technical means of deficiencies in the natural conditions of existence. The attitude underlying this is seen by Blumenberg to lie in theoretical curiosity, the history of which he studies in detail, from its roots in antiquity through the Christian judgment on it as a sinful *curiositas*, down to its rehabilitation and redefinition in the transition from the Middle Ages to the modern age.

The use of a theodicy as key to the construction of the whole history of Christian theology is part of Blumenberg's conception that the modern age originated in opposition to theological absolutism. It makes the genesis of this absolutism comprehensible, and at the same time provides a foil to the way the modern age overcomes the deficiencies of nature by constantly transforming it through human activity. The idea of progress takes on "the vanished role of theodicy" (p. 37). This is the model case for Blumenberg's thesis of the "identity of function" of substantially antithetical ideas which replace each other in the course of history.

But the question of theodicy never had such a simple significance for the history of Christian theology.[4] Christianity came

---

[4] As early as the end of the second century Irenaeus introduced human freedom into his theology of creation, not for the sake of theodicy, but as the essence of the way man is the image of God (*Apodeixis* 2.1). The unity of the redeemer God with the creator, which he maintained against gnostics of every school, did not yet make it necessary for him to justify God with regard to the wickedness and evil in the world. By the time of Clement of Alexandria, at the beginning of the third century, the situation had changed. In his "Miscellanies" (*Stromateis* I, 82ff.) Clement deals with an argument which, as he says, was advanced against Christians from every side: Anyone who does not prevent something is (causally) guilty of it.

to terms in a decisive way with the evil and wickedness in the world not by removing responsibility for the world from the creator, but by belief in the reconciliation of the world by the God who took upon himself the burden of its guilt and misery and so set men free from it. It is strange that in Blumenberg's book this central Christian theme is scarcely mentioned. It found its most far-reaching expression in the idea of the incarnation, of which Blumenberg once admits in passing that it signified a "infinite increase in man's regard for himself" (p. 584). Belief in the incarnation maintained the primitive Christian consciousness of the presence of eschatological salvation, which had already been characteristic of the message of Jesus.[5] Consequently, the delay of the parousia did not represent the catastrophe for Christianity which it has often been claimed to be. Rather, the basic theme of the presence of salvation now became for the first time the central issue. The affirmation of

---

Against this Clement explicitly states that only the doer is guilty. But in the case of the wickedness and evil in the world this is not primarily man, but the devil, who according to 83.2 "was the free master of his decisions". Only after this does Clement give an assurance that for the evil actions of men and their consequences no blame falls on God, since the soul is free (84.1). This argument, a somewhat lame one in view of the superior power of God, hints at the direction in which the problem was to be treated in later Western theology, in Augustine and in scholasticism: Not to prevent something does not mean to do it: God only "permitted" sin, "allowed" it, but did not positively will it. This was supported by such considerations as that God could not will sin, because everything he wills, by the very fact that he wills it, is in accordance with his will and is therefore not sin. The inadequacy of such arguments in the face of an omnipotent God, who does not guard his creatures against falling into sin, is clear enough. Blumenberg rightly emphasizes, pp. 88 f., that Augustine's doctrine of absolute predestination made the problem even more acute; and other writers agree. His assertion that such an argument in fact seeks to save God at the expense of man is however anachronistic, since it does not take seriously the fact that for theological tradition it is the devil who is primarily guilty. The characterization of the problem of theodicy as the main theme of the history of Christian theology, at the expense of every other. is an extremely questionable procedure.

[5] See U. Wilckens, "Zur eschatologie des Urchristentums. Bemerkungen zur Deutung der jüdisch-christlichen Überlieferungen bei Hans Blumenberg" (*Beiträge zur Theorie des neuzeitlichen Christentums*: Festschrift for W. Trillhaas, 1968, pp. 127–42).

the present world, implicit in belief in the incarnation, meant that the assimilation of the cosmology of antiquity by the Christian theology of creation no longer represented a break with the principle of Christianity. The maintenance of belief in creation[6] in the face of extreme gnosticism, and the positive acceptance of a contemporary understanding of the world, were rather made possible and encouraged by belief in the presence of salvation in the form of the incarnation, even though the Christian theme of repentance, the transformation of what now exists for the sake of its redemption, was often allowed to fall into the background.

Belief in the incarnation of God for the redemption of humanity did in fact bring with it "an infinite affirmation of the human regard for the world". In his idea of the "sonship" of man made available by Christ, Gogarten rightly recognized here the decisive positive link between Christianity and the modern self-understanding of man. On the other hand, he merely constructed this link in dogmatic terms, and did not examine in detail the form it actually took in the history of thought. Blumenberg, who discusses the historical course taken by the problem in minute detail, unfortunately underestimates the scale on which the doctrine of man was affected by belief in the incarnation; he notes this only in passing. In fact it is difficult to fit into his conception, for according to him a growing theological absolutism so far forced man into meaninglessness that a humanist self-assertion was possible only in opposition to the theological system. Even in the theology of the early Church the incarnation was regarded as the consummation of what was begun in the creation of man. The second Adam fulfilled the destiny of man to be the image of God. As a result, a unique position in the cosmos is attributed to man, even as a creature. In him – a foreshadowing of the incarnation – the material and spiritual worlds are united, and we find as early as the end of the second century, in Clement of Alexandria, the

---

[6] Its independent significance was previously evaluated quite differently by Blumenberg; cf. his article "Licht als Metapher der Wahrheit" in *Studium Generale* 10, 1957, pp. 432–47.

idea that man is the purpose of the creation of the world as a whole. Only with this idea does the biblical statement that man has domination over the world as the image of God achieve its full significance. Now Blumenberg says of medieval scholasticism that it showed "a general tendency to give less and less weight to the stoicizing statement of the patristic age, that the world was created for the sake of man" (p. 132). But this is a misunderstanding. Whereas in the patristic age the idea of man as the purpose of creation existed side by side and unreconciled with that of a hierarchy of creatures, in which man was subordinate in rank to the angels, in scholasticism the anthropocentric point of view came to prevail. Blumenberg appeals to a passage in Anselm of Canterbury, according to which man was created in order to make up the number of elect which had been reduced by the fall of Lucifer (pp. 132f.). This train of thought, which goes back to Augustine, does in fact place man in a position subordinate to that of the angels. But scholasticism characteristically refused to follow Anselm and Augustine on this very point. During the twelfth century the view came to be accepted that man was created for his own sake, not for the sake of the angels.[7] For Nicholas of Cusa to describe man as a "second God", *secundus deus*, is altogether in line with this tendency to see man at the head of creation, in the sense of an interpretation of man's status as the image of God inspired by belief in the incarnation. Was it not this that first achieved the independence of man with regard to the cosmos which has always been the presupposition of modern thought and modern science? The ancient world saw man as part of the structure of the cosmos, even where it saw him as its centre, as a microcosm or *logos*-being. Only when he was linked with the transcendent creator God was it possible for man to stand back from the world in a way which enabled him to transform

---

[7] In the twelfth century Anselm of Laon wrote that man was created *propter se*, not *propter restaurationem angeli*. In Rupert of Deutz we read *non homo propter angelos, imo propter hominem quemdam angeli quoque facti sunt sicut et cetera omnia*. On this and similar utterances from this period (down to Thomas Aquinas on II *Sentences*, dist. 1, qu. 2, art. 3), cf. M. Chenu, *La théologie du douzième siècle*, 1957, pp. 52ff.

the world according to his own ideas and for his own purposes.

None of this of itself necessarily prevents the emancipation of man, which Christian anthropology made possible in a positive sense, from first being realized as a self-assertion against theological absolutism, as in Blumenberg's arguments. But the absolutism of the Augustinian doctrine of predestination, which makes the decision concerning man's election or rejection a matter for a hidden act of divine choice, prior to any attitude adopted by man, did not go unchallenged throughout the Middle Ages. With very few exceptions, e.g. Peter Lombard, when scholastic theologians were dealing with the doctrine of predestination, they chose to make rejection at least, if not election itself, dependent upon divine foreknowledge of the human decision.[8] This semi-Pelagian watering down of Augustine's doctrine of predestination had at least the advantage of leaving the decision concerning man's salvation to his historical confrontation with the grace of the gospel, instead of keeping the two separate. But even Duns Scotus, who emphasized so strongly that election was a matter of pure grace, by contrast derived man's rejection from the guilt of those rejected, foreseen by God. It is in fact in contradiction to his explicit statements for Blumenberg to ascribe to him the conception of "the undeservedly rejected" as the expression of "the complete absolutism of the divine sovereignty" (p. 140).[9] This detail is characteristic of the perverse way in which "theological absolutism" is constructed in Blumenberg's book. The false impression is created that in scholasticism man and his history were "a matter of indifference" (p. 138) for the will of God, so that it was only possible for man to assert himself by rejecting the absolutism of grace. That the divine love is directed to man from eternity was expressed by Duns

---

[8] The relevant texts are discussed in detail in my study *Die Prädestinationslehre des Duns Scotus im Zusammenhang der scholastischen Lehrentwicklung*, 1954.

[9] Cf. Duns Scotus' *Commentary on the Sententiae*, Book I, dist. 41 (Opera Omnia, ed. Vatic. Vol. VI, pp. 315ff., esp. pp. 332ff.) and my study just mentioned, pp. 90ff.

Scotus in the very idea which Blumenberg so strangely mis-
understands (pp. 137f.), that God decided to unite man with
himself through the incarnation from eternity, and not merely
as a way to do away with the interference of sin.[10]

The voluntarism of the late Middle Ages is very far from the
anti-humanist tendency which Blumenberg attributes to it. Its
exponents were always concerned to maintain both the freedom
of God and the freedom of man, by contrast to extreme
Aristotelian conceptions of a closed cosmic order, which left
room neither for free action on the part of God nor for the
freedom of man.[11] By contrast with this system of cosmic
necessity, which found expression in the belief of the times in
fate and the stars, late medieval voluntarism defended not
only the freedom of God but also that of man.

This means that we must pass a different judgment upon the
relationship of the modern age to the late Middle Ages from
that of Blumenberg. The modern age did not come about
through an act of humanist self-assertion against the absolutism
of grace in the Christian idea of God. It is true that its origins
were characterized by a break with medieval thought. But the
issue here was not the omnipotence of God and the freedom of
his grace, but the positivism of the ecclesiastical system of
salvation, the ecclesiastical authority which for the late Middle
Ages was incapable of rational justification.

One of the insoluble dilemmas of late medieval theology was
that its voluntarist understanding of God no longer enabled it
to relax the rigid system of church authority and set it in
motion. Instead, it arrived at a superficial justification of this
positivism of authority as an act of divine power. But the
matter could not be left here forever. For the rigidity of the
ecclesiastical order made it all the more difficult to perceive
the personal will of God which was supposed to be its origin.
It is consequently characteristic of the late Middle Ages that

[10] Cf. Karl M. Balić, "Duns Scotus' Lehre über Christi Prädestination im
Lichte der neuesten Forschungen", *Wissenschaft und Weisheit* 3, 1936,
pp. 19–35.
[11] I have discussed this at greater length in a review in *Zeitschrift für
Kirchengeschichte* 69, 1955, pp. 355–60.

at many points a tendency developed towards a direct personal relationship with God, by-passing the ecclesiastical order of salvation, or treating it as irrelevant to the relationship of the individual to God. This is found in the mysticism of Eckhart and Tauler, but also in the Augustinianism of Thomas Bradwardine, and not least in Luther's doctrine of direct access to God by faith; and it can also be traced in the thought of Nicholas of Cusa. All these movements posed questions which went beyond the positivism, the authoritarian character, of the existing order of salvation.

This discontent with the positivism of the ecclesiastical order of salvation, the rationality of which had been destroyed by nominalist criticism, is of course not enough to explain the break with the Middle Ages. The rise of the modern age cannot be understood in the abstract terms of the history of ideas. The Reformation, and still more, the historical catastrophes which came about in its train – the fragmentation of Christianity and the wars of religion of the sixteenth and seventeenth centuries – were needed to make the break with the Middle Ages a final one. Not until Christianity had broken down into separate denominations, and each had sought in vain, during the wars of religion, to maintain its absolute claim against the others, was there a spread of a general weariness with the traditional authorities, which, because they were now numerous, had lost their credibility. As a result, a new common ground for the social life of men was sought in nature and reason, in the state and in general morality, and the denominational authorities and their disputes were ignored. Yet only rarely, and in Protestant countries hardly at all, did criticism of the traditional authority lead to a break with Christianity. This may be associated with the fact that Protestantism was able to legitimize the tendency to emancipation from traditional authorities: the direct access of the Christian layman to God, which required no spiritual mediation other than an occasional one, justified the abolition of the privileges of the clergy over the Christian people. In this sense the ideas of the Reformation resulted in a positive evaluation of the emancipation of the modern age, a

Christian legitimation of the modern age. It is astonishing that Blumenberg has not discussed the role of the Reformation in the rise and the self-understanding of the modern age.[12] If he had done so, it would have been difficult for him to deny any positive link between the modern age and Christianity. But if the relationship of the modern age to Christianity is not merely one of antithesis, but also one of real continuity, so that the modern age is quite justified in claiming a Christian legitimation for itself, then there is a new relevance for the category of secularization. A term of some kind is required for the themes of Christian tradition which the modern age has adopted, and for this purpose the category of secularization has the advantage that it also indicates the change which took place in the course of this appropriation.[13] Secularization need not necessarily be a polemical theological concept, as Blumenberg supposes. Just as the secularization of church property and the secularization of clergy took place within the Reformation as the consequence of Reformation principles, so too secularization in a wider sense can be understood positively as a consequence of the Reformation, that is, as the removal of the privileges of the clergy in favour of the Christian people. Seen in this light, secularization is an expression of the coming of age of the Christian layman. This shows that it is a characteristic tendency of the modern age in its struggle against the principle of authority both in religious and political life. Of course not every process of secularization has favoured Christian maturity.

---

[12] This remarkable and significant situation is pointed out also by G. Rohrmoser, *Emanzipation und Freiheit*, 1970, pp. 14ff. See also M. Elze, "Christliche Wurzeln der modernen Naturwissenschaften" in *Christentum und Gesellschaft*, ed. W. Lohff and B. Lohse, 1970, p. 194.

[13] So too K. Löwith in his defence against Blumenberg's attack on the theory of secularization, which was aimed at him too: *Philosophische Rundschau* 15, 1968, pp. 195–201. Löwith rightly stresses, moreover (p. 197), that Blumenberg's account (pp. 18f.) of the concept of secularization as an identity of substance, which was simply appropriated from the original owners, places on his opponents "a burden of proof which he himself admits he cannot sustain"; for historical continuity can naturally never be understood as an identity of substance remaining untouched by historical change.

Secularization can also bring about a break with Christianity altogether. In this sense, these processes are ambiguous. But the motivation of their genuine significance is entirely Christian. This makes it justifiable to speak of a Christian legitimation of the modern age in its emancipation from traditional authorities. Humanist emancipation is not as such a position opposed to Christianity. Rather, in spite of all the tendencies associated with it to turn away not merely from the authoritarian medieval form of Christian tradition, but also from Christianity itself, it represents a phase in Christian history in which the "infinite increase of man's regard for himself" has for the first time come fully to prevail.

7

ESCHATOLOGY AND THE EXPERIENCE OF MEANING

A Lecture delivered to the congress on the Future of Religion at Nijmegen on 23 March 1972, and published in *Toekomst van de Religie: Religie van de Toekomst?*, Uitgeverij Emmaus (N.V. Desclée de Brouwer), 1972, pp. 134–148.

I

UNTIL very recently observers of the intellectual situation of our times took it for granted that there was no future for religion in the modern world. The religious renaissance of the immediate post-war years was followed by a new wave of secularism which gave fresh voice to criticisms of religion from the most various sources. These criticisms found their way into theology itself, through the adoption of Bonhoeffer's call for a "non-religious interpretation" of the Christian message, a call now regarded as prophetic. It seemed that the substance of the Christian message would be saved for mankind now and in the future only by its transformation into a non-religious form. This transformation usually amounted to an interpretation of Christianity in terms of ethics, social ethics, and, more recently, often of social revolution. It was often forgotten, however, that Bonhoeffer's call for a non-religious interpretation of the Christian message was motivated not only by an awareness of the secularity of the modern experience of the world, but at least equally by Karl Barth's theology of revelation, which saw the Christian message and Christian faith as in direct conflict with all religion. What was taking place was an attempt by apologetics to rescue Christianity from the attacks of the modern criticism of religion without having to present a defence against its arguments. Theology might feel that it was being particularly modern in its approach by making use of the arguments of the criticism of religion. At the same time this process dealt with the competing claims of non-Christian religions. The criticism of religion of course applied only to the latter, for the Christian message itself was to be regarded not as religion, but as a testimony to revelation. In this way dialectical theology contributed to the hardening of the prejudice that the time of religion and religions was past. Inevitably, it was not long before this attitude reacted against Christianity itself, whenever there was any serious attempt to extirpate the remnants of religion. As is well known, the most important victim of this purification of Christianity from religion was the idea of God. But the parodoxes of the God-is-dead "theology" reduced to absurdity the thesis of the non-religious character of the Christian revelation. Instead of the end of religion – or even as its decisive phase – it was now the end of Christianity which suddenly seemed imminent, or at least the end of the central content of faith in the Christian tradition. For a few years it seemed as though the religious potential of Christianity was to be devoted solely to social criticism and revolutionary action.

More recently, there have been signs of a reversal of this tendency.

First of all, there is a widespread disappointment with the passion for social revolution. Hopes for the realization of true humanity by changes in the system of society have grown perceptibly more modest. The confidence that at a stroke all could be changed, man's domination of man could be brought to an end, human need might no longer be manipulated, and the alienation and conditioning of life by economic interests could be overcome, turned for many people into scepticism.

Secondly, this resulted in a tendency to withdraw from social commitment into private life. This was not always into the private sphere of the bourgeois family, but often into the community experience of a group which was able to support the insecure individual. The hippy movement, as well as the drug craze and the attempt to go one better than drugs in religious emotion, seem to form part of the backwash of this tendency. When Jesus is recommended as the "greatest trip", this is in the first place a remarkable confirmation of the

Marxist diagnosis of religion as the "opium of the people". This renaissance of religious ideas and concepts in the underground of society was a sensation only because religion had previously been supposed to have no future, and because its remnants were associated almost exclusively with an out-dated establishment.

Thirdly, however, the renewal of religious life in the subcultures of society is important as a sign that for many reasons, and in the most various circumstances, there is renewed questioning concerning the meaning and purpose of life. In a situation of material satiety people may well ask whether that is everything that life offers. The emigration in the last ten years of many young people from prosperous families into hippy groups and other marginal social groups is evidence in itself of this implicitly religious motivation. Other similar forces found their expression in the movement for social revolution, and have been released once again by the disillusionment of at least the short-term expectations associated with it. In the USA a particular role seems to have been played by the disintegration of "civil religion", the shattering of the nationalist faith in America's world mission, the power of which was broken by the war in Vietnam. Like nationalism in Europe in the past, but associated in the USA with a belief in the world mission of democratic ideas, the conviction of America's humanitarian vocation certainly provided for many Americans a sense of purpose and direction into which their daily life could be integrated. But for many groups in American society, the war in Vietnam deprived this belief of its innocence. And while it is easy to underestimate the healing effects of forgetfulness, it is not so easy to explain Vietnam as an unfortunate accident. But the disintegration of civil religion reopens the questions concerning the meaning and purpose of life which in the past found an answer and explanation in nationalism. Without this process it is scarcely possible to explain why a renewal of religious ideas and concerns which originated in a handful of marginal groups should have found so sustained a response in American society.

II

The words "future" and "hope" are prominent amongst the key words of a new religious sensibility. But it is doubtful whether the central impulses of religious revival are concentrated in these particular concepts. For the flight from the world and emigration from society seem to have played a part which must not be underestimated in the return to the ideas and concerns of religion, and "the future" and "hope" can hardly serve as permanent watchwords for such tendencies. A "theology of hope" may of course briefly have performed the function of compensating for specific disappointed hopes of the short-term achievement of the humanizing of society, so that a commitment to hope and the future could be maintained in spite of the disappointment of its secular aims. Jürgen Moltmann has recently argued a link between the rise of the "theology of hope" and the impulses of the Kennedy era. But the effect of his book has been not so much that of an ideological glorification of the political ideals of that period, with the corresponding phenomena in socialist countries such as Czechoslovakia, but rather that of a compensation for increasing uncertainty and disillusionment with such ideals. But here the theology of hope has not only provided an other-worldly consolation for the politically disappointed, but has also strengthened and renewed political hope by the power of Christian hope. This makes clear the function of the ideas associated with the future and with hope within the theme of religion. World-rejecting forms of hope have existed within Christianity, but in its authentic sense, the Christian future hope has worked against the tendency in religion to flee from the world. The future of the God who is to come is also the future of the world, and a Christian who even now is living in the full sense in confidence in the coming of the kingdom of God, does so only when he takes account, not only in his private life but also in political thought and action, of the presence of the kingdom, however much appearances and human resistance still deny the presence of the kingdom of God.

Thus Christian belief in the future can serve as a corrective against the tendencies to flee the world which are so easily associated with the life of religion, and which also threaten the religious renewal which has its roots at the present day in revivalist marginal groups in Western society, and particularly in the USA. Thus Christian eschatology can make an important contribution to preventing a further breach between faith and the world and maintaining the association between the religious renewal and the tasks involved in shaping the future of this world. This of course assumes that there is some point of contact between the secular concern for the future and the concerns of religion. For if the attitude to the future in secular experience such as is expressed in technologically orientated futurology provides no access to the ideas and concerns of religion, then any connection with a religious view of the future remains external and irrelevant to it. In the rest of this lecture, therefore, I shall concentrate upon the relationship between Christian eschatology and the secular experience of the future. I must first of all clarify what kind of future is really at issue in Christian eschatology.

III

The Christian hope is directed towards the coming of the kingdom of God and towards participation in the new life it brings. All other "last things" in Christian tradition are related to this, particularly the resurrection of the dead and the judgment of the world. What kind of future is this? The concern is everywhere, even in the expectation of an end of the present world and a new creation with man, the future of man.

This can be demonstrated in the first instance by looking at the central conception of the kingdom of God. This is a kingdom of peace and righteousness, such as Isaiah (2.1–5) expects in the coming messianic kingdom, which will bring to reality the righteous will of God expressed in the God-given law of Israel. The book of Daniel associates the fulfilment of this hope of political salvation with the expectation of direct rule by God himself, by contrast to the kingdoms of the world, based upon human rule. Consequently, in the book of Daniel (7.13) the kingdom of God is symbolized by the figure of a human being, while the nature of the kingdoms of the world is expressed in animal symbols: not until the kingdom of God comes will there be a basis for a truly human society. Of course peace and justice are goals which every political order seeks to bring about. But under the ordinances of human rule these goals are constantly perverted into their opposite. This is why the rule of God himself is necessary, so that both the righteousness of God, and with it man's social being, can be brought to reality. But to bring to reality the righteousness of God requires a revision of the present unjust relationships amongst men, in which violence and deceit so often triumph. If the righteousness of God is to be realized not merely in a future generation, but in all men, it requires some form of compensation in the world to come, a judgment of the dead, and for this the resurrection of the dead is necessary. Finally, the perfect society of the kingdom of God also requires a change in the natural conditions of existence; it requires a new heaven and a new earth.[1]

Thus the eschatological conceptions of early Judaism, which were taken over as such by primitive Christianity, were directly concerned with the future of mankind. Do they consist of prophecies of particular individual happenings which are to come about at some time in the course of events, preceded and followed by a period of time? In my opinion this is to misunderstand the meaning of the eschatological prophecies of the future. They are of course concerned with a real future, but in a different sense from predictions on the basis of natural laws,

[1] This resumé of the eschatology of early Judaism of course ignores a great many details, and in particular does not discuss the question of the relationship between the kingdom of God and the messianic kingdom, which takes a very different form in the various apocalyptic writings. The selection of the four conceptions mentioned in the text (the kingdom of God, judgment, resurrection and the end of the world) implies the view that they form the essential elements of early Jewish eschatology. By contrast, the question of the relationship between the kingdom of God and the messianic kingdom is of lesser importance.

forecasts of political developments or the intuitive foreknowledge of contingent future events. The eschatological prophecies of the future formulate the conditions of the final realization of man's humanity as a consequence of the establishment of the righteousness of God, which is essential to man's being as such. The realization of man's being as such requires a community in which everyone has his own proper place, so that in it the conflicts between the individual and society, between individual interests and the interests of society, are overcome. If the unity of man's being as an individual and a member of society is an indispensable condition for the realization of his humanity, it is not sufficient for a balance to be struck in some future order of society between the individual and society, even if this could be supposed possible under the present conditions of human existence, where the common interest must be discerned and furthered by individuals who repeatedly do so from the point of view of their private interests. But even if it were possible to establish the unity of men's individual and common interests in a future society, how then would people of previous generations participate in the destiny of man realized in such a future society? The possibility of all human individuals participating in the perfect society in which the destiny of mankind is realized is unimaginable without a resurrection of the dead. And for everyone to participate in the life of the society in the way appropriate to him is inconceivable unless a balance is struck by a judgment of the world which takes place beyond and outside it. Thus the association of judgment, the resurrection of the dead and the realization of a perfect society in the concept of the end of the world and of history, as they have existed hitherto, is in accordance with the idea of the consummation of man's destiny in the unity of its individual and social aspects.

If, then, the statements of early Jewish eschatology concerning the future are intended to formulate the conditions for the realization of man's destiny in the unity of its individual and social aspects, then in the future of the kingdom of God we are concerned with the true and essential future of man. The eschatological statements concerning the future tell us nothing of the happenings by which, in the material course of events, this essential future of human nature is to be realized. The eschatological hope leaves such questions open. In particular, no answer is given to the question of the relationship between the idea of a new creation of the natural world, as the condition of the realization of human nature, and the physical processes with which we are familiar. Are these processes to come to an end, and are they to be replaced by something quite different? Do these physical processes continue, or will they lead beyond the stage which the realization of human nature has at present reached? Must we suppose a "curvature" of time, analogous to the "curvature" of the dimension of space in the theory of relativity? All of these ideas are worth discussion. They are mentioned here only to show that the conceptions found in eschatological statements concerning the end of the world, in the sense of the future of human nature, relieve theology of any need to settle for any one particular conception of the end of the world. But they do not mean that the eschatological future ceases to have any connection with real time, or does not differ from the present and the past.

Does this interpretation of the eschatological conceptions developed in the biblical traditions amount to an anthropological reinterpretation of the eschatological language of the Bible? This would be so only if it could be shown that historically the statements concerned did not have the function here attributed to them. Of course the eschatological conceptions in the scriptures are not formulated as conditions for the realization of human nature. The way they are formulated does not exclude the anthropological perspectives of our own age. But may not the perspectives of a later period reveal something in traditional texts which has hitherto lain unnoticed? Only when the statements of tradition are so forced that they are made to say something different from what can be shown to be present in them, can we properly say their meaning has been altered.

IV

Can the anthropological interpretation of the traditional eschatological conceptions contribute to the understanding of their religious significance? And will it make clear the relevance of the future in general to the ideas and concerns of religion?

In order to answer these questions we must discuss the experience of meaning and significance. We do not mean here the conviction that life has a positive meaning. Rather, the categories of "meaning" and "significance" are formal structural elements in all human experience. These can be limited neither to the semantic relationship between propositions and their objects, nor to the intended meaning of purposeful action. Not only action but also received experiences possess a meaning. Indeed, meaning is primarily apprehended in received experiences. As Dilthey has shown, all experience is a matter of a relationship between part and whole. Even if we speak of the "significance" which is attributed to the individual phenomenon, though always in relationship to a context, and of the "meaning" which the totality makes, but which can also be attributed to the individual phenomenon in its relationship to the whole, a strict distinction is difficult. Thus words "signify" something, but what they signify is always established in any individual case by their "use in language", that is, in the context of the sentence. Sentences mean something; not only in themselves however, but also and at the same time as elements in the wider context of a text or utterance which in itself represents a larger totality of meaning, and in its turn points towards larger structures of meaning in which the position and importance of an utterance or text (its meaning) can vary greatly.

Like the words in a sentence, individual events possess significance in the context of a situation in life. In so far as an event cannot be taken in itself in isolation, but is related to the context of a situation in life or a way of life, Dilthey calls it an "experience". We experience the events which come upon us in so far as we always relate them in one way or another to the whole of our life, as it is present to us in memory and in expectation – that is, we relate it to ourselves. But the whole of our personal life is still in the process of becoming – as long as our life lasts. It exists in a historical process which is not as yet concluded. At any given present moment we are merely anticipating the still incomplete totality of the course of our life. The experiences that take place as life proceeds will correct this anticipation, and in the process of the history of our lives the identity of our self can become problematic. At the same time the standing and importance, the significance, of previous experiences is altered. What formerly seemed insignificant may perhaps appear later as of fundamental importance; and the reverse may be true. The final significance of the events of our life, Dilthey once said, can be measured only at the end of our lives, in the hour of our death. Because of the historical nature of the experience of meaning, that is, because the whole of life is a historical process, the future, and particularly the ultimate future, has a decisive function in the question of the meaning of our life as a whole and of the final significance of individual experiences. The final significance, the real *nature* of the individual things that have happened to us, but also of our own actions, is decided only in the final future of our life, because only then does the whole of life, which forms the horizon for the meaning and significance of all the individual factors in it, at last take shape.

Two further comments: the final future which constitutes the totality of life and is decisive for the final significance, the true essence of all the individual factors in it, cannot be identical with death. Death brings life to an end, and reduces the structure of its meaning to fragments. Of course the death of the individual makes apparent the totality of his life to a degree of completeness which was hitherto impossible; but it is not death which constitutes this totality. Here again our previous distinction between the true and essential future, and the external events which bring about its realization, becomes important. Only the essential future brings existence to the totality which has already been experienced in anticipation in man's confidence in himself. Only the essential future has a liberating effect upon the present by contrast to the unknown future dangers which threaten life, but in which the essential future, though still hidden, may be contained.

Secondly, even with the death of an individual the totality of his life is not yet manifested. For the meaning of the individual life as a whole is also conditioned by its context in the life of the society of which he is a member. Thus the image of the dead, as is most clearly seen in the case of the great figures of mankind, continues to change even after their death as the interpretation of their life and their work continues to develop. The social conditioning of the individual, which for the sake of simplicity we ignored in the above analysis of the experience of meaning, has to be taken into account at every point. It is an essential element in every experience of the self, for the individual possesses his identity only according to the way he is recognized in society, or in the struggle to obtain a recognition which is denied him. The anticipation of the totality of the individual life, which supplies the individual with confidence in himself at any given moment, always extends, therefore, to the social unity in the context of which the individual lives, and looks beyond his own particular society to its place in the life of mankind. The essential future of the individual, on which depends the ultimate decision concerning the meaning of his life and the significance of individual elements in this life, cannot therefore be separated from the essential future of mankind as a whole. And this is the relationship which is expressed in the eschatological conceptions of the Judaeo-Christian tradition, where the decision concerning the life of the individual is put back to the end of all the previous history of humanity, when resurrection and judgment take place, and is associated with the consummation of mankind in the community of the kingdom of God.

V

The analysis of the structure of the meaning of human experience and its historical nature, therefore, places the conceptual world of eschatology in a wider context. It also lays the foundation for its connection with the ideas and concerns of religion. For religion is concerned with the totality of the meaning of life. This realization has been strongly emphasized in the modern sociology of religion by Thomas Luckmann, who draws upon the conceptions of the sociology of religion in Max Weber and Emile Durckheim. According to Luckmann, the constructions of Weber and Durckheim, which differ so much from each other, have their common denominator in the fact that both use the concept "religion" for the totality of meaning of the social order.[2] Luckmann himself follows E. Voegelin in holding that the claim of religion to embody the true and valid order of the life of human society relates every order of society in a "symbolical transcendence" to something which goes beyond itself: to a spiritual order which can be understood as the "universal meaningfulness of human social existence".[3] This is not the place to discuss in more depth Luckmann's thesis that in modern society the autonomy of the individual and the sphere of private life have become "the new social form of religion and at the same time its basic content".[4] In spite of important elements of truth in it, this thesis is unsatisfactory, because in fact it fails to explain the integration of the individual into the social context, which according to Luckmann is supposed to be the specific sociological achievement of religion. But the assertion which is Luckmann's starting point, that "the universal basic social form of religion . . . is originally none other than the structure of meaning of the social order, that is, the inner form of the world view of a society",[5] remains independent of this thesis.

Neither Luckmann, Weber nor Durckheim were aware how close this thesis was in substance to Dilthey's analysis of the

[2] T. Luckmann, *Das Problem der Religion in der modernen Gesellschaft*, 1963, p. 13.   [3] *Ibid.*, p. 35.   [4] *Ibid.*, p. 73; cf. pp. 68ff.   [5] *Ibid.*, p. 36.

experience of significance and meaning. Here, because of the dependence of the parts upon the whole, there must be assumed for every concrete experience a totality of meaning, even if it is only posited implicitly. And it is only this totality of meaning which makes it possible to define the significance experienced in any single thing that happens to one, or associated with any individual action – even if this totality of meaning is only anticipated, and may change as experience proceeds, just as may the individual significance which has been experienced. The similarity between this totality of meaning, which according to Dilthey's analyses is implicit in all historical experience, and the concept of religion in the sociology of religion, is remarkable. Even more surprising is that it is in considerable agreement with one of the classical theological analyses of the concept of religion, Schleiermacher's theory of religion, as developed in his *Discourses on Religion* (1799).[6] In view of this agreement, it is no longer possible for the claims made by the sociology of religion for the concept of religion to be dismissed as no more than an external and sociological aspect of religious life, which does not touch upon the nature of religion.

In the second discourse, "The Nature of Religion", Schleiermacher describes religion in the categories of the part and the whole: "Religion is just the acceptance of each separate thing as a part of the Whole, of each limited thing as an exhibition of the Infinite."[7] This concept of the whole, or the infinite, constantly recurs in the discourse. It largely corresponds to Schleiermacher's concept of the "Universe" which must be restricted neither to nature, nor to mankind and its history, but includes and goes beyond both in the totality of meaning which transcends and comprehends everything that now exists. This

[6] This agreement can be explained in part by the connection between the theory of religion in the *Discourses on Religion* and the problems of the relationship between the individual and society in Schleiermacher's theory of the social contract from the same year 1799. I am grateful to Matthias Riemer for drawing my attention to this connection.

[7] First edition, 1799, p. 56; ET *On Religion*, trs. J. Oman, repr. 1958, p. 279. This English translation was based upon the considerably amended third edition. References to this translation are given where relevant.

concept of the totality of meaning is perhaps the most accurate definition of Schleiermacher's concept of the Universe. Schleiermacher regards the distinctive feature of the religious outlook as that of "seeing in every particular and finite thing the infinite, its impression, its manifestation".[8] Thus in everyday experience individual and finite things are no longer related to the infinite, the Universe, but are taken as they are, although they exist only "by the definition of their limits, which must be as it were dissected out of the infinite".[9] This can be translated into the terminology of Dilthey's analysis of meaning as follows: The totality of meaning implicitly and tacitly assumed in everyday life in any apprehension of the significance of individual things, actions or events is made explicit in religious experience and in the religious consciousness, in such a way, moreover, that the individual phenomenon is experienced *as* a manifestation of the totality of meaning. In religious experience, however, the totality of meaning itself is only a theme in an indirect way, and attention is directed to the deity which is the basis and guarantee of this totality of meaning. This is associated with the fact that the apprehension of the "dimension of depth" or "ground of being" sustaining all concrete experience, to use Tillich's metaphor, is experienced as its self-revelation; or in Schleiermacher's words "the influence of the thing perceived on the person perceiving"[10] is experienced as an "operation of the Universe upon us".[11] At this point Schleiermacher's description is in need of slight correction; for it is not the totality of meaning of the Universe which is experienced as acting upon us, but the unity of a divine reality which actually constitutes and unites this totality of meaning.[12]

The theory of religion in the *Discourses on Religion* laid the

---

[8] *Ibid.*, p. 51. Cf. pp. 277 and 48.   [9] *Ibid.*, p. 53.
[10] *Ibid.*, p. 55. ET p. 278.   [11] *Ibid.*, p. 56. ET p. 48.
[12] Schleiermacher did not realize the constitutive function of the idea of God for the idea of the Universe, but rather saw the idea of God as a possible but not indispensable individual view of the Universe (*Reden*, pp. 124ff.), although he was aware of the connection between the concept of the Universe acting upon us ("as originally acting") and the idea of God ("the form of a free being") (p. 129).

foundation for a description of religious experience as the experience of meaning. But Schleiermacher had not yet taken into account the structure of human experience as a historical process, which was later worked out by Dilthey in his analyses of historical experience. In the *Discourses on Religion* the history of mankind is already one of the principal objects of religion; it is declared to be the highest manifestation of the Universe.[13] But no consequence is drawn from this for the analysis of the form of religious experience itself. The history of mankind remains one way among others of looking at the Universe, even though it is the greatest of them. The theoretical framework of Schleiermacher's theory of religion is determined by the idea of individuality, by the point of view of numerous individual manifestations of the Universe, not by a preoccupation with the historical process of experience.

If Schleiermacher's theory of religion is taken further in the direction of Dilthey's analyses of the historical nature of the human experience of meaning, it can be seen that the totality of meaning which religious experience apprehends as present in individual phenomena is itself involved in the historical process. For this very reason it is still subject to dispute as history proceeds. It is constituted as a totality only by an ultimate future which definitely decides the total meaning of historical reality. All present experience of meaning, and especially religious experiences of the presence of an all-embracing meaning (Schleiermacher's "Universe") within the individual phenomena of life, must therefore be understood as *anticipations* of the total meaning of reality which cannot be definitely decided until that ultimate future. Thus it is a consequence of a growing awareness of the historical nature of human life that the future has come to have essential significance for man's awareness of meaning. In the political sphere this is expressed in the ideas of a more just society in the future, by contrast to orders which can be legitimated only as something handed down by tradition. To this must be added the growing public significance accorded to scientifically based predictions,

[13] *Op. cit.*, pp. 99ff., cf. p. 100.

up to and including modern futurology. Within religion, the
first steps have barely been taken towards a decisive break-
through to the primacy of the future. The formative power of a
past which is regarded as the norm is particularly strong here,
either in the form of a mythical primeval history, as a revelation which has taken place once for all, or as a confessional
identity with a single historical foundation which is supposed
to be valid henceforth. But such religious views come into
conflict with the fundamental modern experience of continuous
historical change. Thus the historical nature of the human
experience of meaning can be adopted and exploited by a
religious vision only if it conceives of the future as essential to
the totality of meaning of human life and of reality as a whole,
and is thereby capable of according positive significance even
to changes in the historical world and in the religious consciousness.[14]

[14] Here the essential future of man which constitutes the totality of
meaning of the social world in which he lives comes to have the position
of the "central point" which according to Schleiermacher's fifth *Discourse*
is the basis of the individual unity of a particular religion and distinguishes
it from others (p. 260; ET p. 223). Its function is "to select some one of
the great relations of mankind in the world to the Highest Being, and, in a
definite way, make it the centre and refer to it all the others" (pp. 259f.;
ET p. 223). But since Schleiermacher regarded the themes and concerns of
religion only from the point of view of man as an individual, not from that
of a historical process of the religious Universe itself, he did not recognize
the central or basic outlook of a religion as the outlook which in any given
case integrated the totality of meaning itself. If he had done so the choice
of it would not longer have had the appearance of "a merely arbitrary
proceeding" and would have been explicable on the basis of the experience
of meaning of a particular society. Secondly, Schleiermacher separated the
Universe as such, in the manner of the Platonic *chorismos*, from the forms
of its individual manifestation. This is no longer possible nowadays, when
it is recognized that only this central or basic outlook can constitute the
totality of meaning of the Universe in its present form. Thirdly, in the
definition in Schleiermacher of the distinctive characteristics of the Christian
religion – in the *Discourses* by the more general conception of corruption
and redemption (p. 181), and in the *Glaubenslehre* (Doctrine of Faith)
by its connection with the "redemption brought about by Jesus of
Nazareth" (§ 11) – he does not go into the constitutive significance of the
eschatological future. From this point of view the "central point" of the
Christian religion could be defined as the presence of the essential future of
man mediated by Jesus of Nazareth.

VI

Under different historical circumstances, the experience of history as the medium through which God made himself known already led, in Israelite prophecy and in post-exilic apocalyptic, to a concentration upon the future, that is, upon the future of the kingdom of God. The conditions under which this occurred differed from those of the modern age in so far as that at that time there was no doubt about the dimension of divine reality as such, nor about the authoritative mediation of God's self-revelation. In a patriarchal society integrated by the authority of tradition and traditional institutions, there was no need for constant recourse to the general nature of man and to what could be based upon it, in order to achieve a social identity in the formation of opinion. This is the case, however, in modern society, because from its origins it has had to achieve its unity in the face of a plurality of religious traditions and inherited world views, and did so by declaring these conflicts to be private matters. But for religion to be reduced to a private matter is in contradiction to its essential function, that of maintaining an immediate awareness of the meaningful unity of reality as a whole and of its divine origin. As the result, religious communions in the modern age have either tried, in contradiction to the basic tendencies of the modern age, to establish the authority of their confessional form in public politics, or else have been obliged through their theology to find a basis for their religious ideas in the general nature and concerns of man. Under the conditions of modern society, the easiest way to do this was by asserting private individual experience itself to be the location of the concerns and issues of religion. The classical and most effective example of this is pietism. But it is becoming increasingly clear that this approach cannot give a permanently convincing demonstration of the general validity of religious concerns and ideas, but can at best preserve its right to plough its own narrow furrow. And because doubt has been cast upon the awareness of moral norms, even the phenomenon of the experience of guilt can nowadays no longer provide the basis for the assertion of the general human validity of religion. If such a general validity is not to be renounced, it can best be maintained by the analysis of the experience of meaning, beginning with the individual experience of meaning, which can very rapidly be shown to be intimately involved in the apprehensions of meaning which are at work in society and which mediate the processes that integrate it. This anthropological perspective establishes the distinction between the way in which the primacy of the future for historical experience has been expounded in this lecture, and the concentration upon the future of the kingdom of God in the thought of post-exilic Judaism. It is in the context of the latter, and in a certain sense as its culmination, that the message of Jesus must be understood, with its demand that the whole world in which men live must be understood and lived solely on the basis of the future of the kingdom of God. Our considerations have shown the relevance of this demand in the quite different context of the problems at issue in modern religion, seen as problems of the experience of meaning. This point of view brings to light certain aspects and implications of the eschatological message of Jesus which have hitherto remained unnoticed, such as the necessity of thinking of the God of the coming kingdom as himself a future God, as the power of the future, which will bring into being the essential future of man. Here Jesus' message of the love of God is seen as an expression of the presence of the coming kingdom in the mission of Jesus himself, which gives to men, in spite of their remoteness from God, a participation even now in the coming kingdom, in spite of the hostility of the world and their own failure as a result of this hostility. Paul and John used the term "freedom" to describe the presence of salvation to Christians; as an expression of the power of the future to determine the present this takes on a new significance: in the event of freedom the essential future of man is already present. With regard to the essential significance of the future for freedom it is ultimately not difficult to arrive at an understanding of God, the power of the future, as the origin of freedom. There is an important link here with the preoccupation of the modern age with freedom as emancipation from traditional forces; while as a basis for the freedom of the modern age which is capable of preserving it from lapsing into impotent subjectivism, the idea of God can once again be maintained in the face of modern atheist criticism.

But is not the fact that Christian faith is bound to the past history of Jesus irreconcilable with such a theological orientation towards the future? Such doubts are justified with regard to views which lay a one-sided emphasis upon the future at the expense of the present and the past. But such antitheses usually ignore the fact that the definite content of their anticipations of the future is always mediated by present and past experience. The significance of the past for every new present which is integrated into the processes of tradition and assimilation depends upon how far this past history contains a still unspent future, that is, upon how far it is able to illuminate the experience of the present which follows it, with regard to the future. This is true of the history of Jesus in a special and unrepeatable way, because the God of Jesus, as the God of the coming kingdom, is himself the power of the future, of the essential future of man, and is therefore the origin of the freedom through which men transform their traditions and renew their historical world.

INDEX OF AUTHORS